D0206385

JOURNAL FOR THE STUDY OF THE PSEUDEPIGRAPHA
SUPPLEMENT SERIES
9

Editor
James H. Charlesworth

Associate Editors
Philip R. Davies
James R. Mueller
James C. VanderKam

JSOT Press
Sheffield

MYSTERIES
AND
REVELATIONS
Apocalyptic Studies since
the Uppsala Colloquium

Edited by

John J. Collins
&
James H. Charlesworth

Journal for the Study of the Pseudepigrapha
Supplement Series 9

BS
1705
.M670
1991

Copyright © 1991 Sheffield Academic Press

Published by JSOT Press
JSOT Press is an imprint of
Sheffield Academic Press Ltd
The University of Sheffield
343 Fulwood Road
Sheffield S10 3BP
England

Printed on acid-free paper in Great Britain
by
Billing & Sons Ltd
Worcester

British Library Cataloguing in Publication Data

Mysteries and revelations: apocalyptic studies
since the Uppsala colloqium.—(JSP
supplement, ISSN 0951-8215; 9).
    I. Collins, John J. (John Joseph), 1946-
    II. Charlesworth, James H. (James Hamilton),
    1940- III. Series
    228.015

ISBN 1-85075-299-0

JESUIT - KRAUSS - McCORMICK - LIBRARY
1100 EAST 55th STREET
CHICAGO, ILLINOIS 60615

CONTENTS

PREFACE

This collection of essays had its origins in a symposium at the Society of Biblical Literature meeting in Anaheim on November 19, 1989, which marked the tenth anniversary of the Uppsala Colloquium on Apocalypticism, August 12-17, 1979. Four of the essays (those of Collins, Stone, Himmelfarb, Hultgård) were presented in Anaheim. They are complemented here by the essays of David Hellholm (who chaired the Anaheim meeting), George Nickelsburg, Gabriele Boccaccini and James Charlesworth.

The Uppsala Colloquium attempted to address all aspects of apocalypticism in the ancient Mediterranean world and Near East. The objectives of the present collection are much more modest. The focus is primarily on Jewish apocalypticism, and six of the eight essays deal with Jewish materials. A seventh, by Anders Hultgård, deals with a Persian text that is of great potential importance for the emergence of Jewish apocalypticism. The eighth, by David Hellholm, is a methodological essay.

The opening essay, by John Collins, is a survey of the study of apocalypticism in the decade after the Uppsala Colloquium. It is concerned especially with the relation between the literary genre apocalypse and the broader phenomenon of apocalypticism. The survey of recent work is supplemented by an appendix, which deals with the contribution of Helge Kvanvig on apocalyptic origins, and by the essay of Gabriele Boccaccini on the work of Paolo Sacchi and the Italian school. The essays of George Nickelsburg and Michael Stone each focus on a particular apocalyptic book, *1 Enoch* and *4 Ezra* respectively. Both scholars draw on two decades of research on these books in the preparation of commentaries in the Hermeneia series. Nickelsburg describes the world view of *1 Enoch*. His essay complements the opening article by illustrating what is meant by apocalypticism, or an apocalyptic world view, as distinct from the literary genre. Stone's essay marks one of the more exciting new directions in the study of apocalypticism to emerge since the Uppsala Colloquium, by inquiring into the religious experience of the author. This kind of question was not entertained under any of the categories of the Uppsala conference ('World of Concepts', 'Literary Genre', or

Sociological Phenomenon'). Yet Stone shows how it bears on the literary understanding of an apocalypse, since it determines the kind of coherence we can expect in a work of this sort. Martha Himmelfarb's essay is in a similar vein. She also raises questions relating to the religious experience implied in visionary literature. This is surely one of the areas where we can hope for significant progress in the coming decade. Jim Charlesworth's essay points to another area that might profitably be explored in the future: the role of folk tradition in apocalyptic literature. While the apocalypses were regarded as evidence for folk beliefs by scholars such as Bousset at the beginning of the century, recent scholarship has tended to view them as scribal phenomena. Without denying the scribal element in the composition of this literature, Charlesworth argues that there is also a significant component that is derived from folk tradition.

Anders Hultgård has contributed an important study of a Persian apocalyptic text. Scholarly opinion has veered wildly on the relevance of Persian material for the study of apocalypticism. For the *Religionsgeschichtliche Schule*, Persia was the *fons et origo* of apocalypticism. More recent scholarship has tended to dismiss the Persian material as late. Hultgård presents a balanced perspective, which recognizes the difficulty of relating the Persian texts to the pre-Christian period, but also shows that they cannot be dismissed as easily as some have tried to do.

David Hellholm's essay stands apart from the others by reason of its methodological character. Hellholm is developing a new approach to apocalyptic texts through the methods of text linguistics. The difficult and abstract character of these methods have hitherto curtailed their impact on general biblical studies. Yet Hellholm's work is one of the most significant developments in the study of apocalypticism in the last decade, and it will undoubtedly demand increasing attention.

In this volume, then, we hope to provide not only a retrospective survey of major developments and debates of the past decade, but also a sampling of new directions that will be important in the closing years of this millennium.

John J. Collins

CONTRIBUTORS

John J. Collins
Department of Theology, University of Notre Dame, Notre Dame, IN 46556, USA

Gabriel Boccaccini
Department of Oriental Studies, University of Turin, Italy

George W.E. Nickelsburg
School of Religion, University of Iowa, Iowa City, IA 52242, USA

Michael E. Stone
Department of the History of Jewish Thought, The Hebrew University, POB 16174, Jerusalem 91161, Israel

Martha Himmelfarb
Department of Religion, Princeton University, 613 Seventy-Nine Hall, Princeton, NJ 08544-1006, USA

James H. Charlesworth
Princeton Theological Seminary, CN 821, Princeton, NJ 05842-0803, USA

Anders Hultgård
Uppsala Universiteit, Teologiska Institutionen, Box 1604, 751 46 Uppsala, Sweden

David Hellholm
Institut for Bibelvitenskap, University of Oslo, POB 1023, Oslo 3, Norway

GENRE, IDEOLOGY AND SOCIAL MOVEMENTS IN JEWISH APOCALYPTICISM

John J. Collins

1979 was a landmark year in the study of apocalypticism. In addition to the international conferences at Uppsala[1] and Louvain,[2] it saw the publication of several major studies: the study of the genre in *Semeia* 14,[3] an influential article by Jean Carmignac,[4] and the first of a series of studies on apocalypticism and the problem of evil by Paolo Sacchi.[5] Christopher Rowland's *The Open Heaven* was also completed, though not published in that year.[6] This outpouring reflected a buildup of interest in the subject over the previous decade, and involved both attempts to take stock of the field and attempts to chart new courses.

Some trends and points of convergence were evident in these studies of 1979. There was widespread agreement that a distinction should be made between the literary genre apocalypse and the wider, looser categories of 'apocalyptic' or 'apocalypticism'.[7] The primary distin-

---

1. D. Hellholm (ed.), *Apocalypticism in the Mediterranean World and the Near East* (Tübingen, 1983).
2. J. Lambrecht (ed.), *L'Apocalypse johannique et l'apocalyptique dans le Nouveau Testament* (BETL, 53; Gembloux, Leuven, 1980).
3. J.J. Collins (ed.), *Apocalypse. The Morphology of a Genre* (*Semeia* 14; Missoula, MT, 1979).
4. 'Qu'est-ce que l'apocalyptique?', *RevQ* 10 (1979–81), pp. 3-33.
5. 'Il "Libro dei Vigilanti" e l'apocalittica', *Henoch* 1 (1979), pp. 42-92.
6. *The Open Heaven. A Study of Apocalyptic in Judaism and Early Christianity* (New York, 1983). J. Gruenwald's study, *Apocalyptic and Merkavah Mysticism* (AGJU, 14; Leiden, 1980), appeared the following year.
7. This distinction was already made by K. Koch, *The Rediscovery of Apocalyptic* (SBT, 2/22; Naperville, IL, 1972) and taken up by P. Hanson, 'Apocalypse, Genre', 'Apocalypticism', *IDBSup*, pp. 27-34. See also M.E. Stone, 'Lists of Revealed Things in the Apocalyptic Literature', in F.M. Cross, W.E. Lemke, and P.D. Miller, Jr (eds.), *Magnalia Dei: The Mighty Acts of God* (Garden City, NY, 1976), pp. 439-43; 'Apocalyptic Literature', in M.E. Stone (ed.), *Jewish Writings from the Second*

guishing mark of the genre was that the material was presented as revelation. Several of these studies emphasized the 'vertical' aspects of apocalypticism: the interest in mysteries and in the heavenly world.[1] This emphasis was largely in reaction against the one-sided emphasis on eschatology which had dominated study of the field in the past. The change in emphasis corresponded to a shift in the focus of the study of apocalypticism, away from the alleged 'dawn of apocalyptic'[2] in prophetic texts of the post-exilic period to the Pseudepigrapha, and especially to the Enoch corpus, which had been thrust to the fore by the publication of the Aramaic fragments from Qumran.[3]

However, the Uppsala Colloquium represented, quite deliberately, a very wide spectrum of views. The participants were drawn from diverse fields and had diverse ideas of what was meant by apocalypticism. After some 25 papers, which had not been circulated in advance, there was one session devoted to seeking consensus. When the participants voted *contra definitionem, pro descriptione*,[4] in a phrase often quoted since then, this did not represent a consensus on proper procedure, but was an expression of fatigue and a recognition that much more time would be needed to mediate the differing viewpoints. The final resolution was a diplomatic evasion of the issue at the end of a very stimulating, but exhausting, conference.

Consensus, of course, is rarely found in scholarly discussion, and the disagreements on the subject of apocalypticism are scarcely greater than those in other areas of biblical studies. There is, at least, general agreement on the corpus of relevant literature. The most heated debates are not so much over the understanding of this material but over the proper use of terminology.

The basic problem here lies in the propensity of scholars to select some feature of an apocalyptic writing that happens to interest them, and arbitrarily declare it to be the essence of 'apocalyptic' or apocalypticism. So the introductory essay in a recent volume on *Apocalyptic and the New Testament* notes (with approval) that 'scholars who have

---

Temple Period (CRINT, 2/2; Philadelphia, 1984), pp. 392-93; M.A. Knibb, 'Prophecy and the Emergence of the Jewish Apocalypses', in R. Coggins, A. Phillips and M. Knibb (eds.), *Israel's Prophetic Tradition: Essays in Honour of Peter Ackroyd* (Cambridge, 1982), pp. 160-61.

1. So especially Rowland, Gruenwald. Note also the subsequent studies of I. Culianu, *Psychanodia I* (Leiden, 1983); and C. Kappler (ed.), *Apocalypses et voyages dans l'au-delà* (Paris, 1987).

2. P.D. Hanson, *The Dawn of Apocalyptic* (Philadelphia, 1975).

3. J.T. Milik, *The Books of Enoch* (Oxford, 1976).

4. Hellholm, *Apocalypticism*, p. 2.

explored the relationship between apocalyptic and Jesus or the apostle Paul, like Schweitzer and Käsemann, have avoided basing their research on assumptions drawn from a study of the literary genre and have instead focused on apocalyptic as *a theological concept*.[1] The advantage of 'a theological concept', from this point of view, is that it is not constrained by the evidence of the ancient apocalyptic literature, 'much of which is indeed abstruse and fantastic',[2] but can be defined by the theologian, in whatever way is most convenient for the explication of Jesus or Paul. Whether or not this theological concept accurately reflects the thought of Jesus or Paul, it can only compound the terminological confusion in modern scholarship. There can be no consensus in the definition of a term such as 'apocalyptic' unless we accept the constraints of a specific body of evidence. The observation of Klaus Koch two decades ago remains true: the word 'apocalyptic' refers first of all to a body of literature, and any analysis of the phenomenon must begin with an analysis of the literature.[3] This is not to say that apocalypticism should be reduced to the literary genre, or viewed only as a literary convention. It is simply to affirm the methodological necessity of a common starting point. The term 'apocalyptic' refers first and foremost to the kind of material found in apocalypses. To use the word in any other way is to invite terminological confusion.

The Discussion of the Genre

My own contribution to the debate in 1979 was concerned with the definition of the literary genre, as part of an SBL task force whose findings were published in *Semeia* 14. We proposed a definition that was based on a combination of form (narrative framework, revelation mediated by an other-worldly being) and content (disclosure of supernatural world and of eschatological future). Ten years later I would, inevitably, do some things differently. In *Semeia* 14, we proposed a sixfold typology. We distinguished two broad types: the 'historical' apocalypses such as Daniel, and the heavenly ascents, often associated with Enoch. That distinction is, I think, fundamental, even though we

---

1. R.E. Sturm, 'Defining the Word "Apocalyptic": A Problem in Biblical Criticism', in J. Marcus and M.L. Soards (eds.), *Apocalyptic and the New Testament. Essays in Honor of J. Louis Martyn* (JSNTS, 24; Sheffield, 1989), p. 37 (emphasis added). Similarly M.C. de Boer, 'Paul and Jewish Apocalyptic Eschatology', *ibid.*, p. 187.
2. Sturm, 'Defining the Word', p. 37.
3. Koch, *Rediscovery*, p. 23.

find mixed types (e.g. the *Similitudes of Enoch*). I would not go so far as Martha Himmelfarb, who would argue that we have two different genres here, although I appreciate the basis for her argument.[1] We further divided each of these types into three sub-types, on the basis of their eschatology. While I think these distinctions were accurate, I have found them less significant in my further work, and I would not now insist on them. In the Jewish apocalypses, at least, the main distinction is between the eschatology of the 'historical' works and that of the ascents, and so the twofold typology is adequate. In my own discussion of the Jewish apocalypses I identified some partial texts (e.g. Daniel 7–12, *Jubilees* 23) as apocalypses. I would now speak simply of the dominant genre of these works as wholes. I would also allow for cases of mixed genre (e.g. *Jubilees*) which have significant affinities with more than one genre. Finally, I would include a rather general statement of function, in the definition, a point to which I will return below. I regard these points as relatively minor modifications of the analysis in *Semeia* 14.

There has been considerable discussion of the genre in the last decade. Among the more noteworthy contributions should be mentioned the text-linguistic studies of David Hellholm on Revelation and the *Shepherd of Hermas*.[2] While insights from this approach have helped clarify some points in the general discussion, such as the importance of distinguishing between different levels of abstraction, it has not, as yet, been widely adopted. For many scholars it remains more mysterious than the texts it seeks to clarify,[3] but I would like to suspend judgment on it until a greater body of such studies becomes available. Instead I would like to focus on two issues that concern the relation between the genre and the broader phenomenon of apocalypticism. First is the question whether the apocalypses have a significant common content, which implies a world-view that was distinctive in the ancient world. Second is the historical development of the genre and its relation to specific social groups or movements.

---

1. M. Himmelfarb, *Tours of Hell: An Apocalyptic Form in Jewish and Christian Literature* (Philadelphia, 1983), p. 61.

2. D. Hellholm, 'The Problem of Apocalyptic Genre and the Apocalypse of John', *Semeia* 36 (1986), pp. 13-64; *Das Visionenbuch des Hermas als Apokalypse: Formgeschichtliche und texttheoretische Studien zu einer literarischen Gattung* (ConNT, 13.1; Lund, 1980).

3. The ambitious study of D.F. Mazzaferri, *The Genre of the Book of Revelation from a Source-Critical Perspective* (BZNW, 54; Berlin/New York, 1989) fails to grasp even the rudiments of Hellholm's approach.

1. *Form and content*

In an article published in 1979, at almost exactly the same time as Semeia 14, the late Jean Carmignac argued that 'l'apocalyptique' is a literary genre that describes heavenly revelations by means of symbols: in short, that it is essentially a literary style and that there is common content in only the most general terms.[1] A number of scholars have taken similar positions. Christopher Rowland proposed that 'apocalyptic seems essentially to be about the revelation of the divine mysteries' and emphasized the diversity of the contents.[2] Relying on Rowland's survey, John Barton drew the conclusion that 'the attempt to find any unifying theme among all the apocalypses that are extant is doomed to failure'.[3] He would allow that the adjective 'apocalyptic' has meaning ('concerned with the disclosure of secrets'), but finds it too broad to be useful. The noun 'apocalyptic' (and presumably 'apocalypticism') is for him devoid of content and it makes no sense to speak of an apocalyptic movement. At the Uppsala conference Hartmut Stegemann also argued that *Apokalyptik* is only a literary phenomenon, concerned with the revelation of secrets.[4] He allowed, however, that the term might also refer to the *Wirkungsgeschichte* of apocalypses, e.g. to the influence of the Enoch tradition on the Qumran community.

The issue here is not a theoretical one of how a genre should, in principle, be defined. Genres may be defined in various ways and on various levels of abstraction. It is possible to identify a corpus of texts which are 'revelations of heavenly mysteries', but that corpus will be much broader than that usually associated with the word 'apocalypse'. The real issue here is whether there is a sub-group of revelations which can be defined on the basis of content, or to put the matter another way, whether those texts which are generally regarded as apocalypses (Daniel, *1 Enoch*, Revelation, etc.) have significant common content which distinguishes them from other revelations. With the exception of Carmignac, scholars do not call all the visions in the Hebrew Bible 'apocalypses'. The analysis of the genre in *Semeia* 14, which was based on content as well as form, argued that there is indeed a common content, which is broadly constitutive of a worldview, which was both distinctive and significant in late antiquity.

1. Carmignac, 'Qu'est-ce que l'apocalyptique?', p. 20.
2. Rowland, *The Open Heaven*, pp. 70-72.
3. J. Barton, *Oracles of God. Perceptions of Ancient Prophecy in Israel after the Exile* (London, 1986), p. 201.
4. H. Stegemann, 'Die Bedeutung der Qumranfunde für die Erforschung der Apokalyptik', in Hellholm (ed.), *Apocalypticism*, p. 498.

content

To be sure, the content common to all the apocalypses is fairly abstract and general. The mysteries they disclose involve a view of human affairs in which major importance is attached to the influence of the supernatural world and the expectation of eschatological judgment. Apocalypses may contain all sorts of data, about cosmological secrets, halachic instructions or sapiential reflection, which is all highly important for the interpretation of the individual texts, but the co-ordinates of the world-view are set by the orientation to the supernatural world and the eschatological expectation. Scholars such as Rowland or Barton, who see only the variety of contents, miss the forest for the trees. They are also misled by a tendency to equate eschatology with the kind of public historical crisis envisaged in Revelation, and a failure to recognize the importance of personal eschatology, the judgment of the dead, which is of crucial importance in both the 'historical' apocalypses and in the heavenly ascents. This world-view, with its eschatological dimension, is historically much more specific and limited than the phenomenon of dreams and visions, or the interest in the revelation of mysteries.

I would emphasize that the world-view that is common to all the apocalypses is much broader and less specific than what is usually called apocalypticism in modern scholarship. The latter is usually based only on the 'historical' type of apocalypse such as Daniel and Revelation, and often involves the hasty generalization of motifs that are relatively rare (e.g. the division between the two ages in *4 Ezra*). If apocalypticism is understood as the world-view of the apocalypses, then it is a broad world-view, within which several more specific ideologies and movements can be identified. At the very least we need to distinguish between the 'historical' type of apocalypticism, typified by Daniel and Revelation, and the more cosmic orientation of the heavenly ascents. These smaller groupings may well be more helpful in interpreting a particular text. Nonetheless, two points should be made:

1.   In the interest of consistent terminology, it is better to retain 'apocalypse' as the inclusive term, which embraces different sub-groups, than to restrict the label arbitrarily to one sub-group. A definition of 'apocalypse' or 'apocalypticism' which excludes either Daniel and Revelation on the one hand, or the heavenly ascents on the other, is confusing rather than helpful.

2.   The content of the genre as a whole is still distinctive, at least in the context of Judaism through the first Christian centuries. Ben Sira, 1 Maccabees, Josephus, the Mishnah, all attest forms

of Judaism that are clearly distinct from apocalypticism, even on the broadest definition of the latter. Obviously, the distinctiveness of the apocalyptic world-view decreases with time. The category is more useful with reference to the second century BCE than to the second century CE. Most scholars, however, would grant that the world-view of the Book of the Watchers differs significantly from anything that preceded it in the Jewish tradition (despite the efforts of Margaret Barker to argue that it represents the traditional religion of Jerusalem).[1] There is greater continuity with the Hebrew prophets in the case of Daniel, but there too there was significant novelty, both in the degree of interest in supernatural powers and in the eschatological hope for resurrection and judgment.[2]

2. *The historical development*

The question of distinctiveness leads us to the second major issue in the current discussion, the historical development of both the genre and the world-view.

The definition of the genre proposed in *Semeia* 14 might be described as a 'common core' definition: it attempts to extract characteristics which are common to all exemplars of the genre. The range of material surveyed was essentially the same as in the Uppsala conference: the Mediterranean world and the Near East over a period of roughly 500 years. This attempt to find a core of defining characteristics is certainly a common way of defining a genre, perhaps the most common.[3] It has been challenged, however, both in the general field of literary criticism and in its application to the apocalypse genre, on the grounds that it is ahistorical.

In his helpful introduction to the theory of genres, *Kinds of Literature*, Alastair Fowler has argued that genres are 'positively resistant to definition' and that the expectation of necessary elements or defining characteristics, which is almost universal among critics

1. M. Barker, *The Older Testament. The Survival of Themes from the Ancient Royal Cult in Sectarian Judaism and Early Christianity* (London, 1987).

2. On the relation of the early apocalypses to traditional Israelite religion, see my essay, 'The Place of Apocalypticism in the Religion of Israel', in P.D. Miller, P.D. Hanson and S.D. McBride (eds.), *Ancient Israelite Religion. Essays in Honor of Frank Moore Cross* (Philadelphia, 1987), pp. 539-58.

3. For a survey of concepts of genre in literary criticism, see A. Fowler, *Kinds of Literature. An Introduction to the Theory of Genres and Modes* (Cambridge, MA, 1982), pp. 37-53.

writing about genre, is 'without any sufficient basis'.[1] For Fowler, genres are looser historical entities, held together by 'family resemblances' and genetic connections.[2] A young Dutch scholar, E.J. Tigchelaar, has argued for a similar view of genre in the case of the apocalyptic literature, although as yet he has not worked out its application at any length.[3] Three issues may be distinguished here: (a) the possibility of definition, (b) the importance of diachronic development in the understanding of the genre, and (c) the genetic dimension.

(a) *The possibility of definition.* Fowler's contention that 'genres are positively resistant to definition' does not withstand serious scrutiny. What cannot be defined cannot be distinguished and so cannot be recognized at all. If Fowler can recognize a genre 'tragedy' he must have at least an implicit definition which enables him to distinguish tragedies from other dramas. His own resistance to definitions is due in large part to the inconsistency of traditional usage. 'Oedipus at Colonus' is traditionally called a tragedy, although it lacks most of the classic characteristics of the genre. Similarly, in the Jewish Pseudepigrapha, the *Apocalypse of Moses* (a variant of the *Life of Adam and Eve*) is not an apocalypse in any modern sense of the word, and the *Testament of Abraham* is not a testament. To say that traditional usage is not consistent, however, is not to say that consistent usage is impossible. In the context of modern scholarship, genres are analytical categories, which do not necessarily coincide with the use of genre labels in antiquity.

(b) *Diachronic development.* We must readily agree with Fowler's insistence that genres have a diachronic dimension, and change over time. Definitions are necessarily synchronic, and some critics have inferred that the definition of apocalypse in *Semeia* 14 is ahistorical.[4] This charge seems to me to misunderstand the purpose of a definition. Beginning with the work of Koch, the study of the literary genre was an attempt to focus the discussion on specific texts, in reaction against

---

1. Fowler, *Kinds of Literature*, p. 39.
2. The 'family resemblance' approach to the apocalyptic genre was already advocated by J.G. Gammie, 'The Classification, Stages of Growth, and Changing Intentions in the Book of Daniel', *JBL* 95 (1976), p. 193.
3. E.J. Tigchelaar, *Apocalyptiek: begrip en onbegrip* (Groningen, 1985); *idem*, 'More on Apocalyptic and Apocalypses', *JSJ* 18 (1987), pp. 137-44.
4. So F. García Martínez, 'Encore l'apocalyptique', *JSJ* 17 (1987), p. 229; Tigchelaar, 'More on Apocalyptic and Apocalypses', p. 138; K. Rudolph, 'Apokalyptik in der Diskussion', in Hellholm (ed.), *Apocalypticism*, p. 775.

vague generalizations about the 'essence of apocalyptic' or theological concepts. The definition of the genre in *Semeia* 14 did not include any statement of function. It has been widely criticized on this point,[1] but reluctance to posit a single function for the genre arose precisely from an awareness of the variety of historical settings in which it might be employed.[2] The paradigm of the genre is like a grammatical paradigm, helpful for analyzing particular statements, but not in itself the vehicle of meaning. Meaning is found in statements, in which the grammar is actualized and applied. Now it is quite true that grammatical paradigms also have a function: to clarify grammar and enhance communication. In the same way the genre apocalypse can be said to have a function, for example, 'to legitimate the transcendent authorization of the message'.[3] I would now accept the amendment to the definition of the genre offered in *Semeia* 36, in the light of the suggestions of Hellholm and Aune: an apocalypse is 'intended to interpret present earthly circumstances in the light of the supernatural world and of the future, and to influence both the understanding and the behavior of the audience by means of divine authority'.[4] This definition of the function of the genre, however, is rather different from those which have prevailed in previous study, e.g. 'for the consolation of a group in crisis'. The more specific functions, which tie the genre to precise social settings (such as 'a group in crisis'), fit some apocalypses but not all. It does not seem to me that social setting can be inferred from literary genre. I would still want to emphasize that the genre can accommodate a considerable range of social settings, and that these have to be established by historical study.

A definition, then, serves not only to identify the common elements, but also to provide a foil against which the variations in particular works can be highlighted. My own study of the Jewish apocalypses, *The Apocalyptic Imagination*, differs from other books on the subject, such as those of D.S. Russell[5] or Christopher Rowland,[6] precisely in

---

1. See Hellholm, 'The Apocalypse of John and the Problem of Genre', *Semeia* 36 (1986), pp. 69-70.

2. This point is appreciated by Tigchelaar ('More on Apocalyptic and Apocalypses', p. 138). In contrast, García Martínez ('Encore l'apocalyptique', p. 229) misses the point completely. He accuses me of lumping together the different kinds of settings when my point was precisely the opposite: they should be distinguished (*The Apocalyptic Imagination* [New York, 1984], pp. 17-32).

3. Aune, 'The Apocalypse of John', p. 87.

4. A. Yarbro Collins, 'Introduction: Early Christian Apocalypticism', p. 7.

5. D.S. Russell, *The Method and Message of Jewish Apocalyptic* (Philadelphia, 1964).

6. Rowland, *The Open Heaven*.

the attempt to deal with the individual apocalypses in their historical context. Synchronic and diachronic elements are complementary aspects of the study of a genre, and should not be regarded as mutually exclusive.

Nonetheless, the call for more attention to the diachronic developments can be fruitful, and certainly points the discussion in the right direction. This is most obvious in the case of the earliest apocalypses, such as Daniel and the *Book of the Watchers* in *1 Enoch*, which are experimental compositions, where 'features belonging to other genres are assembled into a new work of art'.[1] The eventual emergence of 'apocalypse' as a genre label, at the end of the first century CE, was possible because the literary forms had attained a measure of stability. We should be wary, however, of attempts to explain all differences between individual works by developmental theories. The differences between the *Book of the Watchers* and *4 Ezra* are due less to their respective places in the development of the genre than to the fact that they were informed by different theological traditions and were written in very different circumstances. The development of a genre is not mechanical and cannot be plotted on a straight line.

(c) *The genetic dimension*. Family resemblances derive from biological relationships. By analogy, 'in literature, the basis of resemblance lies in literary tradition. What produces generic resemblances... is tradition: a sequence of influence and imitation and inherited codes connecting works in the genre.'[2] There is obvious merit in this observation. In the apocalyptic literature, we can speak of an Enoch tradition and a Daniel tradition, the latter including Revelation and *4 Ezra*, and the influence of both traditions on the *Similitudes of Enoch*. Such tracing of particular developments is certainly necessary, but it can be seen as complementary to the 'common core' type of definition rather than as an alternative to it.

Some recent critics, however, would use the criterion of genetic relationships to restrict the field of apocalypticism to Jewish and Christian material. According to Tigchelaar, 'Seeing genre as a historical group with family resemblances restricts the generic analysis to texts which are genetically related'.[3] He would exclude 'the so-called Greek and Roman apocalypses' from the discussion, pending proof of genetic connections. F. García Martínez has argued even more vehemently against the perspective of the *religionsgeschichtliche*

1. Tigchelaar, 'More on Apocalypses and Apocalyptic', p. 139.
2. Fowler, *Kinds of Literature*, p. 42.
3. Tigchelaar, 'More on Apocalypses and Apocalyptic', p. 141.

Schule which was presupposed both in the Uppsala Conference and in *Semeia* 14. For him, one of the 'firmly established results' of the Uppsala Conference is that the 'history of religions' approach must be abandoned, because it leads to confusion.[1]

This attempt to confine the genre to Jewish and Christian material cannot be justified on either historical or literary grounds. Alastair Fowler, a leading proponent of the 'family resemblance' approach, issues an important caveat:

> In generic resemblance, the direct line of descent is not so dominant that genre theory can be identified with source criticism. We need to leave room for polygenesis. . . and for more remote influences. . . Codes often come to a writer indirectly, deviously, remotely, at haphazard, rather than by simple chronological lines of descent.[2]

In fact, the genesis of the genre apocalypse in Judaism remains uncertain.[3] There are obvious lines of continuity with prophetic visions, but also with Babylonian dream interpretation. Some of the most stimulating contributions of the last decade have explored possible genetic connections between Babylonian material and *Enoch* and Daniel (VanderKam, Kvanvig).[4] The relationship between Jewish and Persian apocalypses remains in dispute, but at present the evidence does not permit us to rule out a genetic connection there.[5] Influence of Greek and Roman material remains a live possibility throughout the history of the genre in Judaism and Christianity. The *religionsgeschichtliche* approach to apocalypticism has always focused on the eastern Mediterranean world in late antiquity where historical relationships are distinctly possible. It has never extended its phenomenological horizons to include, say, the Nordic Voluspa.[6] A truly phenomenological study of apocalyptic and related materials without restriction of time and place might well be interesting, but that is not what was attempted at Uppsala. Even an approach that is focused on

---

1. García Martínez, 'Encore l'apocalyptique', pp. 228-29. Nonetheless he has contributed to the volume edited by Kappler, *Apocalypses et voyages dans l' au-delà*, which is clearly conceived from a history-of-religions perspective.
2. Fowler, *Kinds of Literature*, p. 43.
3. See my comments in *The Apocalyptic Imagination*, pp. 19-32.
4. J.C. VanderKam, *Enoch and the Growth of an Apocalyptic Tradition* (CBQMS, 16; Washington, 1984); H. Kvanvig, *Roots of Apocalyptic: The Mesopotamian Background of the Enoch Figure and of the Son of Man* (WMANT, 61; Neukirchen-Vluyn, 1988).
5. See the essay of Anders Hultgård in this volume.
6. *Pace* García Martínez, 'Encore l'apocalyptique', p. 228, citing Lars Hartman.

genetic relationships cannot afford to treat the Jewish and Christian material in isolation.

The most notable and influential attempt in the last decade to treat apocalypticism as a single tradition has been that of the Italian scholar Paolo Sacchi.[1] Sacchi's work has been primarily focused on the Enoch corpus, but it is presented as an approach to Jewish apocalypticism as a whole. Instead of surveying the entire field and looking for common elements, he starts from a particular text, the *Book of the Watchers*, which he takes to be the oldest apocalypse. He then attempts to discover the key to the system of thought in this book and finds it in the explanation of evil, in the idea that evil is before human will as the consequence of an original sin, which has irremediably corrupted Creation. This idea, then, becomes for Sacchi the essence of apocalypticism. He can trace its influence clearly in the Enoch corpus, and he finds it in somewhat different form in *4 Ezra* and *2 Baruch*. Sacchi also finds a place for Daniel in this trajectory, although this is disputed by his disciple, Gabriele Boccaccini.[2] His ideas have been used by García Martínez to argue that apocalypticism has a generative role in the sectarian writings from Qumran.[3]

There is no doubt that Sacchi has pointed to an issue of major importance in several apocalyptic texts and his work is especially helpful in understanding the Enoch material. As an approach to the phenomenon of apocalypticism, however, it has serious disadvantages. Even if the *Book of the Watchers* is the oldest apocalypse, it does not follow that it should be normative for the notion of apocalypticism.[4] As Sacchi himself notes, it is in many ways distinctive, and atypical of the corpus. If we were to restrict the corpus of apocalyptic works to a tradition genetically connected with the Book of the Watchers we would have a very small corpus, excluding even *4 Ezra* and *2 Baruch*, which Sacchi regards as apocalyptic. The origin of evil is not a primary concern of Daniel. Yet Daniel is at least as influential as the *Book of the Watchers* on the later apocalyptic tradition. Apocalyp-

1. Sacchi's essays are now collected in his *L'apocalittica giudaica e la sua storia* (Brescia, 1990).

2. G. Boccaccini, 'E'Daniele un testo apocalittico? Una (ri)definizione del pensiero del Libro di Daniele in rapporto al Libro dei Sogni e all'apocalittica', *Henoch* 9 (1987), pp. 267-99.

3. F. García Martínez, 'Les traditions apocalyptiques à Qumrân', in C. Kappler (ed.), *Apocalypses et voyages*, pp. 201-35.

4. See the criticisms of Tigchelaar, 'More on Apocalyptic and Apocalypses', p. 143.

ticism cannot be defined on the basis of a single book and cannot be restricted to a single strand of tradition.

Apocalyptic Movements

From what we have seen thus far it should be obvious that it is a gross over-simplification to speak of 'the apocalyptic movement'.[1] At the least, we must allow for several movements, at different times, not necessarily connected with each other genetically. Moreover, we should not necessarily posit a community or movement behind every text, although it is the current fashion to do so. There is little evidence that a movement, apocalyptic or other, lies behind a work such as *4 Ezra*.

The main difficulty in speaking about 'apocalyptic movements' in ancient Judaism does not lie in the meaning of the term, but in the lack of social documentation. A movement might reasonably be characterized as apocalyptic if it shares the world-view typical of the apocalypses. The most straightforward example would be a community which used apocalypses as its typical form of expression. The 'chosen righteous' of the Enoch tradition may be a case in point, although we can say very little about them as a community.[2] A movement or community might also be apocalyptic if it were shaped to a significant degree by a specific apocalyptic tradition, or if its world-view could be shown to be similar to that of the apocalypses in a distinctive way. The Essene movement and Qumran community would seem to qualify on both counts. The point at issue here is not the presence of apocalyptic materials in the Qumran library, which is not necessarily significant, but their role in the major sectarian rules, CD and 1QS, which must be taken as authoritative statements of the self-understanding of the sect.[3]

The analogies between *1 Enoch*, *Jubilees* and CD have been rehearsed repeatedly in recent years. It has even been argued (unjustifiably in my opinion) that *Enoch* and *Jubilees* are Essene.[4] CD explicitly alludes both to the *Watchers* (CD 2.18) and to *Jubilees* (CD

---

1. In fairness to W. Schmithals, *The Apocalyptic Movement: Introduction and Interpretation* (Nashville, 1975), it should be noted that the book originally appeared as *Die Apokalyptik: Einführung und Deutung* (Göttingen, 1973).

2. See my discussion in *The Apocalyptic Imagination*, pp. 56-63.

3. See my essay 'Was the Dead Sea Sect an Apocalyptic Community?', in L. Schiffman (ed.), *Archaeology and History in the Dead Sea Scrolls* (JSPS, 8; Sheffield, 1990), pp. 25-51, with primary reference to CD.

4. P.R. Davies, *Behind the Essenes. Ideology and History in the Dead Sea Scrolls* (BJS, 94; Atlanta, 1987), pp. 107-34.

16.3-4), and the line of influence is not in dispute. For our present context it will suffice to point to the Discourse of the Two Spirits, which forms the metaphysical backdrop of the *Community Rule* (1QS 3–4). Here human life is understood as an arena of conflict between spirits or angels of Light and Darkness, which will culminate in an eschatological finale, with 'everlasting blessing and eternal joy in life without end' for the one party and 'shameful extinction in the fire of the dark regions' for the other. The doctrine of the Two Spirits is not derived from *Enoch* or Daniel, and may well be indebted to Persian sources, but the world-view is quintessentially apocalyptic, in its orientation to the supernatural world and its eschatological expectation.

To say that Qumran was an apocalyptic community is not, of course, to describe it exhaustively. As we have seen, apocalypticism allows for many variations and can be combined with various theological traditions. Qumran can be called a halachic community as well as an apocalyptic one. Equally, there is no reason to take Qumran as a paradigm for the social setting of apocalypticism. The designation 'apocalyptic', however, draws attention to an important aspect of the world-view of Qumran, which serves to relate it to some strands of ancient Judaism and to distinguish it from others.

Conclusion

The study of apocalypticism in the past decade has had to sail between the Scylla of those who would identify it with a highly specific tradition and the Charybdis of those who would empty it of all content. Both extremes should be avoided. 'Apocalyptic' is an ambivalent term, insofar as it refers to different kinds of material, but it is not significantly more ambivalent than other terms such as 'prophecy' or 'wisdom' that we freely use to characterize the ancient literature. The way to overcome the ambiguity is not by rhetorical flourishes banning all use of the term (and thereby making room for other demons worse than the first),[1] but by qualifying it and making distinctions where necessary. The use of the term should be controlled by analogy with the apocalyptic texts, and not allowed to float freely as an intuitive 'theological concept'.

There has been a good deal of work over the last decade on matters of definition and categorization. There are still disputed issues in these areas, but there has been substantial progress. At this point in time,

1. E.g. P.R. Davies's adoption of the term 'millenarian' ('The Social World of the Apocalyptic Writings', in R.E. Clements [ed.], *The World of Ancient Israel* [Cambridge, 1989], p. 253).

the greater need is surely for detailed study of particular texts.[1] At the time of writing, one major commentary on an apocalyptic text (*4 Ezra*)[2] is in press, and two others (*1 Enoch* and Daniel)[3] are nearing completion, all in the Hermeneia series. It is to be hoped that these studies will move the debate on apocalypticism to a new level of specificity, since the debates about definitions and terminology are, after all, only prolegomena to the study of the texts.

Appendix

A NEW PROPOSAL ON APOCALYPTIC ORIGINS

One of the more noteworthy shifts in the study of apocalypticism over the last decade or so concerns the vexed question of the origins of the phenomenon. Scholars such as Otto Ploeger and Paul D. Hanson had approached this issue from the area of post-exilic prophecy and attempted to trace the gradual development of apocalyptic eschatology. The alternative approach of von Rad had also looked for apocalyptic themes in the Hebrew Bible, in this case in the wisdom literature. The publication of the Enoch fragments from Qumran, however, gave a new direction to the discussion. It was now apparent that *1 Enoch* rather than Daniel contained the earliest full-blown apocalypses, and there was obvious discontinuity between this material and Hebrew prophecy. Most recent research on apocalyptic origins has worked backwards, by trying to trace the clues in the books of *Enoch* and Daniel as to the matrix in which these specific traditions developed.[4] In both cases, there are indications that point in the direction of Babylon and the eastern Diaspora. Daniel is supposedly an exile in Babylon, and the stories in Daniel 1–6 recount his exploits at the Gentile court. The figure of Enoch has been shown to be modelled to a great extent on Mesopotamian prototypes.

The Mesopotamian background of the Enoch figure was lucidly demonstrated by James VanderKam in his 1984 monograph, *Enoch*

---

1. Compare Kappler, *Apocalypses et voyages*, p. 47.
2. M.E. Stone, *Fourth Ezra* (Hermeneia; Minneapolis, 1990).
3. By G.W. Nickelsburg and the author, respectively.
4. See my essays, 'The Place of Apocalypticism in the Religion of Israel', in *Ancient Israelite Religion. Essays in Honor of Frank Moore Cross* (ed. P.D. Miller *et al.*; Philadelphia, 1987), pp. 539-58; and 'Daniel and His Social World', *Int* 39 (1985), pp. 131-43.

and the Growth of an Apocalyptic Tradition.[1] VanderKam especially underlined the analogies between Enoch and Enmeduranki, king of Sippar, who appears seventh in the Sumerian King List, as Enoch appears seventh from Adam in Genesis.[2] Sippar was center of the cult of Shamash, the sun god. Enoch was associated with the solar calendar. Most importantly, Enmeduranki was the founder of a guild of diviners and a recipient of heavenly revelations. He was taken into the divine assembly and shown the tablets of the gods. Enoch also claimed to have seen the heavenly tablets. Other signicant analogies were noted between Enoch and Utuabzu, the seventh sage, and Utnapishtim the Flood hero, who was taken to live with the gods. All of this suggests that the figure of Enoch as revealer of heavenly mysteries was developed as a Jewish counterpart to Babylonian mythological heroes. The most natural setting for such a development, at least in its earliest stages, was in the Exile or subsequent eastern Diaspora.

VanderKam's study was independently confirmed by the Oslo dissertation of Helge Kvanvig, which was completed in 1984, before VanderKam's book appeared.[3] Kvanvig also emphasizes the Mesopotamian background of the Flood, which also figures prominently in the Enoch tradition and takes on the character of an eschatological paradigm. His study, however, is along the same lines as that of VanderKam and is an extension rather than a correction of it. The cumulative effect of these two books is to make a strong case that the apocalyptic Enoch tradition had its roots in the Babylonian diaspora.

There is no doubt that at least some of the Enoch apocalypses (the Apocalypse of Weeks, the Animal Apocalypse) were composed in the land of Israel. At some point the tradition must have been brought back from Babylon. VanderKam does not speculate on this development. Kvanvig is characteristically more venturesome. On the basis of links between Enoch and Levi in *Jubilees* and Aramaic *Levi*, he decides that the group consisted of Levites, who were opposed to the Jerusalem priesthood. He further notes that Ezra has to ask Levites from Casiphia, 'the place' (temple?), to supply him with ministers for the house of the Lord (Ezra 8.12). Kvanvig admits that there is nothing whatever to link these Levites to the Enoch tradition, but he suggests a connection nonetheless.[4] Interesting though this suggestion

---

1. CBQMS, 16; Washington, 1984.
2. VanderKam, *Enoch*, pp. 38-45.
3. Kvanvig, *Roots of Apocalyptic*. The first part of this book represents Kvanvig's dissertation. He summarizes his agreements and differences with VanderKam on pp. 319-20.
4. Kvanvig, *Roots*, p. 158.

is, however, it is no more than a shot in the dark. There is a strong case that the Enoch tradition was indeed developed in Babylon, and that its tradents returned to the land of Israel at some point. The Enoch literature in itself, however, provides little evidence of a link with Levi, and there is no evidence that the tradition, apart from the P document, was known in the land of Israel before the third century BCE at the earliest. The sociological matrix of this tradition remains a mystery.

Kvanvig's dissertation is published in conjunction with another monograph-length study of the background of the Son of Man in Daniel 7. This is by far the more original, and controversial, part of his work. He claims to have identified, for the first time, the source of this imagery in an Akkadian composition, *The Vision of the Netherworld*. The claim is of great potential significance: if the primary background both of *Enoch* and the visions of Daniel is Babylonian, this would suggest a common matrix for the two main strands in early Jewish apocalypticism. A Mesopotamian background for Daniel has *prima facie* plausibility, in view of the Babylonian setting of Daniel 1–6. Most recent scholarship, however, has interpreted the imagery of Daniel 7 against the background of the Israelite, and ultimately Canaanite, tradition.

It is to Kvanvig's credit that he focuses the discussion on a particular document. He starts, however, with a dubious principle, declared apodictically, that 'since Daniel 7 is a vision, we are most likely to find the underlying tradition represented in visions' (p. 352). He proceeds to examine two Akkadian Dream Visions, *The Death Dream of Enkidu* (pp. 355-88) and *The Vision of the Netherworld* (pp. 389-441). The latter text was first published by E. Ebeling in 1931[1] and is translated by E. Speiser in *ANET*, pp. 109-10. In it, one Kummaya, in a night vision, sees Nergal, the god of the netherworld, seated on a throne. In attendance are the vizier of the netherworld, fifteen gods in hybrid form and 'one man', whose body is black like pitch and his face like the Anzu bird, wearing a red robe and armed with bow and sword. The terrified Kummaya is brought before Nergal, but a counsellor successfully intercedes for his life. Nergal then asks Kummaya why he has dishonored the queen of the netherworld. He identifies the figure he has seen (presumably the 'one man') as 'the exalted shepherd to whom my father, the king of the gods, gives full responsibility', and also refers to 'your begetter', who 'ate the taboo and stamped on the

---

1. *Tod und Leben nach den Vorstellungen der Babylonier* (Berlin/Leipzig, 1931), pp. 1-19. The text is translated in Kvanvig, *Roots*, pp. 389-92.

abomination'. The dreamer awakes, shaken, and proceeds to give praise to Nergal and his queen.

The Akkadian document is fragmentary and its interpretation is debatable at several points. Kvanvig argues that Kummaya should be identified as a son of Esarhaddon, most likely Ashurbanipal.[1] He takes the 'man' who is 'the exalted shepherd' as Sennacherib, and 'your begetter' as Esarhaddon, who was a rebel king in the sense that he changed his father's religious policies.[2] Kvanvig's study of this document deserves careful attention from Assyriologists, but the identifications are not essential to his main thesis about its relation to Daniel 7.

Kvanvig claims that the Akkadian vision and Daniel 7 show 'close correspondence not only in Gattung, structure of content and imagery, but also in the basic elements of content' (p. 536),[3] and he provides a long list of alleged correspondences. The comparison is a *tour de force*, however, which strains the evidence at every point:

1. *Gattung*

It is true that both documents are night visions, but they are quite different in type. The Akkadian vision is a descent to the netherworld, in a mythic-realistic mode, culminating in an explicit message. The action of the vision involves the dreamer directly. Daniel's vision is certainly not located in the netherworld. It is a symbolic vision followed by an interpretation. Unlike the Akkadian dreamer, Daniel is not involved in the action of his dream. With respect to form, the *Vision* is related to the apocalyptic sub-genre of otherworldly journeys, rather than to the symbolic visions of Daniel.

2. *Structure of Content*

Kvanvig claims that his approach is characterized by attention not only to parallels in separate motifs, but to the way they are combined. He outlines the pattern of content under five headings:[4]

    a.   Action of nature (the winds and the sea in Daniel). There is no parallel in the Akkadian vision at this point

    b.   A series of monsters. Daniel describes four beasts of hybrid form. The *Vision* has fifteen gods. Whether these 'monsters'

---

1. Kvanvig, *Roots,* pp. 433-34.
2. Kvanvig provides a valuable discussion of the theme of rebel king in Akkadian literature (pp. 425-37).
3. Kvanvig, *Roots,* p. 536.
4. Kvanvig, *Roots,* p. 452.

are really analogues is very questionable. In any case the pattern of relationships between the gods and the other figures in the *vision* is completely different from the pattern in Daniel. The Akkadian 'monsters' are deities in attendance at the throne of the divine judge, and correspond to the angelic throne attendants in Daniel rather than to the beasts, which are figures of rebellion.

c. God on the throne. In both visions a god is seated for judgment and surrounded by attendants and by fire. The significance of this parallel is diminished, however, by the facts that fire is very frequently associated with theophanies, and that Near Eastern gods are commonly surrounded by their council. The location of the Akkadian judgment scene in the netherworld constitutes a major difference over against Daniel.

d. The judgment. In both visions the god acts as judge, but that is the extent of the parallel. In Daniel the one being judged is a beast from the sea; in the *Vision* it is the visionary himself. In Daniel, the beast is slain; in the Vision there is a reprieve. The focal point of the Akkadian vision lies in the long speech of the judge, Nergal, to the visionary. There is no analogue to this in Daniel.

e. The ideal ruler, designated as a man. In Daniel, the conferral of an everlasting kingdom on 'one like a son of man' is the culminating point of the vision. In the *Vision of the Netherworld* the 'man' who is 'the exalted shepherd' is an historical figure whose reign is already past. He is introduced to serve as an example and contrast with the visionary's father, but he takes no part in the action of the vision. There is no conferral of the kingdom in the Akkadian work. Still less is there any parallel to the definitive, everlasting kingdom of the 'one like a son of man'. Kvanvig's claim of correspondence in the pattern of content in the two visions is not substantiated. The pattern of relationships between the various figures in the two compositions is entirely different. In contrast, the Ugaritic myths, which many scholars adduce as the background of Daniel 7, present a much better parallel, in so far as they involve a 'rider of the clouds' (Baal) who is subordinate to another divine figure (El) and is opposed by the Sea (Yamm).[1]

3. *Specific motifs*

The correspondence in 'basic elements of content' is also limited. Kvanvig exaggerates the similarity between the monsters by juxtaposing the description of each beast in Daniel with features from several monsters in the *Vision*. So, for example, the first beast in Daniel is a lion with eagle's wings. It is made to stand on two feet and is given a human heart. In the Vision, one god is a lion standing on its hind legs, and several have lion heads, while a god with no lion features has wings. All that can be inferred from this evidence is that Daniel is influenced in a general way by the hybrid forms that are typical not only of this text but of Mesopotamian mythology and art. Again, the fact that a human figure appears in both visions is hardly significant. There is no similarity between Daniel's figure on the clouds and the warrior figure in the *Vision*, either in appearance or in his function in the dream. The expression 'one man' occurs in several Akkadian dream reports, just as human figures frequently appear in biblical visions.

Kvanvig buttresses his treatment of the Son of Man with a discussion of the man from the sea in *4 Ezra* 13.[2] Because of the differences between the two visions, he denies that *4 Ezra* could have used Daniel and argues instead for a 'relationship' with the *Vision of the Netherworld*. In *4 Ezra* the man rises from the sea, as the beasts do in Daniel. Kvanvig argues that the sea must have the same meaning in both visions, and that it represents the Akkadian Apsu, the subterranean waters, which could be the home of both good and bad figures. He follows the Ethiopic version of *4 Ezra* 13.3, reading 'this wind (= רוח, spirit) came out of the sea in the resemblance of a man' rather than having the wind carry up a human figure. He then argues that *4 Ezra* and the *Vision* combine two concepts that are not combined elsewhere: first, the rising of a spirit from the netherworld in the form of a man, and second, 'this man is described in the conventional imagery for divine beings which manifest meteorological phenomena'.[3]

---

1. In view of his professed interest in configurations, it is ironic that Kvanvig does not see that the parallels between Daniel and the Ugaritic myth require explanation (p. 508). I will present the arguments for the Ugaritic background (probably mediated through Israelite tradition) at length in my forthcoming commentary on Daniel in the Hermeneia series.

2. Kvanvig, *Roots*, pp. 514-35.

3. Kvanvig, *Roots*, p. 533.

Here again the evidence is being stretched to the breaking point. The identification of the man with the wind, or spirit, is indeed the *lectio difficilior*, but the Ethiopic version is weak support for such an unusual reading and it can be more simply explained as a translation error. The word for 'spirit' is not actually attested in the Akkadian vision, and is supplied in a restoration by Kvanvig. The supposedly shared meteorological imagery requires a high degree of abstraction. The man in Ezra flies on the clouds; the man in the netherworld resembles the Anzu bird. In fact, all *4 Ezra* 13 has in common with the Akkadian vision is that each involves a human figure. On the other hand, *4 Ezra* explicitly refers to the book of Daniel in 12.11, the chapter immediately preceding the vision of the man from the sea. If we bear in mind that the author was not attempting to reproduce Daniel's vision, but using elements from it to construct his own new vision, then it is surely easier to suppose that he is adapting Daniel 7 in ch. 13 than to posit a hypothetical common source.[1]

Kvanvig goes on to speculate that the traditions from the *Vision* were reapplied to the fall of the Babylonian empire and were picked up by the Jewish tradition in that context. The man in Daniel's vision 'could have been identified as Cyrus, or at least been inspired by his rise to power'.[2] All this is very speculative, and depends in any case on the persuasiveness of the initial comparison between the two visions.

Kvanvig's book, in contrast to VanderKam's, might be accused of 'pan-Babylonian' tendencies, and he builds an edifice on the *Vision of the Netherworld* which that fragmentary text cannot support. The exaggeration of his claims is unfortunate, for he has rendered a valuable service to scholarship by bringing new and important material into the discussion. The *Vision of the Netherworld*, and Babylonian traditions about the netherworld, warrant further examination by students of apocalypticism. Its importance lies, however, not in its alleged influence on the 'Son of Man' passages, but as a precedent for the 'tours of hell' that figure so prominently in later apocalypticism.[3]

Neither VanderKam nor Kvanvig would claim that Mesopotamia is the only source of religio-historical traditions in apocalypticism. Of course the biblical tradition was a major influence. Kvanvig also allows for the mingling of Persian and Babylonian traditions after the

---

1. Kvanvig doubts that *4 Ezra* would have changed so much in Daniel's vision (pp. 522-23), but he does not explain why *4 Ezra* and Daniel would have adapted the common source in such different ways.
2. Kvanvig, *Roots*, p. 554.
3. See the study of this sub-genre by Martha Himmelfarb, *Tours of Hell*.

conquests of Cyrus.[1] These books have shown, however, that apocalypticism cannot be adequately explained exclusively within the confines of native Jewish traditions. While many of the tenets of the old *Religionsgeschichtliche Schule* have been discredited, the religious traditions of the Near East and Hellenistic world remain indispensable for the understanding of apocalypticism.

1. See e.g. *Roots*, pp. 543-49.

2

JEWISH APOCALYPTIC TRADITION:
THE CONTRIBUTION OF ITALIAN SCHOLARSHIP*

Gabriele Boccaccini

1. *The Emergence of a New Approach*

The emergence within Italian scholarship of an original approach to
the phenomenon of apocalypticism is the result of many contemporary
and convergent events. The year 1979 saw in Italy the publication of
the first issue of a new journal of Judaic studies (*Henoch*),[1] the foundation of the Italian Society for the Study of Judaism (AISG),[2] and the
launching of the first collection of Old Testament Pseudepigrapha in
Italian.[3] Credit goes first of all to Paola Sacchi, a leading figure in

---

* This article was written during July 1990 in the course of a six-month stay in
the USA as a Visiting Scholar at Princeton Theological Seminary. I would like to
thank John J. Collins and James H. Charlesworth for the opportunity they offered me
to present this contribution on Italian scholarship. Paolo Sacchi, whose work is the
main source of this article, was even so kind as to suggest some insights by letter.
Michael Thomas Davis, a PhD candidate at Princeton Theological Seminary, helped
me to refine language and style and for this I am very grateful.
    1. *Henoch. Rivista di studi storico-filologici* is headed by a board of directors
formed by the most distinguished Italian scholars in the field of Judaic studies,
namely B. Chiesa, G. Garbini, L. Moraldi, P. Sacchi, J.A. Soggin, G. Tamani, and
A. Vivian. The editorial board is constituted by G. Boccaccini, P.G. Borbone, and L.
Rosso Ubigli. The publisher is Zamorani (Corso S. Maurizio 25, 10100 Torino,
Italy). P. Sacchi was the first chief director and maintained that position until last
year, when he retired and was replaced by the present director, B. Chiesa.
    2. Since 1979, the Associazione Italiana per lo Studio del Giudaismo (AISG) has
been the primary society for Italian scholars in the field of Judaic studies. The Associ-
azione sponsors projects of research dealing in particular with the conservation of the
Jewish heritage in Italy. Every fall it holds its annual conference which includes Italian and foreign scholars. P. Sacchi was the first president and maintained that
position until last year when he retired and was replaced by the current president, F.
Parente.
    3. P. Sacchi (ed.), *Apocrifi dell'Antico Testamento*.

Judaic studies, professor of Hebrew and Aramaic at the Department of Oriental Studies of the University of Turin.[1] His efforts have been supported by a group of his collaborators, principally Liliana Rosso Ubigli and myself. The purpose of the present study is to focus on the Italian contribution to Jewish apocalyptic tradition.

The starting point is a series of studies, dealing with the pseudepigraphon *1 Enoch*. The publication of the fragment 4QEn^a by Milik in 1976[2] proved beyond all shadow of doubt that the dating traditionally accepted by modern research was mistaken. As the text of that fragment was written by a scribe living in the first half of the second century BCE, *1 Enoch* did not, as generally thought, date from the first century BCE, using material going back about a hundred years. *1 Enoch* was much older. Studying the *Book of the Watchers*, the first and oldest book of the Enochic collection, Sacchi was able to identify five different strata, including an even older *Book of Noah*.[3] Such a complex stratification implied a very long redactional process, whose beginning had to reach back to the fifth century BCE.

1 Enoch revealed itself as an exceptional document for our knowledge of the Second Temple period. It is a collection of five books (six, if we consider the *Book of the Giants*). Through a consistent system of literary connections, allusions, and quotations, each book consciously refers to the preceding one(s). When an editor living towards the end of the first century BCE brought them together into a single volume, he was aware that they belonged to the same tradition of thought, in spite of the often strong theological differences between one book and the other.

The identification of such a long and important tradition, covering five centuries in the history of Jewish thought, raised a series of questions. What is the generative idea of this tradition? Which other documents are related to this tradition? What is the relationship between this tradition and the other traditions of Jewish thought in the Second Temple period? As *1 Enoch* is generally referred to as an 'apocalyptic' document, a rethinking of the meaning of this term was immediately necessary. It became impossible, for example, to speak of

1. Dipartimento di Orientalistica, Universita di Torino (via S. Ottavio 21, 10100 Torino, Italy).

2. J.T. Milik, with M. Black (ed.), *The Books of Enoch: Aramaic Fragments of Qumran Cave 4* (Oxford, 1976).

3. P. Sacchi, 'Il "Libro dei Vigilanti" e l'apocalittica'.

an 'apocalyptic' phenomenon born at the beginning of the second century BCE in the wake of the Maccabean revolt.[1]

Sacchi agreed with Carmignac[2] that the adjective 'apocalyptic'
describes the documents that possess the same literary genre as Revelation (named for its *incipit*: *apocalypsis Iesou Christou*). Sacchi also
agreed with Collins[3] who sees, in this literary genre, a linkage of a
certain complex of ideas. The analysis of frequency of the most
recurrent themes in the apocalypses shows that the 'apocalyptic' genre
is an expression of a wide cultural phenomenon that was spread well
beyond the borders of Israel. The apocalypses witness to not only a
form but a content; they are the vehicles of a definitive 'world-view'.

So we can legitimately define and delimit on a formal basis within
Jewish literature a literary *corpus* (the 'apocalypses'), and catalogue
the themes related to this *corpus*, even the related 'world-view'
('apocalypticism'). What Sacchi stressed, however, was that neither the
'apocalyptic' literary genre, nor the 'apocalyptic' world-view constitute a tradition of thought (or even a family of traditions), which may
be compared with 'other' Jewish traditions of thought, such as
Pharisaism, Essenism, and early Christianity.

As emphasized in my 'E'Daniele un testo apocalittico?', the presence
of certain recurring themes, even the same recurring themes, is not
enough for the identification of a tradition of thought. Not only can an
identical form be used by different traditions, but identical ideas (even
the same 'world-view') can assume a different meaning (a role, a
specific weight) in different contexts. It is well put by Sanders when he
writes: 'One may consider the analogy of two buildings. Bricks which
are identical in shape, color and weight could be used to construct two
different buildings which are totally unlike each other.'[4] Two
documents do not necessarily belong to the same tradition of thought
because they share the same literary genre and the same world-view.
An ideological affinity exists only if they have consciously organized
and developed their thoughts out of the same generative idea.

---

1. See D.S. Russell, *The Method and Message of Jewish Apocalyptic*
(Philadelphia, 1964).

2. J. Carmignac, 'Qu'est-ce que l'apocalyptique?', *RevQ* 10 (1979), pp. 3-33.

3. J.J. Collins (ed.), *Apocalypse: The Morphology of a Genre* (*Semeia* 14; Missoula, MT, 1979). Also see by the same author, *The Apocalyptic Imagination* (New
York, 1984); and J.H. Charlesworth, 'The Apocalypse of John: Its Theology and
Impact on Subsequent Apocalypses', *The New Testament Apocrypha and Pseudepigrapha* (Metuchen, NJ, 1987).

4. E.P. Sanders, *Paul and Palestinian Judaism* (Philadelphia, 1977). This quotation from Sanders does not imply agreement with all the aspects of his methodology.

The possibility of a comparative analysis depends on the results of this ideological check. In order to be correct, such an analysis must only be made between commensurable units, that is, between sets defined according to homogeneous criteria. If the apocalyptic phenomenon is only a literary genre (albeit one including its own definite 'world-view'), it can be compared only with other 'forms' of Jewish literature, such as poetry, testaments, halakah, midrash, and hymns, each with its own definite 'world-view'. At the very most we could ask why a certain movement of thought tends to prefer one or another literary genre, that is, one or another 'world-view'. But only an 'apocalyptic' tradition defined according to ideological criteria—if such a tradition does exist—can be compared to other Jewish ideological traditions. Neither Christianity, nor Pharisaism, nor Essenism is a phenomenon defined according to literary criteria.

The study of *1 Enoch* shows that we can also speak of an 'apocalyptic' tradition of thought, which is witnessed first of all by the continuity of the Enochic tradition. The composite and multiform structure of *1 Enoch*, on the other hand, shows how this 'apocalyptic' tradition is expressed historically through different literary genres. The inclusion of a document within the 'apocalyptic' tradition has to be weighed critically according to purely ideological criteria. It should not be taken for granted as the result of a literary affinity. The research on the historical development of the 'apocalyptic' genre (and of its 'world-view'), as well as the analysis of its relationship with the many Judaisms of that time (including the 'apocalyptic' tradition), are both very significant and necessary tasks. Any confusion between the formal (and form-content) level and the ideological level, however, must be carefully avoided.

Sacchi's first contribution on *1 Enoch* was published in 1979 in the opening issue of the journal *Henoch*. The following years were devoted to identifying the inner characteristics of the 'apocalyptic' tradition.[1] The research showed that the 'apocalyptic' tradition is not a homogeneous and static system. We are dealing with a complex and dynamic trend of thought which covers a long period of time, bears developments and deepenings, and therefore cannot be fitted entirely into a unitary scheme or a univocal definition. Yet, in spite of all the differences, it is possible to identify its core in a peculiar conception of

---

1. See the first volume of the *Apocrifi dell'Antico Testamento*; L. Rosso Ubigli, 'Dalla Nuova Gerusalemme alla Gerusalemme Celeste: contributo per la comprensione dell'apocalittica'; P. Sacchi, 'Ordine cosmico e prospettiva ultraterrena nel postesilio. Il problema del male e l'origine dell'apocalittica', and mostly his 'Riflessioni sull'essenza dell'apocalittica: peccato d'origine e libertà dell'uomo'.

evil, understood as an autonomous reality, antecedent even to humankind's ability to choose. This conception of evil is not simply one of so many 'apocalyptic' ideas; it is the generative idea of a distinct ideological tradition of thought, the corner-stone on which and out of which the whole 'apocalyptic' tradition is built.

After having identified in the history of Jewish thought a very ancient 'apocalyptic' tradition, it became possible to compare this tradition with other Jewish (and non-Jewish) traditions of thought. Two articles by A. Loprieno[1] explored the bounds between the Jewish 'apocalyptic' and some Egyptian traditions of thought. In particular, the research on the Jewish wisdom literature immediately revealed itself rich and interesting.[2] The polemical interlocutors of Job, Qohelet and Ben Sira ceased to be anonymous and indefinite. Facing the apocalyptic tradition, the wisdom authors met the challenges of a contemporary tradition, which was bearer of an autonomous and alternative system of thought. For the team of scholars involved with Sacchi in the Italian edition of and commentary on the Old Testament Pseudepigrapha,[3] the 'apocalyptic' tradition has become a familiar and indispensable notion for understanding those ancient documents.

As a result of ten years of research, our understanding of Jewish thought in the Second Temple period has become richer and the debates within Judaism on the eve of the Christian era much clearer. Problems like the origin of evil, the freedom of human will, the sources of knowledge, and the value of the Law for salvation, were not the product of foreign (Hellenistic) influences, but open questions within Judaism itself. Alternative solutions, each deeply rooted in the religious experience of the Jewish people, stood face to face for centuries and would impassion and divide generation after generation, finally leading to the great schism in the late first century CE between Christians and Pharisees.

With the identification of the 'apocalyptic' tradition and of its generative idea, it became possible also to assess the inclusion of other documents within this tradition, according to definitive ideological

---

1. A. Loprieno, 'Il pensiero egizio e l'apocalittica giudaica'; and 'Il modello egiziano nei testi della letteratura intertestamentaria'.

2. See P. Sacchi, 'Giobbe e il Patto (Gb. 9.32-33)'; L. Rosso Ubigli, 'Qohelet di fronte all'apocalittica'; G. Boccaccini, 'Origine del male, libertà dell'uomo e retribuzione nella Sapienza di Ben Sira'.

3. F. Franco, L. Fusella, A. Loprieno, F. Pennacchietti, L. Rosso Ubigli, and P. Sacchi are the scholars who prepared the first volume. P. Bettiolo, G. Boccaccini, M. Enrietti, M. Lana, P. Marrassini, L. Rosso Ubigli, and P. Sacchi worked on the second volume.

criteria. This analysis led Sacchi to exclude the Christian 'apocalyptic' documents (such as Revelation). Christianity is the expression of a related, yet different, tradition of thought. The interpolation of *1 En.* 71.14, belonging to a very ancient phase of its transmission, shows that the 'apocalyptic' tradition was not only earlier but contemporary to first-century Christianity, maintaining its own autonomy. How is it possible to think of Revelation and the *Book of Parables* as belonging to the same tradition, when for the former the 'Son of Man' is Jesus of Nazareth (Rev. 1.12-18) and for the latter that eschatological figure is Enoch (*1 En.* 71.14)? A detailed check[1] also suggested to me that Daniel could not be included within the 'apocalyptic' tradition, and affirmed the deep shift that may exist between documents sharing the same imagery, and even the same world-view.

On the other hand, since his first attempt at a comprehensive history of the 'apocalyptic' tradition,[2] Sacchi included the *Assumption of Moses*, the *Apocalypse of Zephaniah*, *2 Enoch*, *2 Baruch*, and *4 Ezra*, as the commentaries in the second volume of the *Apocrifi dell'Antico Testamento* would agree. The 'apocalyptic' tradition was discovered to be much broader than the Enochic *corpus*. The field of research became the whole Jewish literature in the Second Temple period.

In the 1980s, this approach to the phenomenon of apocalypticism has played a significant role within Italian scholarship. It has strongly shaped even works not directly linked with the Turin group.[3] Also in the international context the interest (if not the agreement over method) has grown. F. García Martínez has taken up some ideas from Sacchi, and argued a generative role for the apocalyptic tradition in the Qumran movement.[4] J.H. Charlesworth deals extensively with the opinions of Italian scholarship in the Italian edition of *The Old Testament Pseudepigrapha and the New Testament*.[5] J.J. Collins speaks about Sacchi's attempt at an ideological definition of apocalyptic as the 'most notable and influential attempt in the last decade'.[6] Unfortunately, the Italian bibliography is not easy to find, and the works it

1. G. Boccaccini, 'E'Daniele un testo apocalittico? Una (ri)definizione del pensiero del Libro di Daniele in rapporto al Libro dei Sogni e all'apocalittica'.
2. P. Sacchi, 'Per una storia dell'apocalittica'.
3. See esp. B. Marconcini, *L'apocalittica* (Torino-Leumann, 1985); and C. Marcheselli-Casale, *Risorgeremo, ma come?* (Bologna, 1988).
4. F. García Martínez, 'Les traditions apocalyptiques à Qumran', in C. Kappler (ed.), *Apocalypses et voyages dans l'au-delà* (Paris, 1987).
5. J.H. Charlesworth, *Gli pseudepigrafi dell'Antico Testamento e il Nuovo Testamento* (ed. and trans. G. Boccaccini; Brescia, 1990).
6. See Collins's article in the present volume.

contains are not translated. Hence, while this body of literature remains almost barred to students of other countries, it is only partially known even by specialists.

The research, of course, is still in the making, and must be assessed in the broader context of an attempt at a comprehensive history of Jewish thought in the Second Temple period.[1] This is the task in which the Italian scholars mentioned are primarily involved. Summarizing the present results of research, we can already speak of four basic periods of apocalyptic tradition. These tentative conclusions are both the framework and the starting-point of our future research.

2. *An Outline of the History of Apocalyptic Tradition*

a. *First period (fifth–end third century BCE)*
The *Book of the Watchers* is the oldest apocalyptic work still extant.[2] The first of its five strata dates back to the fifth century BCE. The author's interest is centered on the problem of the origin of evil, experienced as a reality which involves humankind, but which is metaphysically autonomous. Sin, with all its unhappy consequences, derives from a 'contamination' of nature which involves both human beings and material things (*1 En.* 10.7; 12.4; 15.3; 19.1). Some angels, smitten with love for women, decided to come down to earth and take wives for themselves (*1 En.* 6.7). The sin of the angels took place at the time of Jared, father of Enoch, and damaged irreparably the whole order of nature. God had given powers of generation only to men because they are mortal (*1 En.* 15.4).

According to some unrelated passages present in this stratum, the cause of evil is to be found above all in the fact that the fallen angels taught women those sciences that were celestial secrets, not to be revealed to humankind (*1 En.* 8–9.6). This idea is not followed up, however; astrology, which is here condemned openly, will become in the later *Book of Astronomy* the basis of all sound knowledge.

Giants were born of the union between angels and women; these monstrous beings filled the earth with sorrow. Following the suppli-

---

1. A brief outline of history of Jewish thought in the Second Temple period can be found in P. Sacchi, 'Da Qohelet al tempo di Gesu', *Aufstieg und Niedergang der römischen Welt* 19.2 (1979), pp. 1-32. See also his 'Introduzione' in the first volume of the *Apocrifi dell'Antico Testamento*, and, mostly, his volume *Storia del mondo giudaico* (Torino, 1976).
2. On the *Book of the Watchers* and its relationship with the 'canonical' Pentateuch, see P. Sacchi, 'Il Libro dei Vigilanti e l'apocalittica', and his commentary on *1 Enoch* in the first volume of the *Apocrifi dell'Antico Testamento*.

cations of humanity and the intercession of the faithful angels, God
threw the rebel angels down to hell and killed the giants. These
measures were not enough, however, to prevent the spread of evil; the
souls of the giants continued to roam freely on the earth (*1 En*. 16.1)
in the form of evil spirits, inciting humankind to evil deeds and
causing damage of every kind.

This account of the fall of the angels was used also by the author of
Gen. 6.1-4 in a brief and demythologized summary; this shows he was
familiar with the myth but did not agree with its interpretation. The
giants were not evil spirits but simply 'the mighty men that were of
old, the men of renown'.

Some scholars maintain that the *Book of the Watchers* is a longer
version of the Genesis story. But the demythologized and very abbre-
viated form of the latter makes it obviously of later date; without the
text of the *Book of the Watchers* we would not understand the tiny
passage in Genesis. The Genesis text can no longer be attributed to J,
but rather to a post-exilic editor.

In the vision of things expressed in the *Book of the Watchers*,
humanity appears at one and the same time as cause and victim of sin,
possibly more victim than cause. In *1 En*. 10.8 it says: 'all sin (or each
sin) must be attributed to Asael', that is, to the leader of the fallen
angels, who later will be called the Devil.

In the subsequent strata of the *Book of the Watchers*, the angelic sin
will be duplicated and pushed further back in time. If the contamination of nature, and therefore the thrust of evil against humankind, was
a product of the time of Jared, the sin of Cain is not explained (*1 En*.
22.7). Other angels sinned even before the Watchers sinned by having
sexual intercourse with women. On the fourth day of creation, the
angels of the seven planets that revolve around the earth carried their
planets outside the orbit ordained by God, damaging creation from the
beginning. Adam was put into a universe already contaminated. This
theme is not touched upon, however, in the *Book of the Watchers*.

Another new element is the concept of the immortality of the soul.
The soul of the dead person no longer descends without being judged
into Sheol, where the just and the unjust alike live a life that is a non-
life, far from the light of the sun and the radiance of God. The souls
of the dead gather in a valley to the extreme west of the earth, where
the just and the unjust are clearly separated, and the just are sheltered
from the attacks of the Evil One. It is from here that the souls will
come forth at the time of the Last Judgment, which will ratify for all
eternity the state of both the blessed and the damned (*1 En*. 22).

Already in his lifetime the individual lives in a two-dimensional universe. Its real world is not this world, but the one in which his soul will continue to live. This world is dominated by evil and will be destroyed at the end, when God wills it, but the just are already saved in the hands of God, waiting to reach the valley in the west where there is no longer suffering or sin. Given these notions, Qohelet's strong criticism against those who believe in the immortality of the soul can be seen to make good sense.[1]

In the final stratum of the work there is a radical change. The better world is no longer far away in the west, open to the souls of the just, but is placed at the end of history and destined for those just who are there in that moment of time. The concept of immortality of the soul loses importance. God will save humanity in this world and not in a spiritual dimension (*1 En.* 25.6).

In the second book of the Enochic collection, the so-called *Book of Astronomy*,[2] sinfulness comes to coincide with humankind's status as creature ('No one of the flesh can be just before the Lord; for they are merely his own creation', *1 En.* 81.5). The book seems to assign *ab aeterno* to each his own individual destiny, to the extent that Enoch can read it in the 'tablets of heaven' (*1 En.* 81.2). Individual responsibility is gravely compromised, salvation is entrusted to an extraordinary intervention by God, and the idea of the Covenant is emptied of all substance. Ben Sira's reflection on the origin of evil, humankind's free will, and the principle of retribution was directed mainly against the apocalyptic tradition.[3]

b. *Second period (second century BCE)*

The *Book of Dream Visions*,[4] written about 163 BCE, presents itself as a story of humankind from the beginning down to the author's own lifetime. History is predetermined and revealed to Enoch in two dream visions.

---

1. On the relationship between Qohelet and the apocalyptic tradition, see L. Rosso Ubigli, 'Qohelet di fronte all'apocalittica'.

2. On the *Book of Astronomy* see P. Sacchi, 'Testi palestinesi anteriori al 200', and his commentary on *1 Enoch* in the first volume of the *Apocrifi dell'Antico Testamento*.

3. On the relationship between Ben Sira and the apocalyptic tradition, see G. Boccaccini, 'Origine del male, libertà dell'uomo e principio retributivo nella Sapienza di Ben Sira'.

4. On the *Book of Dream Visions*, see P. Sacchi's commentary on *1 Enoch* in the first volume of the *Apocrifi dell'Antico Testamento*.

The thought of the *Book of Dream Visions* is more systematic than those of the *Book of the Watchers* and the *Book of Astronomy*. There is a leading rebel angel (he now could be called the Devil), who is the true and proper principle of evil. He is a creature who took advantage of his liberty to rebel against God and to encourage other angels and human beings to do the same. Neither the intervention of the good angels to reduce the rebels to impotence (*1 En.* 87–88), nor the Flood is able to eradicate evil from the earth. The three sons of righteous Noah are not the same; only Shem is like his father, while Japheth is violent and Ham is profoundly evil (*1 En.* 89.9). History witnesses a continuous expansion of evil, with no way for humankind to oppose its spread. The vision scrupulously goes over the various episodes of the ancient history of Israel, but no reference is made to the Covenant on Sinai. The idea of the Covenant presupposes a recognition of the individual's freedom of choice between obedience and transgression. In the *Book of Dream Visions* the idea that the individual can be responsible for its own salvation is simply unthinkable; only God's intervention can oppose evil. The ideal of the just person who fulfills the Law is replaced by the figure of the elect who is chosen and justified by God.

After the Babylonian exile the situation collapses; the seventy angels, who were entrusted by God to watch over and govern Israel, transgressed in such a way that the entire history of Israel in the post-exilic period unfolds under a demonic influence (*1 En.* 89.59ff.).

God limits himself to watching the dramatic succession of events. History has to follow its course until the final catharsis when the divine judgment is pronounced and the world is purified of evil. God's wrath can thus be laid to rest and the Messiah, prototype of a new humanity, is to guide the eschatological reign. There is no further question of the immortality of the soul. The world that is blessed and free from evil is the world to come.

Against this view, the contemporary book of Daniel tries to show that the decline of history is neither the consequence of an angelic sin, nor the effect of an evil force, but the right punishment by God for the transgression of the Covenant. Through the concept of resurrection the author stresses that the Law remains, even in a condemned history, the criterion of an individual's judgment.[1]

---

1. On the relationship between Daniel and the *Book of Dream Visions*, see G. Boccaccini, 'E'Daniele un testo apocalittico? Uno (ri)definizione del pensiero del Libro di Daniele in rapporto al Libro dei Sogni e all'apocalittica'.

c. *Third period (first century BCE–early first century CE)*

The third apocalyptic period bears witness to a serious internal crisis. The apocalyptic tradition now faces the problem of human responsibility. The *Epistle of Enoch*[1] is peremptory in tone. At least in the form in which it has come down to us, it no longer speaks of fallen angels, but stresses the responsibility of humankind for sin. 'In the same manner that a mountain has never turned into a servant... likewise, neither has sin been sent upon earth. It is humankind who have themselves created it, and those who commit it are destined to be accursed' (*1 En.* 98.4). The author maintains, however, that the whole history is predetermined and that sin is an evil force, and not simply a transgression or the consequence of human freedom. Only in the fourth apocalyptic period will there be an attempt to reconcile the responsibility of humankind for sin and the general contamination of nature.

In particular, the third apocalyptic period develops the theme of mediation. Between God and humankind superhuman figures (such as the Son of Man in *1 Enoch*, or Melchizedek in *2 Enoch*)[2] appear, to whom the apocalyptic writers give functions which were formerly seen as God's prerogatives. The idea that it should be God himself, who at the Great Judgment condemns sinners, seems to be repugnant to the apocalyptic writers of this period. The more the Judgment is seen as terrible and inexorable, the more the function of Judge is taken away from God and given to others. In the *Epistle of Enoch* it will be the Watchers themselves (*1 En.* 91.15) who exercise judgment over humankind. It is in the *Book of Parables*, however, that this theme is most highly developed. Its author abandons the broad outline of human history as predetermined by God that characterizes the *Book of Dream Visions* and the *Epistle of Enoch*, and returns to a vision of things closer to that of the early phase of apocalyptic tradition. Predestination no longer has its place in history but only in the fate of the individual: 'The Lord of the Spirits created the distinction between light and darkness, and separated the spirits of the people' (*1 En.* 41.8). The

---

1. On the *Epistle of Enoch* and the *Book of Parables*, see P. Sacchi, 'Enoc etiopico 91.15 e il problema della mediazione', and his commentary on *1 Enoch*, in the first volume of the *Apocrifi dell'Antico Testamento*.

2. On Enoch and Melchizedek as superhuman figures, see L. Rosso Ubigli, 'La fortuna di Enoc nel giudasmo antico', and C. Gianotto, *Melchizedek e la sua tipologia*. On *2 Enoch* in particular, see Sacchi's commentary in the second volume of the *Apocrifi dell'Antico Testamento*.

influence of the Essenic doctrine of the two spirits seems apparent here
(cf. 1QS 3.15-19).[1]

The attention of the author is drawn to the heavenly world again,
where both the faithful angels and the souls of the just dwell. Evil
came about by the sin of the angels and, guided by the *Book of Dream
Visions*, the author distinguishes the angel who committed the first sin
(the Devil) from the fallen angels (*1 En.* 54, 55, and 59); the judgment
seems only to look at the latter and never at the former (*1 En.* 61.8).
Even this idea probably owes its existence to the influence of the
Essene tradition, for which the Devil is created as such by God and,
therefore, cannot be judged for what he has done. A new concept of
evil appears in the *Book of Parables*. It is linked to an idea that was
first expressed in the *Book of the Watchers* but was not taken up again;
the cause of evil is not a contamination of nature but rather the disclosure of heavenly secrets, those concerning science and the arts and
above all the construction of arms (*1 En.* 64.1-2).

The gaze of the author is above all directed toward the present, and
he identifies the wicked as all those who wield some sort of power in
the world. Science has given power to some human beings: that is, the
ability to oppress other human beings. The powerful of this world are
the only sinners and their sin, as is said repeatedly, is above all else a
sin of pride (*1 En.* 48.8-10).

The just person is the reverse of the sinner. As the sinner is the one
who has the power to oppress, so the just is the one without the
strength to defend himself. The fact that an individual lives in either of
these conditions does not seem to depend on anything else than God's
choice. It is not by chance that the just is usually called 'the chosen
one'.

But the climax and most characteristic element in the thought of the
Book of Parables is the figure of an eschatological savior called the
'Son of Man', which depends obviously on the vision in Daniel 7. The
Son of Man has the power to reveal the true justice of God. This
evidently does not coincide with what has already been revealed, that is
to say, with the Law (*1 En.* 48.1-3). The Son of Man will cast down
kings from their thrones, rub the faces of the powerful in the dust, fill
them with shame and make their seats into darkness (*1 En.* 46.4-6).

The Son of Man was created before the stars (*1 En.* 48.3), he will be
the light of the people and the hope of all who suffer. This Son of Man
is also called Messiah (*1 En.* 48.10) and thus the messianic function is

---

1. On the Dead Sea Scrolls, see L. Moraldi, *I manoscritti di Qumran* (Torino,
1971; 2nd edn, 1987).

welded on to that of the Son of Man. There will be a final and ineluctable Day of Judgment for evildoers and the world to come will be then inaugurated, a world in which 'the Lord of the Spirits will live above humankind and these will live, eat, sleep and rise with that Son of Man' (*1 En.* 62.14).

This figure of the Son of Man meets the demands existing in Jewish thought and turns them into a fairly coherent system. Already in the book of *Jubilees*, written in the second century BCE and ideologically very close to Essenism and to the apocalyptic tradition,[1] God had foreseen that he himself would dwell on earth with humankind (*Jub.* 1.26). Now, in the *Book of Parables*, God remains in heaven, but his representative will be seen on earth and will dwell for ever among humankind. On the other hand, the Judgment of destruction and condemnation will not be carried out directly by God, as foreseen in the earlier periods of the apocalyptic tradition, but by his representative. Mercy is claimed as the fundamental attribute of God (*1 En.* 50.4); the violent realization of his justice is the duty of his Messiah.

These ideas are fundamental for an understanding of Jesus and his movement. In particular, the Christian concept of the Son of Man depends strongly on the *Book of Parables*. However, there is a very important development. The eschatological judge of the apocalyptic tradition turns, in Jesus' teaching and in his own self-consciousness, above all into him who 'has the authority on earth to forgive sins' (Mk 2.10; Mt. 9.6; Lk. 5.24).[2]

d. *Fourth period (late first and early second centuries CE)*

If the third apocalyptic period shows traces of Essene doctrine, the fourth is explicable mainly in the light of problems arising from the Christian and Pharisaic traditions. We cannot understand the last developments of the Jewish apocalyptic tradition apart from the Pharisaic reaffirmation of the centrality of the Law in the life of Israel on one hand, and the messianic speculations of Christianity on the other hand. In *2 Baruch*,[3] dating from towards the end of the first century, there is an attempt to clarify the relationship between the idea

---

1. On the book of *Jubilees*, see Sacchi's commentary in the first volume of the *Apocrifi dell'Antico Testamento*.

2. On Jesus' conception of the Son of Man, see P. Sacchi, 'Il messianismo ebraico dalle origini al II sec. d.C.', *Quaderni di Vita Monastica* 38 (1988), pp. 14-38.

3. On *2 Baruch* and *4 Ezra* see P. Sacchi, 'L'apocalittica del I sec.: peccato e giudizio', and the commentaries by P. Bettiolo and P. Marrassini respectively in the second volume of the *Apocrifi dell'Antico Testamento*.

of predestination and the demands of human freedom and responsibility.

Predestination is limited to the plane of history in general, which unfolds according to a divine plan and is divided into twelve periods. The author's concept of history is expressed in ch. 53 through 'the vision of light and dark waters'. According to the usual line of apocalyptic thought, the dark element gets stronger and stronger until the Messiah appears. He has superhuman traits like the Son of Man in the *Book of Parables* and the New Testament. This Messiah appears both at the beginning and at the end of history, but shares neither in creation (unlike the Gospel of John) nor in the Last Judgment (unlike the *Book of Parables*). The idea of *mediation*, which was so important for the third apocalyptic period as well as for Christianity, disappears. The superhuman Messiah limits himself to condemning to death on Mt Zion the last earthly king, prior to the resurrection and the Last Judgment (*2 Bar.* 3).

With regard to sin, the author knows the myth of the sin of the angels and women (*2 Bar.* 56.10-13), but is unaware of its implications. He also knows the sin of Adam (cf. Paul), but stresses that Adam was simply a bad model for those who would come after him (*2 Bar.* 18.2). The angels themselves sinned by following the example of Adam (*2 Bar.* 56.10-11). The relationship between humankind and angels is reversed: sin began with humankind and not with angels, and it is stressed that the angels sinned 'because they were free' (*2 Bar.* 56.11); humankind and angels are both free.

The last of the great Jewish apocalypses is that of *4 Ezra* which, according to most recent research, belongs to the beginning of the second century rather than to the end of the first. It is the most complex of all the apocalyptic works, and its comprehensibility is obscured by the strong emotion displayed by the author.

The work is shot through with a profound pessimism about the fate of humanity. Rather like Job, the author complains to God about his injustice toward humankind in general and the Jews in particular. He does not understand why such a terrible disaster has overtaken Jerusalem, and no more does he understand why all humankind should be enveloped in the catastrophe of sin. The work gives the impression of a meditation on the unhappiness of humanity, but the unhappiness the author has in mind is not that of suffering and death, but rather of the final destiny of humankind which for him, with few exceptions, is eternal perdition.

The angelic sin has vanished off his horizon; the fall of the angels is not even mentioned. The emphasis is on the sin of humanity, but above all the sin of Adam. The former depends on the latter, in contrast to *2 Baruch*. At the center of our author's meditation is the Law (*4 Ezra* 8.19-20; 9.31-32). In his justice God offered the Law to all humankind, but only Israel accepted it; such is the meaning of its election. This implies the damnation of all pagans because they have refused the Law. The situation of the Jews is no better, however. They certainly possess the Law, but they transgress it. No one is without sin; this is the recurring idea. No one can save himself because the individual is fully responsible for his evil deeds (*4 Ezra* 3.8; 7.72, 104, 127; 8.56-58).

On the other hand, in juxtaposition with the idea that humankind is entirely free and therefore entirely responsible, the author of *4 Ezra* places the idea that Adam, besides the gift of free will, had something else even more powerful. According to the Latin text, which is the language in which *4 Ezra* has come down to us, Adam had a *cor malignum* ('evil heart'), which gave rise to the sin (*cor enim malignum baiulans primus Adam transgressus est*: 'led by his evil heart, Adam first transgressed', *4 Ezra* 3.21).

The concept of an evil heart corresponds closely with the *yeser hara'* of the rabbinic tradition, but the idea held by the author differs from it because he considers it a truly evil (if not satanic) power, stronger than the individual's capacity to choose. 'Adam was defeated by it, as were also all who were born of him. It produced an everlasting disease: the Law was in the people's heart along with the evil root. What was good disappeared and the evil remained' (*4 Ezra* 3.21-22). The Flood was useless; even after it the evil heart was still in the world. The gift of the Law on Sinai was unable to bear fruit (*4 Ezra* 3.20, 27). Nothing remains except to curse Adam and in a certain sense also the One (God) who is ultimately responsible for the situation: 'It would have been better if the earth [this term is an euphemism for God] had not produced Adam, or at least having produced him, had restrained him from sinning... Adam, what have you done? When you sinned, the fall not only affected you, but also us who are your descendants. What good is it to us, if an eternal age has been promised to us, but we have done deeds that bring death?' (*4 Ezra* 7.117-19).

God's reply does not show a way out, nor give a more realizable hope. 'This is the meaning of the struggle in which everyone born on earth has to engage; if he is defeated he shall suffer the consequences, but if he is victorious, he shall receive what I have promised' (*4 Ezra* 7.116-28).

So, without being able to offer an answer to the questions raised in the course of its long history, the apocalyptic tradition goes downhill.

The success of Christianity and Rabbinism as the two winning Judaisms of antiquity would depend strongly on their ability to meet the questions of a questioning generation with more coherent and reassuring words.

3. *Conclusion*

This brief outline shows how rich an ideological approach to the phenomenon of apocalypticism can be. We have identified not only a literary genre or a world-view, but also a tradition of thought: that is, one of the Judaisms of the Second Temple period. We do not know what this tradition was called or what it called itself in ancient times. The fact that a large number of the 'apocalypses' belongs to this tradition, not to mention the weight of (ab)use which has given an ideological sense to the term as well, authorizes Sacchi's decision to denote this tradition of thought 'apocalyptic'. Another label might be chosen, of course; VanderKam for example suggests using the term 'Enochic tradition'.[1] The same tradition of thought, however, also continues in documents where the figure of Enoch is not central, or is even missing (*2 Baruch, 4 Ezra*). *2 Enoch* is a case in point. In the first section of the document the protagonist is the revealer, Enoch, while in the final section—where there is no longer a revealer—the leading figure becomes Melchizedek. The changing of protagonist does not disturb the ideological continuity.

While the term 'apocalypse' denotes a peculiar literary genre and 'apocalypticism' the world-view of the apocalypses, the 'apocalyptic' tradition cannot be defined as the tradition of thought of the apocalypses. It is rather one of the Jewish traditions of the Second Temple period, which, like other contemporary traditions, was influenced by apocalypticism and wrote apocalypses.

The fact that most works of the apocalyptic tradition are actually apocalypses does not mean that these two sets are coincident, nor that this tradition is a sort of 'subgroup' of an 'apocalyptic' corpus defined according to literary criteria. The documents belonging to the apocalyptic tradition are neither all, nor only apocalypses; some of the major apocalypses (such as Daniel or Revelation) belong to different (if not opposite) traditions of thought.

Within the 'apocalyptic' literary genre, the 'apocalyptic' world-view, and the 'apocalyptic' tradition, there is the same relationship as

---

1. J.C. VanderKam, *Enoch and the Growth of an Apocalyptic Tradition* (Washington, DC, 1984).

within the genre 'halakah', the 'halakic' world-view, and the Rabbinic tradition. Although most material of the Rabbinic tradition is 'halakic' in shape and content, we find the genre 'halakah' even in other Jewish traditions of thought (Essenism, Early Christianity, Philo, etc.). On the other hand, the Rabbinic tradition knows (uses and is influenced by) other literary genres and other world-views (including the apocalyptic one).

Perhaps calling a literary genre, a world-view, and a tradition of thought (three distinct and non-overlapping categories) by the same adjective 'apocalyptic' may appear to be a slipshod use of terminology. Yet this choice has had the great merit of making us more aware of the necessity of further specification in the use of the term 'apocalyptic'. It has prevented us from inappropriate comparison between incommensurable sets. We have learned, above all, that using 'apocalyptic' in absolute terms may be today (after at least a century of overuse) radically misleading. We should *always* specify whether we mean the apocalyptic literary genre, the apocalyptic world-view, or the apocalyptic tradition.

The problem is not terminological. It deals with method. Terms may be interchangeable; hermeneutical categories such as literary genre, world-view, and tradition of thought are not. The call to a better methodological clarity in the study of the 'apocalyptic' phenomenon remains valid, whatever the labels we decide to use in cataloguing the different aspects of this complex phenomenon.

4. *Selected Italian Bibliography (1979–89)*

1979

Sacchi, P., 'Il "Libro dei Vigilanti" e l'apocalittica", *Henoch* 1, pp. 42-92.
Ubigli, L. Rosso, 'Alcuni aspetti della concezione della "porneia" nel tardo giudaismo', *Henoch* 1, pp. 201-45.

1980

Ubigli, L. Rosso, 'Le apocalissi intertestamantarie', *Parole di Vita* 25, pp. 335-48.

1981

Sacchi, P. (with F. Franco, L. Fusella, A. Loprieno, F. Pennacchietti, and L. Rosso Ubigli), *Apocrifi dell'Antico Testamento. Vol. I: Achicar, 3 Ezra, Giubilei, 1 Enoc, Testamenti dei Dodici Patriarchi* (Torino).
Ubigli, L. Rosso, 'Dalla "Nuova Gerusalemme" alla "Gerusalemme celeste". Contributo per la comprensione dell'apocalittica', *Henoch* 3 (1981), pp. 69-79.
Loprieno, A., 'Il pensiero egizio e l'apocalittica giudaica', *Henoch* 3, pp. 289-317.

1982

Luciani, F., 'La funzione profetica di Enoc (Sir. 44.16b secondo la versione greca)', *Rivista Biblica* 30, pp. 215-24.

Sacchi, P., 'Ordine cosmico e prospettiva ultraterrena nel post-esilio. Il problema del male e l'origine dell'apocalittica', *Rivista Biblica* 30, pp. 11-33.
Sacchi, P., 'Giobbe e il Patto (Gb. 9.32-33)', *Henoch* 4, pp. 175-83.
Sacchi, P., 'Riflessioni sull'essenza dell'apocalittica: peccato d'origine e libertà dell'uomo', *Henoch* 5, pp. 31-58.

1983
Luciani, F., 'Le vicende di Enoc nell'interpretazione di Filone Alessandrino', *Rivista Biblica* 31, pp. 43-68.
Ubigli, L. Rosso, 'Qohelet di fronte all'apocalittica', *Henoch* 5, pp. 31-58.
Ubigli, L. Rosso, 'Il quadro ideologico delle apocalissi della fine I sec. d.C.', in *Atti del II Convegno dell'AISG (Idice Bologna, 4-5 novembre 1981)* (Roma), pp. 101-12.

1984
Gianotto, C., *Mechisedek e la sua tipologia* (Brescia).
Ubigli, L. Rosso, 'La fortuna di Enoc nel giudaismo antico', *Annali di Storia dell'Esegesi* 1, pp. 153-63.

1985
Sacchi, P., 'Enoc Etiopico 91.15 e il problema della mediazione', *Henoch* 7, pp. 257-67.
Sacchi, P., 'Per una storia dell'apocalittica', in *Atti del III Convegno dell'AISG (Idice, Bologna, 9-11 novembre 1982)* (Roma), pp. 257-67.

1986
Boccaccini, G., 'Origine del male, libertà dell'uomo e retribuzione nella Sapienza di Ben Sira', *Henoch* 8, pp. 1-35.
Loprieno, A., 'Il modello egiziano nei testi della letteratura intertestamentaria', *Rivista Biblica* 34, pp. 205-32.
Sacchi, P., 'Testi palestinesi anteriori al 200 a.C.', *Rivista Biblica* 34, pp. 183-204.
Sacchi, P., 'L'apocalittica giudaica', in *L'ebraismo* (Quaderni della Fondazione S. Carlo) (Modena), pp. 31-47.

1987
Boccaccini, G., 'E'Daniele un testo apocalittico? Una (ri)definizione del pensiero del Libro di Daniele in rapporto al Libro dei Sogni e all'apocalittica', *Henoch* 9, pp. 267-99.
Boccaccini, G., 'Prospettive universalistiche nel tardo giudaismo', in *Testimoni fino all'estremità della terra* (Bologna), pp. 81-98.
Sacchi, P., 'L'apocalittica del I sec.: peccato e giudizio', in B. Chiesa (ed.), *Correnti culturali e movimenti religiosi del giudaismo. Atti del V Congresso internazionale dell'AISG (S. Miniato, Pisa, 12-15 novembre 1984)* (Roma, pp. 59-77.

1988
Grossi, V. (ed.), 'Cristianesimo e giudaismo: eredità e confronti. XVI incontro di studiosi dell'antichità cristiana', *Augustinianum* 28.

1989
Prato, G.L. (ed.), 'Israele alla ricerca di identità tra il III sec. a.C. e il I sec. d.C. Atti del V Convegno di studi veterotestamentari', *Ricerche Storico Bibliche* 1.
Sacchi P. (with P. Bettiolo, G. Boccaccini, M. Enrietti, M. Lana, P. Marrassini, and L. Rosso Ubigli), *Apocrifi dell'Antico Testamento. Vol. II: Salmi di Salomone, 2 Baruc, 4 Ezra, Apocalisse di Mose (Vita di Adamo ed Eva), 2 Enoc* (Torino).

1990
Sacchi, P., *L'apocalittica giudaica e la sua storia* (Brescia, 1990).

3

THE APOCALYPTIC CONSTRUCTION OF REALITY IN *1 ENOCH*

George W.E. Nickelsburg

The collection of texts known as *1 Enoch* is universally considered to be an 'apocalyptic' work.[1] In *Semeia* 14, the members of the SBL Genres Project accept this description, and place the different components of the collection in particular categories of texts in which otherworldly revelation of various sorts was mediated in a variety of ways.[2] In this essay I shall not dwell on the issue of genre as such. I agree that the different parts of *1 Enoch* embody the notion of revelation in different, somewhat stereotyped, literary forms or subforms. I am concerned, rather, to demonstrate that, in the variety of Enochic texts, the claim to revelation plays an essential role in a common world-view or construction of reality. Specifically, in a world that people perceive as the locus of alienation, oppression, and injustice, the seer presents evidence of salvation by transmitting a revelation about the future or the remote places in the cosmos, where the reality and promise of salvation lie hidden. Because revelation is an inextricable part of this world-view, we may justifiably and meaningfully speak of it as an apocalyptic world-view.

It may seem ill-advised to search for an overarching unity in a literary collection as lengthy, diverse, and complex as *1 Enoch*.[3] The multiplicity of its component parts (created by many anonymous 'authors' over a period of more than three centuries), its variety of

---

1. It is mentioned in a list of apocalypses in a work as critical as that of K. Koch, *The Rediscovery of Apocalyptic* (trans. M. Kohl; SBT 2/22; Naperville, IL, 1972), p. 23.

2. See J.J. Collins, 'The Jewish Apocalypses', *Semeia* 14 (1979), pp. 22-28, 37-40, 45.

3. On literary issues, date, and related matters pertaining to *1 Enoch*, see G.W.E. Nickelsburg, *Jewish Literature Between the Bible and the Mishnah* (Philadelphia, 1981), pp. 46-55, 90-94, 145-51, 214-23; and J.J. Collins, *The Apocalyptic Imagination* (New York, 1984), pp. 36-63, 142-54.

literary forms and genres, and the diversity of its subject matter all militate against easy systematization and synthesis. Nonetheless, *1 Enoch* is a consciously shaped compilation of traditions and texts, and it is appropriate to search for internal points of commonality (apart from Enochic attribution in most cases) in which the compilers and editors saw the potential for a unity comprised of diversity. More fundamentally, because successive parts of the tradition developed from and built on one another, some significant unity is to be expected. In fact, comparative analysis indicates that certain motifs, emphases, and interests are repeatedly expressed throughout the collection and are often structured into its diverse literary forms. From these we may extract a set of unifying factors.

1. *The Focal Point: The Coming Judgment*

The oracle that introduces the collection sets the tone for what follows, announcing God's coming judgment and its consequences: blessings for the righteous and curses for the sinners (chs. 1–5). In one way or another, all the major sections of *1 Enoch* and many of their subsections or component parts either provide background for this theme or elaborate on it and give it prominence.

The mythic materials conflated in chs. 6–11 constitute a narrative that begins with an explanation of the origins of major evil in the world and ends with the anticipation of its eradication on a purified earth among a righteous humanity.[1]

The same counterposition of evil and judgment is evident in the account of Enoch's call (chs. 12–16), which focuses on the nature of the angelic sin and announces the divine verdict three times.[2] The myth of angelic rebellion and a companion myth about rebel stars are focal in the account of Enoch's first journey (chs. 17–19), where the goal of the journey and the climax of the narrative are the places of punishment for angels and stars.[3]

The account of Enoch's second journey also structures the notion of sin and punishment into its literary form, but extends it to include the human as well as the divine realm (chs. 21–32). At each station of the journey, Enoch has an interpreted vision that relates to angelic sin or

---

1. On these chapters, see Nickelsburg, 'Apocalyptic and Myth in 1 Enoch 6–11', *JBL* 96 (1977), pp. 383-89.

2. See Nickelsburg, 'Enoch, Levi, and Peter: Recipients of Revelation in Upper Galilee', *JBL* 100 (1981), pp. 575-82.

3. See Nickelsburg, *Jewish Literature*, p. 54.

to human sin or righteousness, and their consequences in the judgment[1]
(cf. also ch. 108). Chapter 33 alludes to Enoch's celestial journeys,
which have been recounted in the astronomical material now
summarized in the *Book of the Luminaries* (chs. 72–82). While this
material is presented in chs. 33–36 and 72–82 almost exclusively in
factual form, it is also used as a point of reference for human error
(2.1–5.4; 80.2-8) and divine punishment (100.10–101.9).

Human activity and its modes, consequences, and judgment are the
exclusive subject matter of chs. 92–105. The counterposition of sin or
righteousness, and punishment or reward, is structured into the
literary forms that constitute the section.[2] For the most part, the
author focuses on sin and its punishment in the great judgment. The
admonitions to righteous conduct and promises of reward are set
largely in the context of their alternatives. The righteous are either
depicted as the victims of sinners, or they are warned to avoid sinful
ways.

The temporal dimension of sin (mainly) and righteous conduct, as
well as the results of such behavior, are recounted from creation to the
judgment, in long and short form, in the *Animal Vision* (chs. 85–90)
and the *Apocalypse of Weeks* (93.1-10; 91.11-17). Chapters 83–84 and
106–107 are narratives about humanity's sin and Noah's righteousness
and their judgment at the time of the Flood.

The *Parables of Enoch* (chs. 37–71) are a separate compilation of
major elements of the Enochic tradition: tours of the celestial phenomena; journeys to the terrestrial places of punishment; stories about
Noah and the Flood. However, the judgment motif is set forth mainly
in Enoch's heavenly visions of the Elect One who will vindicate the
righteous elect and execute judgment on their powerful royal
oppressors.

In summary, there is scarcely a page in *1 Enoch* that is not in some
sense related to the expectation of an impending divine judgment that
will deal with human sin and righteousness, and the angelic rebellions
that are in one way or another related to them.

2. *The Temporal and Spatial Dimensions in* 1 Enoch's *World-View*

1 Enoch's view of reality, with its focus on the coming judgment, has
both a temporal and a spatial dimension. It views the present situation

---

1. See J.T. Milik, *The Books of Enoch: Aramaic Fragments of Qumrân Cave 4*
(Oxford, 1976), p. 35; Nickelsburg, *Jewish Literature*, pp. 54-55.
2. See Nickelsburg, 'The Apocalyptic Message of 1 Enoch 92–105', *CBQ* 39
(1977), pp. 310-15.

in terms of the past and the future; and, alternatively, it sets the locus of human activity in relationship to the heavenly realm and the rest of the cosmos.

The temporal dimension

The temporal dimension in *1 Enoch* is perhaps the most obvious to the reader of biblical literature. The activity attributed to God, the angels, and human beings takes place in past, present, and future. Major angelic rebellions occurred in primordial time, but they impinge upon the world as the authors know it in their own time. For the author of the *Animal Vision*, other angelic sin is presently underway and is evident in Israel's oppression by the nations. Human actions have present and future consequences. The righteous are suffering now at the hands of the wicked. The present actions and attitudes of the righteous and wicked will be subject to scrutiny and retribution at God's future judgment, as will the actions of the rebellious angels. The juxtaposition of present and future is so frequent in *1 Enoch* as to be commonplace. The temporal dimension is most obvious, however, in the *Animal Vision* and the *Apocalypse of Weeks*. These texts arrange events along an explicit temporal continuum that stretches from creation to the eschaton, and each author has a specific notion of when the judgment will occur.

This temporal dimension notwithstanding, the texts in *1 Enoch* devote relatively little space to speculations about the *time* of the end. It may be the case that many of the Enochic authors expected the judgment imminently. The *Epistle*, in particular, expresses the idea explicitly at a number of points.[1] But the calculation and periodization that may undergird such an expectation are explicit only in the *Animal Vision* and *Apocalypse of Weeks*, which constitute a mere 13 percent of the text of *1 Enoch*. Clearly, the authors of the various parts of *1 Enoch* had other interests as they composed their texts.

The spatial and material dimension

The authors of *1 Enoch* depict human and divine activity taking place in a spatial dimension that is far more explicit and emphatically evident than the temporal dimension. What is obvious in *1 Enoch*, once one sees it, is the authors' preoccupation with a world that is described in spatial and material terms, a world that can be experienced, at least in principle, by the five senses.

---

1. See 94.1, 6, 7; 95.6; 96.1, 6; 97.10; 98.16.

This spatial dimension, however, is rarely spelled out with reference to specific geographic locations, and place names are used only of sacred sites: Sinai (1.4; cf. 89.29); Hermon and its environs (6.5; 13.7, 9); Jerusalem, though not by name (26–27; cf. 25.5; 56.7; 89.50, 54-56, 66, 72-73; 90.26-36; 93.7-8, 13). Certainly the authors think of events as occurring in particular places, but it is mainly in the *Animal Vision* and the *Apocalypse of Weeks*, with their recitation of Israelite history, that one can clearly perceive the actions of identifiable people and nations.

The pervasive spatial dimension in *1 Enoch* is present, rather, in the authors' cosmology and mythic geography, and in their references to the nonanimate aspects of creation. It is mainly the places and things in these realms that Enoch sees, smells, hears, tastes, and feels, or to which the readers' attention is called. And to no small extent, the authors emphasize the orderliness and obedience that prevail in this spatial and material realm.

Cosmology is most evident in the *Book of the Luminaries* (chs. 72–82). Here Enoch records what he saw when he visited the heavens and traveled across the vast extents of the terrestrial disk: the portals through which the sun, moon, and stars rise and set; the gates of the winds; the four quarters of the earth; its seven great mountains, rivers, and islands. Throughout, the account emphasizes the order of the creation. The cosmic and meteorological phenomena take place in the way they do because God has structured into the cosmos the places and devices that make possible their orderly functioning.

The cosmological traditions selectively gathered in chs. 72–82 are presupposed and sometimes complemented elsewhere in *1 Enoch*, especially in chs. 1–36. Here the Enochic authors refer back to the cosmological and astronomical traditions, enhance them with accounts of Enoch's journeys, and appeal to the readers' senses by elaborating the narratives with references to the spatial dimension and its components.

The introduction to the *Book of the Watchers* (chs. 1–5) contrasts humanity's faithless disobedience with the orderly obedience that prevails among the heavenly bodies and in the changing of earth's seasons. The repeated introductory words, 'observe' and 'see', are an appeal to the empirical experience of nature. The luminaries in heaven, the clouds, dew, and rain, earth's heat and cold, and the foliage of its trees are the exemplary basis of the author's admonition.

The story of the watchers' rebellion makes both negative and positive references to the components of the created realm (chs. 6–11). The watchers revealed forbidden information about the terrestrial world of plants and minerals, and taught prognostication that was based on the movements of the celestial bodies. The deeds of the giants wreaked havoc on the whole terrestrial realm: human beings, birds, beasts, creeping things, fish, and agricultural produce. In consequence, the earth lay polluted and moribund. Conversely, the author's picture of the future envisions a purified earth, with woods and fields, where a renewed and multiplying humanity will be nourished by the fabulous fertility of wine, grain, and oil.

The mythic account of Enoch's heavenly ascent and call is heavily embellished with references to the concrete, material, and experiential (especially 14.8-18). He hears the summons of the clouds and winds, and is sped on his way by shooting stars, lightning flashes, and winds. He sees and enters a heavenly palace constructed of the elements—fire and lightning flashes, hailstones and snow—and he experiences the heat and cold that emanate from them.[1] These components of the call story, combined with references to the seer's emotional state and physical reactions, constitute a powerfully sensual expression of a religious belief.

Chapters 17–19 reiterate and elaborate on the message of chs. 12–16: the rebel watchers (and the disobedient stars) are doomed to eternal punishment. But here this message is tied to the author's cosmology. The temporal dimension (judgment will take place) is reinforced by reference to the spatial dimension: Enoch travels to the edge of the earth, where he views the fiery places of punishment. Moreover, although the point of the journey account is the pair of interpreted visions that bring it to a climax, the seer cannot bypass the opportunity to document his journey with a string of references to the terrestrial and celestial loci and phenomena that marked the course of the journey. Although the *point* of the section is eschatological, the *medium* of its expression is cosmological. Enoch's journey account makes roughly the same point in the same way (chs. 21–32): cosmology undergirds eschatology. There are places structured into the cosmos that guarantee the coming reality of judgment and the consequent rewards and punishments. God's creation anticipated God's judgment and serves as its instrument. More than in previous sections, however, one finds an appeal to the senses. Enoch sees the cosmic places and realia in detail and marvels over them. He smells the fragrance of the tree of life and the tree of wisdom, and he alludes to the eating of their fruit. The description of the journey to the Far East (chs. 28–31) is a counterpart to ch. 17, but is recounted in botanical

---

1. See Nickelsburg, 'Enoch, Levi, and Peter', pp. 580-81.

rather than cosmological detail. The *Book of the Watchers* ends with summarizing reference to the broader lore about Enoch's journeys through the heavenly sphere (chs. 33–36).

Taken as a whole, the Book expounds a message about the coming judgment. It does so through a variety of literary forms: prophetic oracle, mythic narrative, prophetic call story, journey accounts. In all of these, however, one finds reference not simply to the future when judgment will happen, or to the past when rebellion took place. The temporality of the message is reinforced by repeated reference to the spatial realm and to the things that can be experienced by the senses.

This spatial dimension is also integral to the *Book of Parables* (chs. 37–71). The first and third parables include accounts of Enoch's celestial journeys (chs. 41–44; 60). In the second parable, the book's central message of judgment—carried primarily by the heavenly tableaux which feature the Elect One—is reinforced by accounts of journeys to the terrestrial places associated with judgment and punishment. Running through the book, moreover, are references to the 'earth' or 'land', which is now possessed by the kings and the mighty, but which will be renewed and become locus of salvation after the judgment. This element is reminiscent of chs. 6–11.

Enoch's epistle is composed primarily of the seer's alternating words of doom and promise, which juxtapose the present deeds of the sinners and the present circumstances of the righteous with their future punishment and reward. At one point in particular, however, the cosmic dimension breaks through (100.10–102.3). The elements witness humanity's deeds and enact God's judgment, and heaven and earth will quake and tremble at the final theophany.

Significantly, the concluding chapter of the corpus blends the temporal and spatial dimensions of the Enochic message of judgment (ch. 108). A pair of paragraphs about the doom of the sinners and the blessedness of the righteous (vv. 2-3, 7-10) enclose a brief account of Enoch's vision of the fiery place of punishment. The section and the corpus as a whole conclude with the promise of the judgment, which will send the wicked to the place 'where the days and times are written for them' (vv. 11-15).

3. *Dualism in* 1 Enoch

1 Enoch's construction of reality, with its temporal and spatial dimensions and its populations of divine and human characters, is characterized by several complementary kinds of dualism.

Temporal dualism

The temporal axis in *1 Enoch* is sharply divided between the present time, which will end with the judgment, and a new age that follows. In many different ways, the authors contrast the present time, which is evil or deficient, with the future, which will bring healing and renewal. A plagued, polluted, and ravaged world will be healed, cleansed, and re-sown (chs. 6–11). The time of demonic domination will come to an end (chs. 12–16; 19.1). Those who have suffered or been murdered will be sustained by the fruit of the tree of life (25.5-6). The Israelite flock, devoured and dispersed by gentile beasts and birds of prey, will be restored and gathered, and humanity, divided at the beginning, will be reunited as one people (chs. 85–90). Most pervasively, this temporal dualism is concerned with the issue of divine justice. Life in the present time is marked by injustice, but this will be adjudicated in the future, at the time of the great judgment (see part 1 above). This concern is worked out most explicitly and in greatest detail in the *Epistle* (chs. 92–105), which is dominated by what are effectively descriptions of human sin and suffering. In the present time, the righteous are unjustly victimized by the sinners, who go unpunished. In the grave, both experience the same fate. All that will be overcome, however, when God rewards the righteous for their piety and compensates them for their suffering, and the sinners receive their just deserts. The *Parables* make the same point but focus on the judgment itself and the events related to it.

Cosmic dualism

The spatial dimension in *1 Enoch* is marked by a sharp dualism that has both vertical and horizontal aspects. Heaven is the realm of the divine and earth the habitation of humans. Disaster occurs when the realms are confounded (chs. 6–16). The descent of the watchers results in the pollution of the earth, which now becomes the habitation of malevolent and destructive demons. Conversely, the decimated earth and the remnants of humanity will be delivered when the divine Judge and his faithful entourage descend from heaven to earth to execute judgment. In the meantime, the mechanisms that will facilitate that judgment exist in the heavenly realms and are operative (esp. 89.59–90.19; 92–105 *passim*). Angels record human deeds and act as mediators and advocates in the divine throne room. The books containing the names of the righteous and their rewards are a prominent reality in God's presence. The Elect One stands before God and receives his commission as the agent of judgment (chs. 37–71). Heaven is also the place of the luminaries and the elements. In contrast to most of earthbound humanity, they faithfully follow the commands that God instituted at creation, and when asked, they execute judgment on the wicked (esp. chs. 2; 72–82). 1 Enoch's cosmic dualism has a horizontal aspect. Enoch's journeys carry him across the face of earth's disk. In places uninhabited by living mortals, God's will is carried out, or at least, the apparatus that will execute God's will stands ready (chs. 17–36). On the mountain of the dead, a distinction is made between the souls of the righteous and the sinners. Beyond it, to the northwest, stands the mountain on which the divine Judge will descend and where presently the tree of life waits to be transplanted to the sanctuary. To the extreme northwest are the pits where the rebellious divine beings already suffer punishment. Far to the east is the original paradise, where wisdom is hidden. All in all, Enoch's journeys carry him to places in the cosmos that are removed from human habitation or hidden from human access, where God's created intent is potential or actualized.

Ontological dualism between divine and human
Related to *1 Enoch*'s spatial dualism is the absolute distinction between divine beings and humans. In the case of God, this distinction is emphasized throughout the book by names that denote God's uniqueness and absolute transcendence (the Great One, the Holy One, the Great Holy One, the Lord or God of the Ages, etc.). This transcendence is underscored in a special way in the descriptions of the heavenly throne room in the accounts of Enoch's call (ch. 14) and ascent (ch. 71) and in the references to the eschatological theophany (chs. 1; 102.1-3).

The heavenly entourage shares in God's separateness from humanity, as is indicated by their most frequent title, 'the holy ones'.[1] According to 15.1–16.1, the sin of the watchers consisted precisely in their violation of the absolute distinction between spirit and flesh and their defilement of their holiness.

The disastrous consequences of this angelic rebellion are an integral part of a special aspect of the human–divine dualism, viz. the 'demonic' victimization of humanity. According to ch. 8, angelic revelations lead human beings astray. In chs. 12–16 the ghosts of the dead giants, which are not eradicated because they are spirit, constitute a realm of evil spirits who prey on humanity in a variety of ways. The

---

1. There is no place in *1 Enoch* where we can be certain that the original text used the term 'angels'. The Aramaic texts from Qumran indicate that the ordinary term for these heavenly creatures was 'watchers' (*'îrîn*) and, in their unfallen state, 'watchers and holy ones' (*'îrîn wᵉqadîšîn*), i.e. 'holy watchers'.

Animal Vision adds an additional nuance: the angelic shepherds are responsible for Israel's victimization at the hands of the nations. Through all of this runs the notion that sin and evil, at least in many of their guises, are functions of a spirit realm that is at war with humanity.

The disaster of human life here and now: at the intersection of several dualisms
According to *1 Enoch*'s world-view, then, humanity exists at the intersection of three kinds of dualism. The human situation is defined both as it is and in terms of what it is not. The present age is evil and awaits the time of adjudication, deliverance, and renewal. This world is the scene of sin, violence, victimization, and pollution, and is separated from the heavenly and cosmic spheres, where God's will is done. Humanity here and now is the prey of evil spirits who oppose God and are contrasted with the holy ones in God's heavenly entourage. Thus, the disastrous character of human existence is emphasized by means of dualistic comparisons that are made in temporal, spatial, and ontological terms.

4. *Salvation in* 1 Enoch: *The Resolution of its Dualisms*

By its very structure, *1 Enoch*'s dualism optimistically allows for deliverance or salvation from the situation that is pessimistically described from a number of converging perspectives. Opposed to present injustice and disaster here are the future judgment and salvation that are poised in the beyond.

Salvation in the future, when God intervenes
Most obviously, that deliverance lies in the future, at the time of the judgment and thereafter. To begin with, the conflict in the divine realm will be resolved, as only it can be, through direct divine intervention; God and God's holy ones will exterminate their malevolent counterparts: the rebel watchers, the evil spirits, and the angelic shepherds. Additionally, the wicked human perpetrators of sin and oppression will be judged, removed from this world, and destroyed. Equally important, the defiled and moribund earth will be cleansed and revived. Above all, the new state of affairs will be universal and permanent. All evil, sin, and impurity will be removed from the whole earth, and all the children of the whole earth will be righteous for all the generations of eternity (10.20–11.1; 91.16-17).

Salvation in the present: bridging the dualism through revelation given to the community of the righteous and chosen

Although definitive salvation lies in the future, revelation transmitted in the present time effects a significant resolution of the book's temporal, spatial, and ontological dualism. Such revelation is a pervasive concept in *1 Enoch*, and, in one guise or another, the notion is present in all of the book's component parts, whether it is ascribed to the ancient seer or to those living in the author's own times.[1]

In chs. 1–5, Enoch cites his visions and their angelic interpretations (1.2), and the whole section is presented in the form of a prophetic oracle. Although the narrative in chs. 6–11 is not presented as a revelation, in 10.1-3 God commissions the angel Sariel to teach Noah about the coming judgment and the means that will save him from its destruction. In chs. 12–16 the purpose of Enoch's ascent is to receive an oracle of doom which he is to bring to earth. In chs. 17–19, 20–36, and 108, the function of Enoch's journeys is to receive revelation about the hidden world, and the *Book of Parables* as a whole is the revelation of such heavenly and cosmic journeys. Revelation takes a special form in chs. 83–90, where Enoch's knowledge of the future, which he transmits to Methuselah, has come to him through dreams. In chs. 33–36, astronomical lore is gained in journeys through the cosmos in the company of an interpreting angel. The *Epistle*, alone of the major sections of *1 Enoch*, does not describe Enoch receiving revealed knowledge; however, at several points Enoch explicitly, or implicitly, bases his admonitions on the things he has seen during his journey (93.2, 11-14; 97.2, 7; 98.6; 103.1-2; 104.1, 7-8; cf. 81.1-4).

The salvific function of revelation is explicit in several key texts in *1 Enoch*. In the *Animal Vision* the opening of the eyes of the blind lambs is a first step toward salvation (90.6). Both 5.8 and 93.10 foresee that 'wisdom will be given to the chosen' of the end time, and in 104.12-13, this is identified with the Enochic books. In each case the reception of wisdom is constitutive of salvation or life.[2]

Revelation bridges the book's dualism in several ways. Enoch's revelations about the celestial structures and the movements of the heavenly bodies are a torah that is foundational for correct calendrical observance (chs. 72–82). His cosmological revelations in chs. 17–19

---

1. On the literary forms that embody this notion, see the citations in J.J. Collins, 'The Jewish Apocalypses'.

2. See Nickelsburg, 'Revealed Wisdom as a Criterion for Inclusion and Exclusion: From Jewish Sectarianism to Early Christianity' in *'To See Ourselves as Others See Us': Christians, Jews, 'Others' in Late Antiquity* (ed. J. Neusner and E.S. Frerichs; Chico, CA, 1985), pp. 74-79.

and 21–32 present evidence that judgment is already being exacted and that the places of future judgment are ready for their tasks. His viewing of the heavenly tablets (81.1-4), his witnessing of angelic advocacy (89.59–90.19), and his visions of events in the heavenly courtroom (chs. 37–71) are assurance that the apparatus for the future judgment is already in operation. These revelations are salvific in function because they provide a means of hope in what is, by all appearances, a hopeless world, and because they encourage the righteous to stand fast against apostasy. This exhortative function is explicit in the *Epistle*, where Enoch's revelations are cited as the basis for his repeated admonitions that the righteous should not fear, but be hopeful of vindication.[1] Similarly, in the oracle that introduces the corpus, Enoch's revelations support his promise of future blessing.

Thus the books of Enoch are a corpus of texts that guarantee future salvation on the basis of a present reality to which the seer has been privy and which he now reveals. That seer—in the Book's fiction, Enoch of old, in reality the complement of authors who stand behind these texts—is the bridge between opposing worlds: present and future, earthly and cosmic, human and divine. His revelations, written down, transmitted, and interpreted, are constitutive of the community of the chosen and righteous. Although allegedly received in primordial antiquity, these revelations are promulgated in a present that stands on the threshold of the end time. Functionally, they are eschatological revelation. As the *Animal Vision* and *Apocalypse of Weeks* indicate, they are given at the end of the age (just as Noah received revelation before the first judgment), and this eschatological character further enhances the assurance that the revelations offer. Definitive deliverance will take place soon.

In summary: we may properly use the term 'apocalyptic' to characterize the texts in *1 Enoch*, because the claim to revelation or, indeed, the literary form that presents this claim, is not accidental to the text, but is essential to its world-view, or construction of reality. The authors' revelations are the salvific means by which the readers bridge and overcome the dualisms that are the very nature of reality as they understand and experience it.[2]

---

1. On these admonitions in 96.1-3; 97.1-2; 102.4-5; 104.2-6, see Nickelsburg, 'Apocalyptic Message', pp. 315-18.

2. For a similar approach, see the extension of the *Semeia* 14 definition of 'apocalypse' in A. Yarbro Collins, 'Introduction: Early Christian Apocalypticism', *Semeia* 36 (1986), p. 7.

5. *The Enochic Writings in their Context*

It remains briefly to place the Enochic texts in their context in the history of Israelite religious thought, as it is attested in the post-exilic biblical texts. I have emphasized that the Enochic authors locate human existence at the intersection of a set of dualisms. Temporally and spatially, humanity is placed at a point where it is bereft of divine justice and blessing and where it is victimized by malevolent spirit forces. Earth is not heaven; now is not the age to come. This heaping up of dualisms underscores humanity's pitiful state.

One can make a case for speaking of a developing dualistic eschatology in post-exilic prophecy.[1] Already in Jeremiah and Ezekiel, and increasingly in Second and Third Isaiah, the present is qualitatively contrasted with the future, which is often depicted as a return to first beginnings, whether the Exodus, the covenant, or creation itself.[2] In addition, of course, the prophets think of God as dwelling in heaven with the divine entourage. What the biblical texts lack, however, is the mutual reinforcing of dualisms, which underscores humanity's inaccessibility to divine blessing and salvation. In *1 Enoch*, by contrast, the future—which is not yet—is overlaid by the 'there' that is not here. The Enochic authors provide this spatial axis, in large part, by using material from the 'wisdom tradition' and shaping and nuancing it to serve the eschatological character and purpose of the temporal axis. Moreover, they endow this wisdom material with the authority that derives from revelation. Enoch travels to and sees, and has explained to him, the places and realia of the cosmos which were inaccessible to humans according to authors like Job.[3] It is this combination of dualisms, mediated by repeated claims to revelation, that sets the Enochic texts off from their prophetic counterparts and earns for them the term 'apocalyptic dualism' or 'dualistic apocalypticism'. This set of dualisms is further enhanced by the dualistic myths about the origins of evil in chs. 6–11, which are the presupposition for much of the corpus.

It is a topic worthy of investigation to ask what the driving forces were that fused the prophetic temporal dualism, the spatial dimension of interest to the sages, and the ontological dualism of the myths into a

---

1. I do so in my article on 'Eschatology', to appear in the forthcoming *Anchor Bible Dictionary*.
2. In the case of Second Isaiah, one can really speak of a qualitative difference between the past and the present, which is the moment of salvation.
3. On Enoch's place in the diversity of Persian/Hellenistic Judaism, see M.E. Stone, 'The Book of Enoch and Judaism in the Third Century BCE', *CBQ* 40 (1978), pp. 479-92.

single, mutually reinforcing dualistic construction of reality. Surely experience played a role; people felt alienated and victimized. From the point of view of intellectual and religious history, what is interesting is the fact that they expressed this experience in the dualistic synthesis that we find in *1 Enoch*.

Furthermore, it is noteworthy that the experience which I attribute to the Enochic authors and their communities is widely attributed to the non-Judaic peoples of the Hellenistic age.[1] It would be worth comparing the structure of *1 Enoch*'s thought with that in other texts of the late Persian and early Hellenistic period. Are there dualisms, and how do they work? Does one appeal to revelation as a means to bridge the dualisms?

Whatever the findings of such a comparative investigation, *1 Enoch* is evidence of a watershed in the history of Israelite thought. The coincidence and heaping of temporal, spatial, and ontological dualisms, and their resolution in the claim of revelation, parallel and presage essential elements in the rise of gnosticism and Christianity and in a kind of spirituality that continued through the middle ages and that is still present in substantial sectors of the Christian church.

---

1. For a classical expression of this analysis, see R. Bultmann, *Primitive Christianity in its Contemporary Setting* (trans. R.H. Fuller; New York, 1956).

4

ON READING AN APOCALYPSE

Michael E. Stone

1. *Introductory Matters and Basic Issues*

A decade has passed since the Uppsala symposium, which was one of
those timely events that have it in them to change, or at least to deflect,
the path of scholarship. The Uppsala discussions brought a variety of
social and historical factors to bear on the study of apocalypticism,
conceived in broader cultural, temporal, and geographic terms than
just Jewish, just Palestinian, just Second Temple. Other participants in
the present Symposium will discuss the impact of that broader
chronological and geographical perspective on the study of the Jewish
apocalyptic literature.

I wish to direct my attention, however, to one single apocalypse, for
I have spent a good many years, indeed far more than have passed
since the Uppsala symposium, in the close reading of one particular
apocalypse, that is *4 Ezra*.[1] The result of those years' reading is an
overall interpretation of *4 Ezra* which is new in its emphasis and its
general thrust. Here I shall attempt to set forth basic aspects of that
new interpretation and to consider whether this approach to *4 Ezra* has
any ramifications for the understanding of other apocalypses.

At the outset, two preliminary observations are in order. First, what
I am presenting is hindsight. Here I shall set forth what I did in normative terms, yet I did not start analysing the book after having
conceived of the issues in those terms. Instead, I reached my overall
interpretation through an extended process of methodologically non-
selfconscious agonizing over the meaning of the document. Here I shall

---

1. This is the name commonly used for chs. 3–14 of the work known in the
English Apocrypha as 2 Esdras. These chapters form a single, Jewish work which
was written about 95 CE originally in Hebrew. Issues of original language, text,
transmission, etc. are dealt with in detail in the writer's *4 Ezra* (Hermeneia; Minneapolis, 1990).

extract a systematic description of my approach to the book from the outcome of that agonizing. The second preliminary observation is that this method of interpretation may not prove fruitful for all apocalyptic literature. Of course, that can only be verified by trying to read other apocalypses in a similar way.

The central issue in previous exegesis of *4 Ezra* has been inconsistency. From Richard Kabisch at the end of the nineteenth century down to the recent work of Egon Brandenburger,[1] scholars have endeavored to understand how the varied literary features of the book are related to one another and how the apparently 'contradictory' things that the book says could co-exist in the same work. Other specific issues have been of concern as well, as exemplified by the recent flurry of writing on theodicy and the responsibility for evil,[2] but it is these inconsistencies that have been the gadfly to scholarly concern.

In my view, however, not strict logical consistency but coherency is a controlling category which must guide us in understanding the book. The book made sense to its author, to its readers: our task is to discover how. Concurrently, the book must be regarded as religious literature, not just as a compendium of theological concepts or midrashic traditions, and what it says about the religious experience and social functioning of the pseudepigraphic hero should be taken rather seriously at the social and psychological as well as at the literary levels. From these new methodological sensitivities arises a different way of approaching the delineation of the function of *4 Ezra*.

2. *The History of Scholarship on these Issues*

The new perspectives in interpretation of the book engendered by this approach stand out most strikingly when regarded in light of past scholarship which, as we stated, concentrated on the question of logical inconsistency. I shall outline briefly three different responses to the problem of inconsistency: the literary-critical response of Kabisch and

---

1. For a review of scholarship, see Stone, *4 Ezra* 'Introduction', section 3. See R. Kabisch, *Das vierte Buch Esra auf seine Quellen untersucht* (Göttingen, 1889) and E. Brandenburger, *Die Verborgenheit Gottes im Weltgeschehen* (ATANT, 68; Zürich, 1981).

2. A.L. Thompson, *Responsibility for Evil in the Theodicy of IV Ezra* (SBLDS, 29; Missoula, MT, 1977). A more recent work on the same topic, which I have not yet seen, is T.W. Willett, *Eschatology in the Theodicies of 2 Baruch and 4 Ezra* (JSPS, 4; Sheffield, 1989).

Box,[1] the form-critical and psychological resolution of Hermann Gunkel,[2] and the formal and theological approach of Egon Brandenburger.[3]

Children of their age, Kabisch and Box resolved the inconsistencies they perceived in the book by a source-critical analysis. They viewed *4 Ezra* as a composite of five sources, fairly clumsily put together by a 'Redactor'. In theory, it was literary roughness and inconsistency that betrayed the presence of sources, whose existence was confirmed by supposedly incompatible eschatological conceptions. In fact, as the art was practiced by Box, the argument turned chiefly on the issues of conceptual contradictions, with literary criteria playing only a minor role.

This theory was quickly and tellingly criticized,[4] and the next major contribution to the understanding of *4 Ezra* was made by Hermann Gunkel. He recognized, as have many who followed, that some of the phenomena Kabisch and Box had observed really did exist in the book, in particular the distinction between the first four and the last three Visions. Yet he denied that these phenomena imposed a source theory. His own view was founded upon three arguments: (a) that a more careful reading shows that many of the supposed 'inconsistencies' did not exist; (b) that some of the inconsistencies were caused by the inclusion of oral, traditional materials into the apocalypse, particularly in its eschatology; and (c) that the author's deep and complex nature engendered thought that is not always consistent.[5] 'According to Gunkel', to quote Hayman's apt observation, 'the splitting of the author's being into the man and the angel...corresponds with his inner life.'[6]

1. Kabisch, *Vierte Buch*; G.H. Box, *The Ezra-Apocalypse* (London, 1912). The history of scholarship is set forth in detail in Stone, *4 Ezra*. These were not, of course, the only scholars holding this view, but they are typically representative. The same is true of those authorities cited in the rest of this paragraph.

2. H. Gunkel, 'Das vierte Buch Esra', *Die Apokryphen und Pseudepigraphen des Alten Testaments* (ed. E. Kautzsch; Tübingen, 1900), II, pp. 331-402.

3. Brandenburger, *Verborgenheit*. This was not his first work relevant to the topic, nor is he the only scholar taking this approach. His is the most recent, major exposition of it, however, and I have consequently chosen to concentrate my attention on it.

4. See e.g. the 'Prefatory Note' by W. Sanday in Box, *Ezra-Apocalypse*.

5. Gunkel set his views forth in his introductory comments to his Commentary on *4 Ezra* in 'Das vierte Buch Esra', pp. 331-402.

6. A.P. Hayman, 'The Problem of Pseudonymity in the Ezra Apocalypse', *JSJ* 6 (1975), p. 49. Truly to be inconsistent, therefore, ideas must not just be formally inconsistent. The critic seeking inconsistency must take the other factors into account as well.

The recent works of Wolfgang Harnisch and Egon Brandenburger on *4 Ezra*, though differing from one another in many details, are dominated by a common methodological approach.[1] Both scholars regard the book as the work of a single author (although Harnisch also utilized a modified source theory claiming that Visions 5 and 6 are secondary) and both readily admit that the author used pre-existing sources. Reflecting modern trends in biblical scholarship, they demand quite rightly that the overall interpretation of the book should account for its chief literary features and express the author's intent and ideas. Yet in their isolation of 'chief literary features' and of 'the author's intent and ideas', a deliberate choice may be discerned which reflects their approach and reinforces their argumentation.[2] Our discussion is based on the most recent exposition of the Harnisch–Brandenburger approach, the latter's *Die Verborgenheit Gottes*, published in 1981.

3. *The Character of* 4 Ezra *according to Brandenburger*

4 Ezra, as even a superficial reader knows, is composed of seven parts which are usually called 'visions'. The first three are actually dialogues between the seer and the angel Uriel; the fifth and the sixth are symbolic dreams and their interpretations. The fourth starts off looking like a dialogue, but shifts to an ecstatic experience of heavenly Jerusalem, while the seventh 'vision' tells of the restoration of the Sacred Scriptures, burnt in the destruction of the Temple.

The central problem of the book was conceived by Brandenburger in terms of conceptual and formal issues. One arises from the disputatious dialogue of the first three visions. The views forwarded by the angel in Visions 1–3 are those accepted by the Seer in the *Abschiedsrede* in 14.28-36, while the views urged by the Seer in Visions 1–3 are not taken up at all later in the book.[3]

---

1. Thus note Brandenburger's earlier work, *Adam und Christus: exegetisch-religionsgeschichtliche Untersuchung zu Röm 5.12-21* (WMANT, 7; Neukirchen, 1962) which influenced W. Harnisch. Harnisch wrote a series of articles on *4 Ezra*, and his most substantial contribution is his book *Verhängnis und Verheissung der Geschichte. Untersuchungen zum Zeit- und Geschichtsverständnis im 4. Buch Esra und in der syr. Baruch-apokalypse* (FRLANT, 97; Göttingen, 1969).

2. Naturally, we all are vulnerable to such circularity. Below I use terms such as 'the obvious literary point' or the like; these too beg the question. In the final analysis, only the 'fit' between the theory proposed and the givens of the text can serve as a criterion for the reasonableness of a theory.

3. Another issue is structural: the dialogue breaks off in Vision 4. Furthermore, the relevance of Visions 5–6 to the problem presented by Visions 1–4 and 7 (as Brandenburger conceived it) must be explained.

Brandenburger's approach is based upon the notion that the purpose of the book is to promote the views that are set in the angel's mouth in Visions 1–3 and in Ezra's mouth in the *Abschiedsrede*. These views were identical with the author's own and they are opposed to those argued by Ezra in Visions 1–3. Thus Brandenburger and Harnisch discern two clear, polemically opposed opinions in *4 Ezra*. Both scholars think that these two views or opinions reflect two, polemically opposed social realities, either distinct groups (Harnisch) or 'streams of thought' (Brandenburger).[1] *4 Ezra*, therefore, is before all else a polemic over certain theological issues, and an assertion of those opinions about the theological issues that the author considers to be correct. The actual theological issues at stake are three: (1) theodicy; (2) the redemptive character of Torah, which is unrealizable; and (3) that many are created and only few are saved.

These issues are lengthily debated, Brandenburger maintains, by the seer and the angel in Visions 1–3, but no change in the seer's position results from this debate. In Vision 4, however, the seer undergoes a remarkable transformation: he comforts the mourning woman using the very arguments with which the angel, unsuccessfully, attempted previously to console him. This transformation is designed to resolve a problem in the narrative plot. Visions 5–6 are to be revelations to Ezra, yet in the course of Visions 1–3 Ezra was not moved from his skeptical views by the discussion. Consequently, he can be made worthy of receipt of the revelation to come only by a wondrous transformation which is consequently introduced. Compare Brandenburger! Observe that, although Brandenburger notes that this transformation took place and describes some of its features, he does not seek to explain it. Indeed, he is not concerned with the dynamic of the transformation itself and he energetically denies the relevance of the psychological factors such as were invoked by Gunkel. Because he regards the purpose of the book to be the presentation of a certain point of view, it suffices him to regard the transformation as a technical literary strategy.

The chief structural issues correlative with this basic position are, then: first, the nature and function of the dialogue in the book; second, the role of Vision 4 and Ezra's transformation; third, the relationship of Visions 5–6 to the rest of the book; and finally, the purpose and function of Vision 7. On another level, there is a problem of the relationship between the *personae* of Ezra and the angel. Thanks to

---

1. See Stone, *4 Ezra*, 'Introduction', part 3.

Gunkel and Brandenburger, these issues are to the fore, but Brandenburger has not resolved them.[1]

In response, a number of observations may be made. First, it seems to me patently against the literary truth of the book to maintain that the agonizing dialogues of Visions 1–3 are simply a literary means of forwarding the author's views, which are put in the angel's mouth. Ezra, not the angel, is the dominant 'I' of the first part of the book. Second, Brandenburger regards the book as a carefully crafted theological treatise, yet in it no answer is given, on theological or other grounds, to the difficult issues posed by the seer in Visions 1–3. This tells profoundly against Brandenburger's basic attitude to the book. Third, he ignores all but the testamentary section in Vision 7. This runs against the obvious thrust of the vision, which focuses on the idea of revelation to Ezra as to Moses.[2] Fourth, the relevance of Visions 5–6 to the basic thrust of the book, as conceived by Brandenburger, is unclear. Finally, he can offer no explanation of the transformation of Ezra in Vision 4, just the assertion that it is required by the author on literary grounds.

4. *The Criterion of Logical Consistency*

The problematic issues that Brandenburger's theory attempts to resolve may be described as a series of inconsistencies. Some of these inconsistencies are literary and structural, and they have been discussed above. Others are conceptual and theological. When logical consistency between theological concepts becomes the operative analytical criterion, it produces all sorts of problems. The following is an example. Brandenburger assumes that the purpose of the book is to forward certain points of view and so in the discussion of the first visions he has to isolate just where those points of view are presented. Thus, he makes much of the fact that in those visions certain ideas are set in the angel's mouth. These must be the theological ideas that the author wishes to forward, since he would scarcely have attributed to the angel or to God ideas he considered wrong. Those wrong ideas, which according to Brandenburger the author wishes to controvert, are set in Ezra's mouth.

---

1. The above outline of Brandenburger's views is necessarily sketchy, yet one or two observations on them must be made.

2. Even on grounds of the number of verses, the Farewell Address is far from being a major theme of the chapter, as a simple verse count will show.

Ezra, Brandenburger claims, was unchanging throughout the first three visions.[1] Yet the angel's views in Visions 1–3 are taken up by the Ezra in the *Abschiedsrede* in Vision 7. That implies the transformation in Ezra which is related in Vision 4. Brandenburger regards this transformation as a mere literary strategy, for Ezra must be said to change so as to be worthy of speaking the divine view. Suddenly he changes; all Brandenburger can do is call it a *Mysterium*.[2] But, I would maintain, the transformation is not thereby explained.

Moreover, if the views put in the mouth of God or his angel can only be good, why is Ezra chosen to voice wrong opinions? Ezra, we are told, represents the skeptical, even gnosticizing opponents of the author. Yet Ezra is scarcely an appropriate figure for this. To this obvious initial problem we may add another. Brandenburger, and Harnisch before him, had to regard not Ezra but the angel as the 'myself' of the author in the first three Visions of the book. Yet this contradicts the obvious literary sense of those three Visions in which it is Ezra, not the angel, who is the hero. Can the dispute between Ezra and the angel then be adequately explained as a literary representation of a theological *Auseinandersetzung* which is anchored in social reality? Do Ezra and the angel really represent different points of view having different social bases? Has not a demand for logical consistency led to absurd results? Why? I would deny Brandenburger's interpretation, for the following reasons.

1. First, the transformation as Brandenburger presents it makes no sense. It is *deus ex machina*, which is in no way explained by his own assumptions about the book.

2. The view that the angel is the *dramatis persona* with whom the author identifies in the first four visions runs against literary common sense.

3. If the point of the book is to forward certain theological concepts, then it is quite extraordinary that Ezra's theological counter-arguments are never refuted. All that happens is the unexplained *Verwandlung*. I suggest that although Brandenburger perceived real issues in the study of the book, his

---

1. This was, in fact, not the case, as I demonstrated in M.E. Stone, 'The Way of the Most High and Injustice of God in 4 Ezra', in *Knowledge of God in the Graeco-Roman World* (ed. R. van den Broek, T. Baarda and J. Mansfeld; Leiden, 1988), pp. 132-42.
2. Brandenburger, *Verborgenheit*, p. 87.

analysis does not resolve them because it is based on wrong
assumptions. What sort of alternatives can I offer?[1]

5. *A Search for Coherence*

A significant option is to review the assumptions made about the book.
4 Ezra is clearly the work of a single, consummate literary craftsman.
All explanations must start from this fact. Obviously, from Brandenburger's careful but unsuccessful analysis, *4 Ezra* does not make sense
as a document presenting a theological argument. However, since it
was written by one author, carefully and deliberately, then it may be
assumed to have made sense both to its author and to his readers. How
so?

At one level, we may say that most previous critics tried to make
sense of the book on the basis of the assumption that the propositions
asserted expressly or implicitly by the author are (or should be) consistent with one another as to their content. Where such logical
consistency does not appear on the face of asserted or implied
propositions, it was sought by having recourse either to source-critical
dissection or to structural hypotheses that run against common sense.

Yet already Gunkel, by using psychological criteria, had taken the
important step of seeking factors other than articulated or implied
propositions of the text to give coherence to the work. This possibility
should not surprise us, after all. Humans have produced many writings
the coherency of which is provided by factors outside the explicit or
implied content of their propositions. Indeed, one might maintain with
some plausibility that the purpose of *4 Ezra* is not to provide a consistent presentation of a series of propositions at all. In other terms: At
our point of departure stands the assumption that *4 Ezra* made sense to
its author and readers. If the book does not make sense as a
presentation of a theological argument, then it is not one, but something else![2]

---

1. Brandenburger's book appeared in 1981. At the time I was in the process of
working out crucial parts my own approach to *4 Ezra* and, having heard something of
Brandenburger's work, I resolved to postpone reading it until I finished my own
analysis. Once the draft of my work was completed, I read Brandenburger's book
attentively and integrated it into the results of my own analysis. My major results,
however, were reached in engagement with *4 Ezra*, not with Brandenburger. I am
indebted to K.W. Whitney, with whom I came to see more clearly how this following
part of the present paper should be structured.

2. As Earle Breech said, it is not 'a container for ideas'. See E. Breech, 'These
Fragments I Have Shored Against My Ruins: The Form and Function of 4 Ezra', *JBL*
92 (1973), p. 269.

6. *Religious Experience*

Here, a second factor in our reading of this apocalypse comes to bear. In my commentary, I have demonstrated quite unambiguously that the religious experience attributed to the pseudonymous seer reflects actual religious experience that the author underwent or of which he knew intimately.[1] This may be true of many of the other Jewish apocalypses of the Second Temple period, although it cannot always be proved as convincingly as in the case of *4 Ezra*. This fact has far-reaching implications for the understanding of the book. It makes an enormous difference whether the book is a composition designed to forward certain theological ideas within a literary framework of revelation, or whether the book reflects the author's religious experiences, mediated to us, of course, in a traditional fixed form. In the latter case, then, the author's own experience will be one of the factors providing coherence to the discourse of the book.

When Hermann Gunkel introduced the issue of the author's psychology into the discussion of *4 Ezra*, he proposed that many of the apparent repetitions in the course of the first three visions actually arose from the the author's internal conflicts. The use of a psychological explanation of literary phenomena was energetically rejected by Brandenburger, though he does not clearly say why. We assume that he objects to this approach so strongly because it involves shifting the emphasis of the book from the theological discourse to the psychological dynamic.

As has been noted, the resolution of four central problems in the book will go far towards determining its basic thrust, and here I maintain that the author's own religious experience provides one of the central keys to the reading of the book and a resolution of these problems.

The partners in the dialogues are Ezra and the angel. In Visions 1–3 Ezra is obviously the hero, yet equally obviously the views put by the angel/God cannot have been opposed by the author. I suggest that Ezra and the angel represent two aspects of the author's own internal debate and agonizing over the destruction. In Visions 1–3 his pain and distress are represented by Ezra; the answers he knows intellectually are represented by the angel.[2]

The eschatological information imparted by the angel in the course of the first three visions did not differ in its conceptual content from

---

1. Developed in my commentary on *4 Ezra*. This view was foreshadowed in Stone, 'Apocalyptic, Vision or Hallucination?', *Milla va-Milla* 14 (1974), pp. 47-56.
2. This point is, of course, a development of Gunkel's view.

the information revealed by means of the Dream Visions 5 and 6. Yet in Visions 1–3 that information did not satisfy or assuage Ezra's pain, while in Visions 5–6 it certainly did.[1] Why? What happened? Ezra was not vanquished by the angel's arguments: Brandenburger realized this! Ezra changed radically, but that change is not a literary device designed to create a purified Ezra, worthy of receipt of revelation. It is a real change, an experience of religious conversion undergone by the author.

A major feature of Vision 4 is role reversal. At the start of the experience, the mourning woman plays the role that Ezra did in Visions 1–3, to which Ezra responds the way the angel did in those Visions.[2] This dynamic precipitated a very powerful religious experience in the course of which the seer received enlightenment and fell unconscious. This experience was one of religious conversion. In it, the values and ideas that had previously been externalized in the figure of the angel were internalized by the seer, while his pain was now outside him, seen as the woman, and she is wondrously transmuted into the Heavenly Jerusalem! The theological arguments are never resolved theologically, because they are resolved by the conversion itself. In conversion, doubts and inner struggles become irrelevant. For this reason, the next element in the book is revelatory dream vision and not theological refutation. The angel and Ezra are both positive figures, both part of the author's psyche, of the author's self. So is the woman–Jerusalem. When the author is able to externalize the pain as the woman, and to offer comfort in the person of the seer, that catalyzes the powerful psychological experience. Here is the explanation of the 'mysterious' change; here is the explanation of the incoherent dialogue; here is the explanation for the inconclusiveness of the theological debate!

The arguments by which I support this central assertion are complex, and I certainly cannot enter into them now. Moreover, I am not maintaining that an identical psychological dynamic must necessarily be at play in any other work. I do claim, however, that *4 Ezra* is a good example of a case where a factor outside the theological or propositional consistency of the statements provides a potent key to the understanding of the book. This is religious literature; it consistently

---

1. Witness the end of Vision 6, which is a deliberate reversal of the plaint against God's government of the world, with which Vision 1 opens.

2. He can do this, I would maintain, because in fact his position had been changing, albeit very gradually, in the course of the first three visions. In this matter, too, my view differs from that of Brandenburger; it is set forth in 'Way of the Most High' and in full detail in my forthcoming *4 Ezra*.

describes religious experience, and the mere possibility that such religious experience has an authentic foundation profoundly affects its interpretation.

7. *Social Setting*

A third factor which must be taken into account is the sociological context. Admittedly, it is most difficult to investigate the sociological context/s of the apocalypses in light of ordinary historical sources.[1] We know almost nothing about the circles that wrote them, or their actual historical identification; we are ignorant of how the apocalypses functioned and were used. This is due to lack of information in conventional historical sources, aggravated by the pseudepigraphic mode of writing.

Nonetheless, an approach analogous to that developed in the case of the psychological experience of the apocalyptic author may cast some light on the social role and functioning of the seer. Our point of departure is the various passages which describe the relationship between the seer and the surrounding society. For instance, in 12.42 Ezra is recognized as a prophet by the people, by the social context, and he assents to that role by not denying the people's recognition. The people address Ezra as a 'prophet', and Ezra accepts that title; it is the people's attitude to him that determines his acceptance. From a methodological point of view, the fact that the social context is presented as determinative of religious role is a factor that has never been taken into account in the study of the apocalypses. It is, moreover, significant for the exegesis of the book that this happens only in Vision 5, and not before. Henceforth Ezra conducts himself as a prophet.

Vision 7 is a narrative about a revelatory experience, and its central function is to declare Ezra revealer of the twenty-four books of Sacred Scripture as well as of esoteric teachings. Thus Ezra is assimilated to Moses, he is a perfect revelatory figure, and he is assumed to heaven. The vision opens by drawing the parallel between Ezra and Moses. While both exoteric and esoteric things were revealed to Moses (14.6), in 14.7 Ezra is told that he has had esoteric revelation, that he is to teach this secretly to the wise, and that he is to be assumed. He is to go to instruct the wise (the recipients of the esoteric teaching) and

---

1. M.E. Stone, 'Apocalyptic Literature', *in Jewish Writings of the Second Temple Period* (ed. M.E. Stone; Compendia Rerum Iudaicarum ad Novum Testamentum 2.2; Assen and Philadelphia, 1984), pp. 433-34; M.E. Stone, 'The Question of the Messiah in 4 Ezra', *Judaism and its Messiahs* (ed. J. Neusner *et al.*; New York, 1988), pp. 217-20.

comfort the lowly among the people. Ezra agrees to this, but demands exoteric revelation as well as esoteric, for 'thy law has been burned'. God instructs Ezra to take five men with him and to go to a field. (Note that a group of five men accompany the seer also in *2 Baruch*.) Following the divine command, he assembles the people and addresses them. Then he departs for the field, receives the cup of the holy spirit, drinks it, and dictates his words, which include esoteric and exoteric works, the whole of scripture and an additional seventy books.[1]

So there are three *dramatis personae*: Ezra, the group of five scribes to the people, and the people. Ezra speaks in general terms, urging righteousness and hope. (It is this speech that Brandenburger sees as the very climax of Vision 7.) While in the field, he dictates secret and open teachings to the scribes. It has been observed that in ch. 6 of *Ascension of Isaiah* there is an interesting description of ecstatic activity. Isaiah is in the presence of the king and the princes of Israel. A group of forty prophets is also present and the king summons all the people. Isaiah speaks praises of God and enters a trance in which his spirit is assumed. The three groups are maintained. Isaiah is in the circle of the prophets, who know he is in trance. The people are apart and do not know. They had been sent out of the room when he went into the trance. On his awakening, he recounts his experience to Hezekiah and his son and to the prophets, but not to the people.

It is intriguing to compare this scenario with that in *4 Ezra* and *2 Baruch*. They may be seen as sharing the three players:

the seer	recognized as prophet by the people or the king,
an inner group	which accompanies the seer and is to some extent
	privy to his ecstatic experience,
the people.	

There is a separation of place: the people are apart, and the seer and his inner group are apart.[2] This is true both in *4 Ezra* and in *Ascension of Isaiah*. There is also, at least in *Ascension of Isaiah* and in *4 Ezra*, a distinction between two parts of the seer's experience and communication, that to the people as a whole, and that to the inner circle. In *2 Baruch*, at a number of points, the seer secludes himself with an inner group of five, while the people await their return.

I propose considering the possibility that these features reflect aspects of the actual social functioning of the author. The public

---

1. Compare also the three actors: Jesus, the inner group, and the people in Mk 4; cf. particularly Mk 4.33-34. This is one of a number of examples from the Gospels.

2. The initial impetus for this approach was given to me by A. Roitman in a discussion. The development of the material is my own responsibility.

recognition of Ezra's role as prophet and his responsive acceptance of it may well correspond to the way that the apocalyptic author himself was recognized by his own society (however small that society might have been). The threefold division of people, inner group and seer has many parallels and cannot be viewed as independent inventions by the authors of these three ancient texts. In fact, the seer was surrounded by an inner group, to whom he revealed the esoteric teaching and who participated in some measure in ecstatic experience. At a greater distance was the general society from which the writer/prophet received validation and which he addressed in prophetic style. These considerations become potent factors in the exegesis of the book, as well as in providing insight into the actual functioning of apocalyptic writers.[1]

I may perhaps be permitted one further piece of speculation. In the narrative of the book, Ezra receives his prophetic role from the people. To the people, however, he does not reveal the secret knowledge that has been made available to him: that he uncovers only to the elect inner group. This may reflect a reality in the author's society, that is, the author may have received his own authentication through social recognition and consequently have acted in accordance with fixed, commonly recognized patterns, including two different contexts of revelation. If this was so, then it offers some insight into the functioning of *4 Ezra*. The book's message may have been effective in society because it presents the seer as acting in the way that the author's contemporaries readily recognized as appropriate to prophets and apocalyptic visionaries. The author's personal experience, then, is mediated in a traditional form, and his message gains effectiveness because the pseudepigraphical seer is described as conducting himself in clearly identifiable ways that carry authority.

8. *Concluding Remarks*

In conclusion, then, when we consider what has been presented here, and try to draw more general conclusions from it, the following points may be of broader application.

a.   The category of coherency must be introduced into the discussion and the search after the factors providing coherency should be a central concern of those studying this ancient

---

1. It may also provide something of a key to the understanding of pseudepigraphy, and particularly the author's self-understanding.

religious literature. This is true, of course, in cases of unitary authorship (or powerful unitary redaction).

b.   The apocalypses must be taken much more seriously as religious literature, not just as compendia of theological concepts or midrashic traditions. These are works to be examined in their own right.

c.   Therefore, what the books say about the functioning of their pseudepigraphic heroes should play a significant role in the exegesis and explanation of the books. This is true at various levels of discourse, both social and psychological, as well as conceptual.

5

REVELATION AND RAPTURE: THE TRANSFORMATION
OF THE VISIONARY IN THE ASCENT APOCALYPSES

Martha Himmelfarb

As far as I know, the first person to comment on some of the questions
about the nature of apocalypticism that concerned the Uppsala
Colloquium was Baraies the Teacher, a third-century disciple of Mani.
His words are preserved for us in the Cologne Mani Codex, that
remarkable compilation of information about the life of Mani from the
great apostle himself and from his immediate followers.[1] Although
antiquity is not necessarily an indicator of reliability, I think we have
something to learn from Baraies, who calls our attention to an aspect
of many apocalypses that seems to me quite important, but that has
been given relatively little attention.

One of the sections of the Codex attributed to Baraies contains brief
citations from and summaries of five otherwise unknown apocalypses
ascribed to some of the earliest biblical patriarchs: Adam, Seth (here,
Sethel), Enosh, Shem, and Enoch, in that idiosyncratic order, followed
by several passages from the letters of Paul describing his ascent to the
third heaven and other revelations to him.[2] These excerpts are intro-

1. The Codex is now available with German translation and notes in L. Koenen
and C. Römer (eds. and trans.), *Der Kölner Mani-Kodex: Über das Werden seines
Leibes* (Abhandlungen der Rheinisch-Westfälischen Akademie der Wissenschaften,
Papyrologica Coloniensia, 14; Opladen, 1988). It was originally published and
translated by L. Koenen and A. Henrichs, 'Der Kölner Mani-Codex (P. Colon. inv.
nr. 4780). *PERI TES GENNES TOU SOMATOS AUTOU*', *ZPE* 19 (1975), pp. 1-
85; 32 (1978), pp. 87-199; 44 (1981), pp. 201-318; 48 (1982), pp. 1-59. The first
half of the Codex has been translated into English in R. Cameron and A.J. Dewey,
The Cologne Mani Codex (P. Colon. inv. nr. 4780): 'Concerning the Origin of His
Body' (Texts and Translations, 15, Early Christian Literature Series, 3; Missoula,
MT, 1979).
2. At the head of this section, where the attribution should appear, there is a
lacuna. For the attribution to Baraies, whose words appear elsewhere in the Codex as
well, see Henrichs and Koenen, 'Mani-Kodex', *ZPE* 19 (1975), pp. 80-81 n. 80*.

duced to make the point that Mani stands in a long line of spiritual leaders, each at the head of a community like Mani's.

> Let him who is willing listen and note how each of the forefathers showed his own revelation (*apokalypsis*) to his chosen, whom he chose and gathered together in the generation in which he appeared, and wrote it down to leave to posterity. He made known to them things having to do with his rapture, and they preached about it to those outside . . . So then during the period and course of his apostleship each one spoke concerning what he had seen and wrote it down as a memoir, and also about his rapture (p. 47).[1]

The apocalypses Baraies cites are not otherwise known to us from canon lists or quotations.[2] They show many points of continuity with the preserved Jewish apocalypses and some of the early Christian ones, but they also exhibit a number of parallels to gnostic works.[3] We tend to assume that the extant Jewish apocalypses were written in Palestine and Egypt, although there has been some recent interest in a Babylonian provenance for the earliest Enochic works.[4] Could these apocalypses also be Babylonian? This might account both for Baraies's knowledge of them and our lack of knowledge, as well as for some of their peculiar traits.

As the notes below suggest, the apocalypses attributed to Enosh and Shem seem remarkably similar. I wonder if they are really two separate texts.

1. Parenthetical references are to pages of the Mani Codex. All translations from the Codex are mine; I have consulted the translations of Koenen–Römer and Cameron–Dewey.

2. *The Catalogue of Sixty Canonical Books* (in *New Testament Apocrypha* [ed. E. Hennecke and W. Schneemelcher; trans. R.McL. Wilson; Philadelphia, 1963], I, p. 51) mentions an apocryphal book of Adam without any indication of whether it is an apocalypse; none of the other names found in the Mani Codex appear in the other canon lists published in Hennecke–Schneemelcher (I, pp. 42-52). Nor are there any references under these names in M.R. James, *The Lost Apocrypha of the Old Testament* (London and New York, 1970).

Works attributed to Adam, Seth, and Shem appear among the Nag Hammadi tractates, but it is clear that they are not the apocalypses Baraies quotes. There is a point of contact with the Nag Hammadi *Apocalypse of Adam*, which describes Adam as an exalted figure like the Adam of Baraies's apocalypse. But the Nag Hammadi *Apocalypse of Adam* does not contain an ascent. The works attributed to Seth and Shem do not show any real parallels to the apocalypses Baraies quotes.

3. For example, Seth is of course a particularly important figure for some gnostics; both Enosh and Shem are pondering the nature of creation when their revelations take place (pp. 52, 55); the 'posterity of the Spirit of Truth' (p. 55) to whom Enosh hands down his writing has a gnostic ring to it.

4. J.C. VanderKam, *Enoch and the Growth of an Apocalyptic Tradition* (CBQMS, 16; Washington, DC, 1984).

The content of the revelations in the apocalypses Baraies cites is quite varied, including individual eschatology,[1] cosmology,[2] angelology,[3] and a vision of the heavenly throne room,[4] but at least as far as I can tell from the excerpts and summaries, collective eschatology does not appear.

For Baraies, the patriarchs were apostles, like Paul and like Mani, and his picture of the setting of the apocalypses imposes the pattern of Manicheism on them. 'He made known to them things having to do with his rapture, and they preached about it to those outside. . .' None of the passages he cites gives any indication of a group of followers; indeed the very existence of a group for the earliest of the patriarchs would be problematic.

In his comments, Baraies gives the fact of rapture equal weight with the content of revelation.[5] This emphasis on rapture is especially striking, because Mani's revelations came to him not through ascent but from his heavenly twin. The emphasis on rapture, then, does not represent a reading back of Manichean practice onto the apocalypses, but Baraies's understanding of the apocalypses he knew.

While Baraies singles out only two elements, revelation and rapture, in his discussion of apocalypses, the portions of the apocalypses he chose to quote suggest another. The excerpts and attendant summaries are quite brief, with little detail about the content of revelation, but three of the five passages describe an experience in which the visionary becomes like the angels.

---

1. Individual eschatology is the primary concern of the passage from the *Apocalypse of Enoch*, in which Enoch is taken to see the places where the righteous are rewarded and the wicked punished (pp. 58-60).

2. As noted above, the setting for the revelations of both Enosh and Shem is their consideration of questions having to do with the nature of creation. It therefore seems likely that the apocalypses include cosmological revelations, although none appears in the material quoted by Baraies.

3. Baraies's summary mentions various types of angels as the subject of the revelation to Adam (p. 49).

4. A heavenly throne room descends to Shem as he stands on the high mountain to which he has been carried (p. 56).

5. In the excerpts, all of the patriarchs except Adam are explicitly described as experiencing a supernatural journey, although not necessarily to heaven. Both Enosh and Shem are taken not to heaven but to high mountains (pp. 53, 55), like Ezekiel at the start of his vision of the eschatological temple (Ezek. 40.2). In both apocalypses the verb *harpazo* is used for the mode of transportation. Adam is reported in the summary to have seen various types of angels in the course of his revelation, strongly suggesting ascent, and there is a lacuna in the text at the point in the excerpt where the rapture might have been mentioned (bottom of p. 48).

Adam, we are told in Baraies's summary, 'became more exalted than all the powers and angels of creation' (p. 50). Seth's claim is slightly more modest: 'When I heard these things, my heart rejoiced, and my understanding was changed, and I became like one of the greatest angels' (p. 51). Shem does not claim full angelic status, at least in the excerpt quoted by Baraies. Rather, following great physical agitation, a voice lifts him by his right hand and breathes into him, bringing him 'an increase of power and glory' (p. 57).

No such transformation appears in the portion of the Apocalypse of Enosh quoted, but the description of Enosh's fear when the spirit seized him to transport him is very close to the one associated with Shem's transformation (p. 53),[1] and I would not be surprised if the complete apocalypse included a transformation. The excerpt from the Enoch apocalypse contains a less elaborate description of fear in reaction to the arrival of seven angelic revealers, but without a transformation (p. 59). Again it is possible that the complete apocalypse contained one, since the preserved Enochic apocalypses are so rich in transformations.

The *Book of the Watchers*, almost the earliest of the apocalypses and a work of great influence, contains the first ascent to heaven in Jewish literature. Heaven is here understood as a temple, and although Enoch is not actually transformed when he ascends to the heavenly temple, he is able to stand before God like a heavenly priest, that is, an angel.[2] After his ascent, his journey to the ends of the earth shows that he is indeed a fit companion for angels (*1 En.* 17–36). This claim appears to have its roots in the prophetic claim to participation in the divine council.[3]

In *2 Enoch* the ascent is clearly a reworking of the ascent in the *Book of the Watchers* in combination with the tour to the ends of the earth,[4] and the transformation that Enoch undergoes is in large part a development of themes from the *Book of the Watchers*. Here, as

1. Shem: 'Then the appearance of my face was changed so that I fell to the ground. And my vertebrae shook, while my feet could not support my ankles.' Enosh: 'My heart became heavy, and all my limbs shook. My vertebrae were violently shaken, and my feet did not support my ankles.'

2. For heaven as a temple in *1 En.* 14–16, see G.W.E. Nickelsburg, 'Enoch, Levi, and Peter: Recipients of Revelation in Upper Galilee', *JBL* 100 (1981), pp. 575-90.

3. M. Himmelfarb, 'From Prophecy to Apocalypse: The *Book of the Watchers* and Tours of Heaven', in A. Green (ed.), *Jewish Spirituality: From the Bible through the Middle Ages* (New York, 1986), pp. 149-51.

4. G.W.E. Nickelsburg, *Jewish Literature between the Bible and the Mishnah* (Philadelphia, 1981), p. 185.

Enoch prostrates himself before God's throne in the seventh heaven, God orders the angel Michael to extract Enoch from his body, anoint him with fragrant oil, and dress him in a special garment, a process that suggests priestly investiture. When Michael has done so, Enoch discovers that he has become 'like one of the glorious ones: there was no observable difference' (22.10).[1] After the transformation God reveals to him secrets never revealed before, not even to the angels (ch. 24).

The process of transformation is taken about as far as it can go in *3 Enoch* or *Sefer Hekhalot*, as this hekhalot work is more properly known. *Sefer Hekhalot*, which is formally an apocalypse, reports the revelations of the angel Metatron to R. Ishmael, the hero of many other hekhalot works. Metatron begins the revelations with his own story: he was Enoch son of Jared until God took him to heaven and exalted him over all his creations, making him his second in command (ch. 4; nos. 5-6, 886-87).[2] This is surely the greatest success story ever told, although there are attempts in other works and even within *3 Enoch* itself (ch. 16; no. 20) to reduce Metatron's status, suggesting that not everyone was entirely comfortable with Enoch's success.[3]

According to *Sefer Hekhalot*, Enoch becomes Metatron by growing into a being of enormous size with seventy-two wings (ch. 9; nos. 12, 893). After this transformation God provides his new servant with a glorious throne (ch. 10; nos. 13, 894) and a splendid robe (ch. 12; nos. 15, 896). If the robe is intended to suggest priestly investiture, this is never made explicit. But in his edition of *3 Enoch*, H. Odeberg quoted a reference to eight garments of Metatron from a work entitled *Alphabet of Metatron* found in a manuscript in the British Museum.[4] As P. Alexander notes in his translation of *Sefer Hekhalot*, eight is the number of the high priest's garments.[5] A passage found in only a

---

1. Trans. F.I. Andersen, '2 (Slavonic Apocalypse of) Enoch', in J.H. Charlesworth (ed.), *The Old Testament Pseudepigrapha* (Garden City, NY, 1983), I, pp. 138-39.

2. For *3 Enoch*, chapter references refer to P. Alexander, '3 (Hebrew Apocalypse of) Enoch', in Charlesworth, *OTP*, I, pp. 223-315. For *3 Enoch* and other hekhalot texts discussed here, references introduced by 'no.' are to units of P. Schäfer in collaboration with M. Schlüter and H.G. von Mutius, *Synopse zur Hekhalot-Literatur* (Texte und Studien zum antike Judentum, 2; Tübingen, 1981).

3. The classic passage is *b. Ḥag.* 15a. See Alexander, '3 Enoch', p. 268 n. a.

4. *3 Enoch or the Hebrew Book of Enoch* (Cambridge, 1928), p. 32.

5. '3 Enoch', p. 265 n. a to ch. 12.

single manuscript of *Sefer Hekhalot* (ch. 15B) refers to Metatron's activity in the heavenly temple.[1]

The *Similitudes of Enoch* in its final form includes the transformation of Enoch into the heavenly son of man, a type of angelic figure (*1 En.* 71.14).[2] But the Similitudes' use of material from the *Book of the Watchers* goes in a rather different direction from that of *2 Enoch* and *Sefer Hekhalot*. The transformation is simply announced rather than described, though it is preceded by an experience not unlike the overwhelming physical experience described in the apocalypses of Shem and Enosh (*1 En.* 71.11). As far as I can tell, there are no priestly overtones to this transformation.

Now the transformations of *2 Enoch* and *Sefer Hekhalot* are quite extraordinary. Enoch does not become merely an angel, but an exalted angel. If it were not for the apocalypses of Adam and Seth quoted by Baraies, one might be inclined to treat this sort of transformation as the peculiarity of a couple of ill-understood texts about Enoch. But Baraies shows us that this type of transformation is more widespread. While Baraies's quotations indicate neither priestly elements nor the influence of the Book of the Watchers, they are so brief that it is impossible to draw any certain conclusions.

A somewhat different and more democratic notion of transformation appears in a larger number of apocalypses. Here transformation into an angel or a star—that is, a member of the heavenly host—is promised to the righteous as a reward after death. Daniel describes the fate of the righteous thus: 'Those who are wise will shine like the brightness of heaven, and those who turn many to righteousness, like stars for ever and ever' (12.3). The *Epistle of Enoch* promises the righteous that they 'will shine like the lights of heaven' (*1 En.* 104.2) and 'have great joy like the angels of heaven' (104.4).[3] Later the *Similitudes of Enoch* describes the righteous dead dwelling with angels (*1 En.* 39.5), shining like fire (39.7), while in *2 Baruch* the righteous

---

1. '3 Enoch', p. 303. The manuscript is Bodleian 2257/4 (Neubauer), which is not included in Schäfer's *Synopse*. The passage appears also in a manuscript of the writings of the German Hasidic rabbi, Eleazer of Worms. The idea that Metatron served as heavenly high priest is explicit elsewhere in rabbinic literature (*Num R.* 12.12).

2. See the discussion of the relationship of ch. 71 to the rest of the *Similitudes* in J.J. Collins, *The Apocalyptic Imagination: An Introduction to the Jewish Matrix of Christianity* (New York, 1984), pp. 151-53.

3. Trans. M.A. Knibb, '1 Enoch', in H.F.D. Sparks, *The Apocryphal Old Testament* (Oxford, 1984).

dead are promised first equality with the angels and the stars (51.10), and then splendor even greater than that of the angels (51.12).[1]

In the *Ascension of Isaiah*, Isaiah reports that as he ascends through the seven heavens his glory increases until in the seventh heaven he finds himself fully the equal of the angels. But he remains inferior to the righteous dead (9.37-39).[2] The visionary of the *Apocalypse of Zephaniah* is a dead soul, who, after he is found righteous, dons an angelic robe and joins the angels in their song (ch. 8).[3]

The *Apocalypse of Abraham* similarly suggests that Abraham achieves a kind of fellowship with the heavenly host; the song Abraham sings to protect himself during the ordeal of ascent turns out to be the song sung by the creatures of the divine throne (18.1-3). No relationship between Abraham's experience and the fate of the righteous after death is made explicit, but there is a hint of such an understanding in the mention of Azazel's garment, now set aside for Abraham (13.14). Abraham is never shown putting on the garment, and the garment is probably to be understood as reserved for after death, like the garments mentioned in the *Ascension of Isaiah* (8.26, 9.2).

Experience much like the transformations described in the apocalypses appear in other types of literature from late antiquity as the goal of heavenly ascent. In the hekhalot texts, the culmination of ascent is often the visionary's participation in the heavenly liturgy as a manifestation of his equality with the angels, just as in the apocalypses.[4] At the end of a series of hymns to be used to ascend (or in the terminology of some of the hekhalot texts, to descend) to the divine chariot, R. Ishmael says in *Hekhalot Rabbati*, 'All these songs R. Aqiba heard when he descended to the chariot, and he took hold of them and learned them as he stood before the throne of glory, the songs that his ministers were singing before him' (no. 106). In another section of *Hekhalot Rabbati*, we learn that when the visionary finally

---

1. J.J. Collins, 'Apocalyptic Eschatology as the Transcendence of Death', *CBQ* 36 (1974), pp. 21-43, discusses the fate of the righteous after death in texts from the last two centuries BCE. *2 Baruch* does not fit within this timespan.

2. For a more extended discussion of Isaiah's transformation in the *Ascension of Isaiah*, see M. Himmelfarb, 'The Experience of the Visionary and Genre in the Ascension of Isaiah 6-11 and the Apocalypse of Paul', in A. Yarbro Collins (ed.), *Early Christian Apocalypticism: Genre and Social Setting* (*Semeia* 36; Atlanta, 1986), pp. 97-111.

3. I refer to the chapter divisions in O.S. Wintermute (trans.), 'Apocalypse of Zephaniah', in Charlesworth, *OTP*, I, pp. 497-515.

4. Himmelfarb, 'Heavenly Ascent and the Relationship of the Apocalypses and the *Hekhalot* Literature', *HUCA* 59 (1988), pp. 91-93.

gains admission to the last gate and arrives before the throne of glory, 'he begins to recite the song that the throne of glory sings every day' (no. 251). Remember that the song Abraham recites in the course of his ascent turns out to be the song of the throne of glory.

One goal of the rituals prescribed in the magical papyri is immortality or deification. In the so-called Mithras liturgy the initiate is to say of himself at the culmination of his ascent,

> I, NN, whose mother is NN, who was born from the mortal womb of NN and from the fluid of semen, and who, since he has been born again from you today, has become immortal out of so many myriads in this hour according to the wish of god the exceedingly good—resolves to worship you. . . (*PGM* IV.645-51).[1]

In another text contained in the same papyrus as the Mithras liturgy, the initiate says, 'I have been attached to your holy form. I have been given power by your holy name. I have acquired your emanation of the goods, Lord, god of gods, master, daimon' (*PGM* IV.216-19). After a string of magical words, the instructions conclude, 'Having done this, return as lord of a godlike nature which is accomplished through the divine encounter' (*PGM* IV.220-22).[2] In a system in which there are many deities, 'a godlike nature' probably means something not very different from taking one's place among the angels.

If the experiences described in the apocalypses are similar to those in the hekhalot texts, can the hekhalot texts give us a clue to the settings in which ascent apocalypses were written? The suggestion of continuity between the apocalyptists and the merkavah mystics goes back to Gershom Scholem, who based his argument on the similarity between the visions of the heavenly chariot, reported in rabbinic literature and the hekhalot texts, and those of the apocalypses.[3] The hekhalot texts contain instructions for those who wish to achieve visions of the chariot. Scholem seems to have believed that the visions of the apocalypses represent the actual experiences of their authors, achieved the same way as the later merkavah mystics achieved their visions, although their authors did not choose to record the practices. Following Scholem, Ithamar Gruenwald points to ascetic practices as a

---

1. Trans. by M.W. Meyer in H.D. Betz (ed.), *The Greek Magical Papyri in Translation, Including the Demotic Spells* (Chicago, 1985), pp. 50-51.
2. Trans. by E.N. O'Neil in Betz, *Greek Magical Papyri*, pp. 41-42.
3. *Major Trends in Jewish Mysticism* (3rd edn; New York, 1961), p. 43.

point of continuity between the apocalypses and the hekhalot literature.[1]

Most apocalypses do not refer to such practices, but there are several in which fasting and other types of asceticism do appear. Among the ascent apocalypses, in the *Apocalypse of Abraham*, God commands Abraham to undertake a limited fast for forty days before sacrificing and receiving a revelation (9.7-8), but Abraham exceeds God's command by spending forty days in the wilderness in the company of the angel Iaoel, neither eating nor drinking (12.1-2). The *Ascension of Isaiah* depicts Isaiah as the head of group of prophets living in the wilderness, dressed in sackcloth, and eating wild herbs (2.8-11). The setting in which Isaiah's vision in the *Ascension of Isaiah* takes place (ch. 6) is very close to that of the vision of R. Neḥuniah b. haQanah in the famous passage in *Hekhalot Rabbati* (nos. 198-250): in both the visionary sits in the midst of his circle, reporting on what he sees. Since this scene is often presumed to represent the actual setting of the practice of merkavah mysticism, this parallel is particularly impressive.

But aside from this last parallel the similarities between the practices of the apocalypses and the hekhalot literature are general rather than specific. As to the relationship between the picture in the *Ascension of Isaiah* and *Hekhalot Rabbati*, the passage in *Hekhalot Rabbati* is the only such description in hekhalot literature, although there are many places in which the instructions for ascent suggest that the would-be visionary is alone as he attempts his ascent.[2]

At this point we need to confront head-on a crucial fact that Scholem and others have ignored: the apocalypses are literature, indeed one might even say fiction. Scholem's position assumes that when the author describes the ascent, he is describing his own experience under someone else's name. But the relationship between the author and his hero is not nearly so direct; indeed the visionary takes his identity from traditions about a great figure of the past.

The question of whether the apocalypses represent a reflection of actual experience, whether of transformation or of other visionary phenomena, is an extremely difficult one, and I will only attempt to indicate a few guiding principles for approaching it. The answer is

1. 'Manicheism and Judaism in Light of the *Cologne Mani Codex*', in *From Apocalypticism to Gnosticism* (Beiträge zur Erforschung des Alten Testaments und des antiken Judentums, 14; Frankfurt, 1988), p. 271.

2. See e.g. *Hekhalot Zuṭrati* (nos. 413-19), and the Ozhayah fragment from the Geniza; see P. Schäfer, *Geniza-Fragmente zur Hekhalot-Literatur* (Texte und Studien zum antiken Judentum, 6; Tübingen, 1984), pp. 2a/23-2b/24.

surely different for different apocalypses, and each needs to be considered in its own right.[1]

Pseudonymity and literary connections at first seem to militate
against actual experience, but we must also remember the 'conservative character of mystical experience', in the title of Steven Katz's
essay,[2] the way in which undoubtedly genuine mystical experiences are
shaped and informed, at least in the telling (and that is of course all we
have), by the assumptions of the mystic's tradition.

On the other hand, it is clear that if visionary experience is reflected
in the apocalypses, there are many mirrors between the experience and
the text. Pseudonymity is perhaps the darkest mirror, the one we least
understand. My own guess is that texts that describe a human being
becoming not just an angel, but the most exalted angel of all, are more
literary, and the relationship to experience is less direct, than texts that
describe a somewhat more modest form of transformation.

Now I turn to a somewhat more tractable question, the function of
the theme of transformation in the apocalypses. David Halperin has
recently argued that the ascent of human beings to heaven to take their
place among angels is actually an invasion of heaven, a displacement of
the rightful inhabitants by young upstarts.[3] He is concerned primarily
with rabbinic literature and the hekhalot texts, but he considers the
apocalypses too. For him Enoch's transformation into Metatron in
Sefer Hekhalot is the most striking example of such displacement,
which he reads in Freudian terms as an adolescent fantasy of sur-
passing and displacing adult figures of authority.

It is a brilliant reading, but I do not think it does justice to the range
of uses of transformation in the apocalypses.[4] I suggest instead that
these descriptions of transformation be understood in the context of
some of the major developments of the history of Judaism in the
Second Temple period.

One result of the traumatic break with the traditions of the past
caused by the destruction of the First Temple and the exile, it is often

---

1. Stone's discussion of *4 Ezra* in this volume represents just such a consideration.

2. 'The "Conservative" Character of Mystical Experience', in Katz (ed.), *Mysticism and Religious Traditions* (New York, 1983), pp. 3-60.

3. 'Ascension or Invasion: Implications of the Heavenly Journey in Ancient
Judaism', *Religion* 18 (1988), pp. 47-67; *idem, The Faces of the Chariot: Early
Jewish Responses to Ezekiel's Vision* (Texte und Studien zum antiken Judentum, 16;
Tübingen, 1988), pp. 359-446.

4. For a more detailed discussion of this point, see my forthcoming review of
Halperin, *Faces of the Chariot*, in *Critical Review of Books in Religion* 3 (1990),
pp. 340-42.

argued, is a new feeling of distance between God and humanity, a feeling unknown in the religion of Israel before the exile. Ezekiel's vision of God on a chariot-throne is a response to the fact that the temple, once the center of religious experience, is no longer available. The appeal to creation in the work of the other great prophet of the exile, Second Isaiah, a new departure in prophetic literature, also reflects a sense of distance between Israel and the God of history.

Such distance makes prophecy problematic. In the post-exilic period, there is a gradual movement away from prophecy toward interpretation as a primary mode of religious authority. In Zechariah, a post-exilic prophet, prophecy has become interpretation, visions to be deciphered. This form then becomes one of the central modes of revelation in the apocalypses. Angels are usually the interpreters of these visions. The heroes of the Bible talked with God, but the heroes of the apocalypses, on the whole, talk with angels. The Hellenistic period sees the emergence of angels with names and to a certain extent distinctive identities. God is understood to dwell in the midst of myriads of angels, to whom he delegates the performance of various tasks.

Most attempts to describe the emergence of the angelologies of early Judaism are unable to shake off the feeling that the new developments represent a falling away from the heights of classical biblical religion.

> Fundamentally the whole of angelology was an indication that the figure of God had receded into the distance and that the angels were needed as intermediaries between him, creation and man... This strictly-ordered, pyramid-like hierarchical system probably corresponded to a general religious need of the time, as it exercised a profound influence, not only on the Greek-speaking Judaism of the Diaspora and early Christianity, but through them on gnosticism and indeed on the whole of popular religion in late antiquity, as is shown by its significance for magic. Even neo-Platonism could not escape its influence.[1]

Although he does not quite say so in this passage from *Judaism and Hellenism*, Martin Hengel's language (God 'has receded into the distance', neo-Platonism 'could not escape') strongly suggests that this new development is undesirable. Other scholars make this judgment quite openly.

Drawing on our discussion of the visionary's transformation in the apocalypses, I would suggest a somewhat different way of looking at

---

1. M. Hengel, *Judaism and Hellenism: Studies in their Encounter in Palestine during the Early Hellenistic Period* (Philadelphia, 1974), I, p. 233.

the phenomenon.[1] In *By Light, Light*, E.R. Goodenough speaks of Philo's system as intended to solve 'the problem of the relation of the Unrelated', of how God could 'be brought into relationship with the world, in spite of the fact that He was essentially beyond relation'. Philo's solution to the problem is a variation on the standard ancient answer, to understand God through the image of the sun sending forth its rays, its brightness in no way diminished by the rays.[2]

Whatever the faults in Goodenough's reading of Philo, I suspect that he is correct to see the problem of distance as central to Philo, and, as Hengel too suggests, to many others in late antiquity. Once we have recognized how widely this problem was perceived, we realize that angels are not its cause but an attempt at its solution. The development of a picture of the world in which a large number of angels play so prominent a role should be understood not simply as a reflection of a sense of distance but as an attempt to overcome that distance. The idea that the heavens are full of angels assures human beings of contact with the sphere of the divine, if only its periphery.

What is more, it turns out that the boundaries between human beings and angels are not very clear. Despite its seven heavens and myriads of angels, a text like the *Ascension of Isaiah* does not really reflect a gulf between man and God. The righteous, according to this work, can expect to spend eternity as angelic beings contemplating God himself. To be sure, for most this experience is reserved until after death. But certain exceptional men can have a foretaste of it while still alive, thus serving as examples of the future intimacy with God to which all the righteous can look forward.

Thus Baraies the Teacher teaches us something important in his insistence on the intimate link between revelation and rapture or, one might say, between content and form. It is not only what God reveals to the visionary that is important, but the very fact that God is willing to bring a human being near to him. Under certain circumstances, according to the apocalypses, human beings can cross the boundary and join the angels. Clearly we need to rethink the pessimism so often attributed to the apocalypses.

---

1. For similar conclusions about the role of angelology in early Judaism, see L.W. Hurtado, *One God, One Lord: Early Christian Devotion and Ancient Jewish Monotheism* (Philadelphia, 1988), pp. 22-35. Hurtado traces the negative view back to Bousset.

2. *By Light, Light: The Mystic Gospel of Hellenistic Judaism* (New Haven, 1935), p. 11.

6

FOLK TRADITIONS IN JEWISH APOCALYPTIC LITERATURE

James H. Charlesworth

In my judgment, research[1] has shown that apocalyptic thought originated in the proto-apocalypticism of the latter prophets (esp. Ezek. 38–39, Zech. 5–6, 9–14, and Isa. 24–27, 56–66),[2] and that as apocalypticism developed it was enriched by thoughts derived from other

---

1. Notes to the present article are selective. For bibliographies see J.M. Schmidt, *Die jüdische Apokalyptik* (Neukirchen-Vluyn, 2nd edn, 1976); J.H. Charlesworth (with P. Dykers and M.J.P. Charlesworth), *The Pseudepigrapha and Modern Research with a Supplement* (SBLSCS, 7S; Chico, CA, 1981); C. Rowland, *The Open Heaven: A Study of Apocalyptic in Judaism and Early Christianity* (London, 1982); J.J. Collins, *Daniel with an Introduction to Apocalyptic Literature* (The Forms of Old Testament Literature, 20; Grand Rapids, 1984); M.E. Stone (ed.), *Jewish Writings of the Second Temple Period* (CRINT, 2.2; Assen, 1984); Collins, *The Apocalyptic Imagination: An Introduction to the Jewish Matrix of Christianity* (New York, 1984); Rowland, *Christian Origins: From Messianic Movement to Christian Religion* (London, 1985); Charlesworth (with J.R. Mueller), *The New Testament Apocrypha and Pseudepigrapha: A Guide to Publications, with Excursuses on Apocalypses* (Metuchen, NJ, 1987); C. Kappler *et al.*, *Apocalypses et voyages dans l'au-delà* (Paris, 1987); T.W. Willett, *Eschatology in the Theodicies of 2 Baruch and 4 Ezra* (JSPS, 4; Sheffield, 1989). Also see the chapters in the present book, and Boccaccini's discussion of the Italian School. Among the most valuable collection of essays are the following: M. Philonenko (ed.), *L'apocalyptique* (Études d'histoire des religions, 3; Paris, 1977); L. Monloubou (ed.), *Apocalypses et théologie de l'espérance* (Lectio Divina, 95; Paris, 1977); Collins (ed.), *Apocalypse: The Morphology of a Genre* (Semeia 14; Missoula, MT, 1979); K. Koch and J.M. Schmidt (eds.), *Apokalyptik* (Wege der Forschung, 365; Darmstadt, 1982); D. Hellholm (ed.), *Apocalypticism in the Mediterranean World and the Near East* (Tübingen, 1983); P.D. Hanson (ed.), *Visionaries and their Apocalypses* (Issues in Religion and Theology, 4; London, 1983).

2. I am indebted here to the excellent research published by P.D. Hanson, especially his *The Dawn of Apocalyptic* (Philadelphia, 1975); and his 'Introduction', in *Visionaries*, pp. 1-15.

cultures, especially from Mesopotamia.[1] While the apocalypses, which (except for Daniel and Revelation) are collected together in the Pseudepigrapha,[2] reflect the methods and skills of the scribal schools in Judaism,[3] another dimension of apocalypticism has not been adequately observed. Folklore, especially humor, has helped shape the Jewish apocalypses.[4] Likewise, the bizarre images and symbolic language in the Jewish apocalypses were derived from ancient Near Eastern iconography that antedated them by numerous centuries. The purpose of the present study, therefore, is to argue that Jewish folk traditions—folklore, humor, and inconography—are one element in the development of Jewish apocalyptic thought. Jewish apocalypticism is a learned phe-

---

1. See H.L. Jansen, *Die Henochgestalt* (Oslo, 1939); P. Grelot, 'La légende d'Henoch dans les apocryphes et dans la Bible: origine et signification', *RSR* 46 (1958), pp. 5-26, 181-210; H.D. Betz, 'Zum Problem des religionsgeschichtlichen Verständnisses der Apokalyptik', *Zeitschrift für Theologie und Kirche* 63 (1966), pp. 391-409 (ET by J.W. Leitch in *Apocalypticism* [*JTC* 6 (1969)], pp. 134-56); J.Z. Smith, 'Wisdom and Apocalyptic', *Religious Syncretism in Antiquity: Essays in Conversation with Geo. Widengren* (ed. B.A. Pearson; Missoula, MT, 1975), pp. 131-56; republished in *Visionaries and their Apocalypses*, pp. 101-20; the chapters by T. Olsson, J. Bergman, S.S. Hartman, G. Widengren, W. Burkert, B. Gladigow, J.G. Griffiths, J. Assman, A. Hultgård, and H.D. Betz, in *Apocalypticism in the Mediterranean World and the Near East*; Stone, in *Jewish Writings*, p. 392; and especially J. VanderKam, *Enoch and the Growth of an Apocalyptic Tradition* (CBQMS, 16; Washington, DC, 1984).

2. See the recent comments by Collins in 'Apocalyptic Literature', *Encyclopedia of Early Christianity* (ed. E. Ferguson; New York, 1990), pp. 56-58. Traditionally Roman Catholics label the Protestant 'Apocrypha' as deuterocanonical books; the so-called 'Pseudepigrapha' are therefore 'Jewish Apocrypha'. See the excellent study by R.E. Brown, P. Perkins, and A.J. Saldarini on 'Apocrypha; Dead Sea Scrolls; Other Jewish Literature', in *The New Jerome Biblical Commentary* (ed. R.E. Brown, J.A. Fitzmyer, and R.E. Murphy; Englewood Cliffs, NJ, 1990), pp. 1055-82.

3. See especially the contributions by J.Z. Smith, notably his 'Wisdom and Apocalyptic', in *Visionaries and their Apocalypses*, pp. 101-20. D.E. Orton has shown that in Jewish apocalypticism a 'scribe' denoted not only a 'copyist' or 'author', but also a bearer of revelation. I agree with Orton that 'in the literary apocalyptic context the scribe epithet is always related to the eminent, spiritual and charismatic role of the figure, as the *recipient and mediator of divine revelations*'. I would have written 'almost always'. See Orton, *The Understanding Scribe: Matthew and the Apocalyptic Ideal* (JSNTS, 24; Sheffield, 1989), p. 78.

4. Long ago (in 1903) W. Bousset argued that Jewish apocalypticism produced a 'Literatur der aufsteigenden, ungebildeten Schicht des Volkes, eine Literatur von stark laienhaftem Charakter'. See Bousset, 'Die religionsgeschichtliche Herkunft der jüdischen Apokalyptik', in *Apokalyptik*, p. 134. I am convinced that folk tradition in Jewish apocalypticism is an element in the development of the apocalypses, but reject Bousset's claim that apocalypticism was produced by uneducated lay people. That idea is no longer tenable.

nomenon; but that insight should not hinder us from recognizing that the apocalypses, and apocalyptic writings, preserve Jewish folk tradition.[1]

Preliminary Observations

At the outset I wish to urge that we explore 'proto-apocalyptic' features in non-Jewish texts,[2] such as *The Lamb to Bocchoris, Berossus,* and *Abydenus*, but we must be careful not to transfer the adjective 'apocalyptic' to a text that only vaguely parallels apocalyptic thought.[3] An apocalyptic writing must be able to transfer the reader from a finite, meaningless, world to another eternal, meaningful world; and it must possess an eschatological tone with a correlative disenchantment with history and the present social situation.[4] It is not so much elements that make a writing 'apocalyptic'; it is the scheme and the tone.

I am convinced that the origin of the Jewish *apocalypses* is to be found primarily in Prophecy but also (to a lesser extent) in Wisdom,[5] and that the full-blown Jewish apocalypses are indelibly marked by

---

1. All translations cited, unless otherwise noted, are from *The Old Testament Pseudepigrapha* (2 vols.; ed. J.H. Charlesworth; Garden City, NY, 1983–85).

2. No clear pre-Christian apocalypse has been found outside Early Judaism; see Charlesworth, 'Excluded "Apocalypses"', in *The New Testament Apocrypha and Pseudepigrapha*, pp. 54-55 (plus end notes). See the caveats about the Persian apocalyptic writings by Collins in *Apocalypse*, pp. 207-17.

3. See the comments by J.Z. Smith in *Imagining Religion: From Babylon to Jonestown* (Chicago Studies in the History of Judaism; Chicago, 1982), pp. 90-96.

4. See my discussions of defining an apocalypse and apocalyptic writing in *The New Testament Apocrypha and Pseudepigrapha*.

5. G. von Rad traced the origin of apocalypticism to Wisdom; see his *Old Testament Theology* (2 vols.; New York, 1965) and *Wisdom in Israel* (Nashville, 1972). P. von der Osten-Sacken in *Die Apokalyptik in ihrem Verhältnis zu Prophetie und Weisheit* (Munich, 1969) showed the inadequacies in von Rad's approach. In full-blown apocalypses, like *1 Enoch* (cf. esp. 42.1-3; 49.1; 61.7; 63.2), apocalyptic thought is clearly influenced by wisdom. See F. Dexinger, *Henochs Zehnwochen-apokalypse und offene Probleme der Apokalyptikforschung* (Studia Post-Biblica, 29; Leiden, 1977), pp. 39-43. Also see the significant insights by J. VanderKam in his 'The Prophetic-Sapiential Origins of Apocalyptic Thought', in *A Word in Season: Essays in Honour of William McKane* (ed. J.D. Martin and P.R. Davies; JSOTS, 42; Sheffield, 1986), pp. 163-76. VanderKam concludes that prophecy, broadly defined, was 'probably the decisive stimulus in the evolution of apocalyptic thought' (p. 174).

   I. Gruenwald suggests that we should call Jewish apocalyptic Thought 'Para-Prophecy'. See his 'Jewish Apocalyptic Literature', *Aufstieg und Niedergang der römischen Welt*, II.19.1, pp. 89-118.

influences from Egypt (especially *Test. Abr.*, *2 En.*, *Sib. Or.* 5), Greece and Rome (notably *Sib. Or.* 5, *4 Ezra*), Syria (*Sib. Or.* 7), and Babylon (perhaps *Sib. Or.* 4 and *1 En.*). Judea and Galilee play a major role in almost every apocalypse, whether the provenience is somewhere in Palestine or the Diaspora.

We must distinguish between the literary genre (the apocalypses themselves), related phenomena and documents (apocalyptic is an adjective not a noun), and the social dimensions of the apocalyptic groups (apocalypticism).[1]

Folklore[2]

Many stories in Jewish apocalyptic literature evolved from conversations around the campfire, the hearth, or anywhere else where Jews would customarily gather to relax and talk, especially after work. In folklore fact and fiction 'mingled freely',[3] producing creative histories,[4] and 'in its own way, non history'.[5] Folklore and humor—and of course the physical relaxation and psychological release gained from laughing—served as a catharsis from physical labors and the psychological oppressions caused by insensitive ruling Jews, like John Hyrcanus and Alexander Jannaeus, hostile enemies, like Antiochus Epiphanes and Pompey, and oppressive tyrants, especially Herod the Great. Jews were certainly not too serious to enjoy and master the art

---

1. See Hanson, 'Introduction', in *Visionaries*, pp. 1-5; esp. p. 8. On the social dimensions of Jewish apocalypticism, see Nickelsburg, Hengel, Meeks, and Kippenberg in *Apocalypticism in the Mediterranean World*; also see L.L. Grabbe, 'The Social Setting of Early Jewish Apocalypticism', *JSP* 4 (1989), pp. 27-47.

2. Dov Noy defines Jewish folklore 'as the creative spiritual and cultural heritage of the Jewish people handed down, mainly by oral tradition, from generation to generation by the various Jewish communities'. See Dov Noy, 'Folklore', in *Encyclopedia Judaica*, VI (1971), cols. 1374-1410; the quotation is in col. 1375. Also see cols. 1408-10 for a helpful bibliography. In this paper I have tried to tighten this loose definition (see the section below entitled 'Motif-Index of Folklore and a Refined Methodology').

3. H.A. Fischel, 'Diaspora, Fact and Belief', *Bulletin of Indiana School of Religion* 53 (1963), p. 1.

4. See D. Mendels, '"Creative History" in the Hellenistic Near East in the Third and Second Centuries BCE: The Jewish Case', *JSP* 2 (1988), pp. 13-20. Mendel's observations are consonant with the ones I am now making about folklore.

5. Fischel, 'Story and History: Observations on Greco-Roman Rhetoric and Pharisaism', in *American Oriental Society; Middle West Branch: Semi-Centennial Volume: A Collection of Original Essays* (ed. D. Sinor; Asian Studies Research Institute, Oriental Series, 3; Bloomington, IN, 1969), p. 60.

of humor;[1] they were dedicated to Torah but they developed 'a subtle and trenchant humor, but not so subtle or trenchant as to wipe out any chance of delight in it'.[2]

While the study of folklore has been seen to be important for biblical studies,[3] the significance of folklore, and humor, in the Jewish apocalyptic literature has not been recognized.[4] This failure seems to result from two misconceptions. First, the apocalypses are judged to be only serious and somber, and denote a pessimistic view of present reality. As has been abundantly clear over the last two decades, the apocalypses are complex, and represent many facets of the culture of Judaism, especially before 135 CE.

Secondly, laughter, as in Abraham's and Sarah's response to God's promise (Gen. 17.17; 18.12), and humorous stories are considered embarrassing, inappropriate, or merely deemed frivolous.[5] Some critics, like Reinhold Niebuhr, reluctantly[6]—but incorrectly—felt

1. E. Berggrav, *Humor og alvor* (Copenhagen, 1954), p. 71, claimed that Jews during the time of Jesus lacked an appreciation for humor.

2. I. Knox, 'The Traditional Roots of Jewish Humor', in M.C. Hyers, *Holy Laughter: Essays on Religion in the Comic Perspective* (New York, 1969), p. 160.

3. See esp. H. Gunkel, *Esther* (Religionsgeschichtliche Volksbucher, 2/19-20; Tübingen, 1916); 'Jakob', *Preussische Jahrbucher* 176 (1919), pp. 339-62; *Legends of Genesis* (New York, 1966); *Das Märchen im Alten Testament* (Religionsgeschichtliche Volksbucher, 2/23, 26; Tübingen, 1917, 1921); S. Niditch, *Underdogs and Tricksters: A Prelude to Biblical Folklore* (San Francisco, 1987).

4. The importance of humor in the shaping of ancient traditions is only slowly being perceived in biblical research; see L. Kretz, *Witz, Humor und Ironie bei Jesus* (Olten, 2nd edn, 1982); J. Jónsson, *Humour and Irony in the New Testament* (BZRG, 28; Leiden, 1985); M.C. Hyers, *And God Created Laughter: The Bible as Divine Comedy* (Atlanta, 1987).

5. Most books on the theology of laughter begin by struggling to show that the enterprise is not irresponsible; as R.C. Cote observes, it is 'safer to spend one's time in "serious" activity than to enter into "frivolity"' (*Holy Mirth: A Theology of Laughter* [Whitinsville, MA, 1986], p. 9). As M.C. Hyers stresses, for most scholars (and others) 'holiness and laughter, like the sacred and the profane, seem to be opposite, if not in opposition to, one another' (*Holy Laughter*, p. 1).

6. As J. Pinchas and L. Davidsohn wrote long ago, 'Daß die Bibel auch Humoristik enthält, ist allerdings früher vielfach übersehen worden, weil man, unter rein theologischen Gesichtspunkten, dieses leichte literarische Genre nicht der Bibel für würdig hielt. Die wissenschaftliche Betrachtungsweise des bibl. Schrifttums hat auch den rein weltlichen Charakter vieler Stücke herausgestellt' (Pinchas and Davidsohn, 'Humor und Witz, Jüdischer', *Jüdische Lexikon* [1927, 1982], II, col. 1687). See also the judicious comments by F.F. Hvidberg in *Weeping and Laughter in the Old Testament: A Study of Canaanite-Israelite Religion* (Leiden, 1962), and the lexicographical discussions in the major reference works on the Hebrew *s̱hq* and the Greek *gelaō*.

forced to admit that it is not possible to 'find much humour or laughter in the Bible'.[1] In the eighteenth century R. Blackmore claimed that 'unbridled wit and humor' was insane and unthinkable in religion.[2] Left unperceived, especially since the demise of humor in religion since the Reformation,[3] are the theological dimensions of humor, expressed, *inter alia*, in the Jewish Simchat ha-Torah and K. Barth's insight that thankfulness is expressed in humor and honor.[4]

This aspect of humor is obvious, but another is equally evident. Humor can be an appropriate way to cope with the inhuman; it can denote an attempt to rise above the anguish that *Fata viam inveniunt*. Throughout the biblical and extra-canonical writings human pride, vain wisdom, selfishness, greed, pretension, and misplaced adoration is treated with humor and comedy.[5]

Recognizing this salvific and cathartic dimension of humor, we are released from the charge of missing the seriousness in early Jewish apocalyptic writings, and are free to begin to perceive how hilarious

1. R. Niebuhr, 'Humour and Faith', *Discerning the Signs of the Times: Sermons for Today and Tomorrow* (New York, 1946), pp. 111-21; the quotation is on p. 111. Niebuhr erred when he stated that Ps. 2.4 is 'the only instance in the Bible in which laughter is attributed to God' (p. 111). God is said to laugh in Pss. 2.4, 37.13, 59.8; Wisdom is said to laugh, according to Prov. 1.26. We have a lot to learn about the use of humor in Early Judaism when we think about the perceptive comment by Niebuhr that 'all the victims of tyranny availed themselves of the weapon of wit to preserve their sense of personal self-respect. Laughter provided them with a little private world in which they could transvalue the values of the tyrant, and reduce his pompous power to the level of the ridiculous' (p. 116). These comments, it seems to me, are apposite for the social setting of *3 Maccabees*.

2. See M.C. Hyers, *The Comic Vision and the Christian Faith: A Celebration of Laughter* (New York, 1981), p. 10.

3. See H. Cox, *The Feast of Fools* (Cambridge, MA, 1969); and J.W. Bastien, 'Humor and Satire', *The Encyclopedia of Religion*, VI, pp. 526-29.

4. K. Barth, *Die kirchliche Dogmatik* (Zürich, 1951), III, 4, p. 745. Here I wish to express appreciation to Jónsson, *Humour and Irony in the New Testament*.

5. Besides the publications already noted, see the following publications (although none includes a study of humor in the Apocrypha, Pseudepigrapha, and Dead Sea Scrolls): F.F. Hvidberg, *Weeping and Laughter in the Old Testament*, see esp. pp. 138-54 (with regard to weeping some of the Pseudepigrapha are discussed, but not with regard to laughter); H. Höffding, *Den store Humor* (Copenhagen, 1916 [this work is a classic]); H. Thielicke, *Das Lachen der Heiligen und Narren: Nachdenkliches über Witz und Humor* (Herderbücherei, 491; Berlin, 1974); Hyers, *The Comic Vision*; W. Thiede, *Das verheissene Lachen: Humor in theologischer Perspektive* (Göttingen, 1986); and Hyers, *And God Created Laughter*.

folk humor was in Early Judaism. For me, a supreme example is found in the *Apocalypse of Abraham*.[1]

If one of our tasks is to seek to indwell the social world of the Jews who produced the apocalyptic writings, we should endeavor to perceive what reaction reading aloud portions of them might cause. Through humor others, Jews and non-Jews, could have been won over to a claim that God protects the Jew (*die Lacher auf seine Seite ziehen*).[2] Humor was a way of attacking the powerful and hostile, without breaking cultural norms for respecting the dignified and the theological and moral restrictions put on anger and hatred.

The Apocalypse of Abraham

The *Apocalypse of Abraham* is a Jewish work of circa CE 100; but it is preserved only in Slavonic versions.[3] In this apocalypse we have a story that is usually not properly assessed. It is often dismissed as another example of Jewish polemics against idolatry. In fact it is a story that incorporates many tales, which are often hilarious, and which probably were once a part of early Jewish audio-oral transmissions. Laughter, rather than pious reference, would have been the normal, and certainly the original, spontaneous response to tales that illustrate the absurdity of idolatry. Only two excerpts from the *Apocalypse of Abraham* shall suffice for the present.

According to ch. 2, Abraham saddles the asses of his idolatrous father, Terah, and takes them to the market in order to sell them. Sharing the journey with some merchants, Abraham is startled when the asses take fright from the sound of the merchant's camels, and throw the gods on the ground. More than the stone gods are shattered. Here is the self-contained tale (2.1-9, according to the translation of Rubinkiewicz with Lunt in *OTP*, I, pp. 689-90):

1. It would be easy to illustrate my point by turning to other works in the *OTP*, especially the *Testament of Solomon*, which, as D. Duling states, is heavily influenced by Jewish folk legends, and is full of tales and types of folklore often associated with Solomon. A. Aarne and S. Thompson in their classical work entitled *The Types of Folktale: A Classification and Bibliography* (second revision; Helsinki, 1962) include examples from the Pseudepigrapha; for example, AT 803, 920, 920A, 926. AT 922A is from the *OTP*; it is '*Achikar*. Falsely accused minister reinstates himself by his cleverness'. One of the funniest passages in the Pseudepigrapha is found in *3 Macc.* 5.1–6.29.

2. See Freud, *Jokes*, p. 103.

3. For caveats on working on Slavic Pseudepigrapha, see my *The Old Testament Pseudepigrapha and the New Testament* (SNTSMS, 54; Cambridge, 1975), pp. 32-36. Also see R. Rubinkiewicz, 'La vision de l'histoire dans l'Apocalypse d'Abraham', *Aufstieg und Niedergang der römischen Welt*, II.19.1, pp. 137-51.

He made five other gods and he gave them to me and ordered me to sell
them outside on the town road. I saddled my father's ass and loaded them
on it and went out on the highway to sell them. And behold, merchants
from Phandana of Syria were coming with camels, on their way to Egypt
to buy *kokonil* from the Nile. I asked them a question and they answered
me. And walking along I conversed with them. One of their camels
screamed. The ass took fright and ran away and threw off the gods. Three
of them were crushed and two remained (intact). And it came to pass that
when the Syrians saw that I had gods, they said to me, 'Why did you not
tell us that you had gods? We would have bought them before the ass
heard the camel's voice and you would have had no loss. Give us at least
the gods that remain and we will give you a suitable price.' I considered it
in my heart. And they paid both for the smashed gods and the gods which
remained. For I had been grieving in my heart how I would bring payment
to my father. I threw the three broken (gods) into the water of the river
Gur, which was in this place. And they sank into the depths of the river
Gur and were no more.

A fresh reading of this story reveals a humorous tale, typical of the
best in Jewish folklore. To laugh at hearing such stories was salubri-
ous, because the Jews' enemies, who were all around them, were
worshipping idols. How absurd, ironic, and humorous is the account of
the reaction of the Syrian merchants.

Another account which probably had been the subject of much
hilarious laughter in antiquity is found in 5.6-15 of the *Apocalypse of
Abraham*. Abraham is preparing Terah's midday meal. In collecting
wood chips for the fire, Abraham finds a wooden god:

And on its forehead was written: god Barisat. And it came to pass when I
put the chips on the fire in order to prepare the food for my father, and
going out to inquire about the food, I put Barisat near the enkindling fire,
saying to him threateningly, 'Barisat, watch that the fire does not go out
before I come back! If the fire goes out, blow on it so it flares up.' I went
out and I made my counsel. When I returned, I found Barisat fallen on his
back, his feet enveloped by fire and burning fiercely. And it came to pass
when I saw it, I laughed (and) said to myself, 'Barisat, truly you know
how to light a fire and cook food!' And it came to pass while saying this in
my laughter, I saw (that) he burned up slowly from the fire and became
ashes. I carried the food to my father to eat. I gave him wine and milk, and
he drank and he enjoyed himself and he blessed Marumath his god. And I
said to him, 'Father Terah, do not bless Marumath your god, do not praise
him! Praise rather Barisat, your god, because, as though loving you, he
threw himself into the fire in order to cook your food.' And he said to me,
'Then where is he now?' And I said, 'He has burned in the fierceness of

the fire and become dust.' And he said, 'Great is the power of Barisat! I will make another today, and tomorrow he will prepare my food.'[1]

Here is another story that was most likely a part of the living folklore of pre-70 Judaism. The story is hilarious; the Jew who created the tale would have been rewarded by peals of laughter as his audience thought about a wooden god who could be so ironically described. The enjoyment would have been enhanced by the recognition that the enemy (perhaps in a camp nearby or just across the inn) actually revered such idols as Barisat.

The intellectual element in Jewish humor distinguishes it from the frivolous joke.[2] Humor and comedy are especially attractive because of the way they expose categories and then demolish them.[3] Jews, especially living during the time when apocalyptic thought was developing, used humor and comedy to articulate essentially the same thought as expressed in the apocalypses. The present powers are not so real, hence magical worlds were imagined, described, and entered. From such distances the ephemeral was laughable and life livable.

As we contemplate the use of folklore and humor in Early Judaism, it is important to recognize its social dimension. Humor contributed to the feeling of covenantal solidarity (its *Zusammengehörigkeitsgefühl*). A joke is told to be heard (and requires 'einen Zuhörer'),[4] and to win over others to your side of a situation. The contagious element in humor is social; another's laughter causes others to laugh even though the reason for the laughter is unknown.[5] Jewish humor, as we have observed, is not frivolous or developed for the sake of the joke. Humor is employed to articulate something serious; and it has a social and historical dimension. P.L. Berger rightly corrects H. Bergson's suggestion that the comic is the discrepancy between the living and the mechanical:[6] 'the comic is a specifically and exclusively *human* phenomenon'.[7] In the excerpts quoted above, we hear Jews expressing

1. *OTP* I, pp. 690-91.
2. As E. Edel stated, 'Im jüdischen Witz ist immer eine gewisse Epik, eine gefällige Breite' (Edel, *Der Witz der Juden* [Berlin, 1909], p. 10).
3. See the insights by W.F. Lynch in 'Comedy', *Christ and Apollo: The Dimensions of the Literary Imagination* (New York, 1960), pp. 91-112.
4. Thielicke, *Das Lachen*, pp. 37-38; esp. p. 38: 'Der Witz ist ein *kommunikatives Gebilde*'.
5. See Thiede, *Das verheissene Lachen*, pp. 23-26.
6. H. Bergson, 'Laughter', in *Comedy* (ed. W. Sypher; Garden City, NY, 1956); Bergson, *La rire* (Paris, 1947).
7. P.L. Berger, 'Christian Faith and the Social Comedy', in *Holy Laughter*, pp. 123-33.

through lore their anguish of having to live in a world created by
Yahweh but experienced as controlled by idolatrous men.
    These colorful tales were carefully created.[1] They probably were
not the product of one solitary author; they reveal an oral-audio
transmission. They evolved out of folklore into narrative. This development probably can be imagined better by examining the tales in light
of the motifs in folklore. Contrary to some erudite opinions,[2] early
Jewish apocalyptic literature is sometimes satirical, playful, and
humorous; it can ridicule the enemy.

Motif-Index of Folklore and a Refined Methodology

The only means to undergird the suggestion that we have before us, in
the *Apocalypse of Abraham,* an example of early Jewish folklore is to
align the excerpted passages with the motifs identified and organized
by S. Thompson. This pioneer in folklore research admitted great
difficulty in answering 'the leading question—what is a motif?' He
replied:

> To this there is no short and easy answer. Certain items in narrative keep
> on being used by storytellers; they are the stuff out of which tales are
> made. It makes no difference exactly what they are like; if they are actually
> useful in the construction of tales, they are considered to be motifs. As a
> matter of fact, there must usually be something of particular interest to
> make an item important enough to be remembered, something not quite
> commonplace.[3]

The search for folklore motifs, essentially the smallest items in a tale,[4]
and their functions in early Jewish apocalyptic literature is enhanced
by another statement by Thompson; the Jewish penchant for being
preoccupied with the other world, the supernatural, is to be attuned to
what 'is normally far enough from the commonplace to form good

---

    1. J. Licht, who does not adequately discuss the element of humor in the biblical
stories, does rightly stress the 'narrator's purely aesthetic intention' (p. 23), which is
missed by the commentators (Licht, *Storytelling in the Bible* [Jerusalem, 1978]).
    2. I. Davidsohn claimed that 'the apocryphal literature, though largely imitative,
aims neither at playfulness nor at ridicule' (*Parody in Jewish Literature* [Columbia
University Oriental Studies, 2; New York, 1907], p. 1).
    3. S. Thompson, 'Narrative Motif-analysis as a Folklore Method', in *Beiträge zur
vergleichenden Erzählforschung (Festschrift für Walter Anderson)* (ed. K. Ranke;
Helsinki, 1955), pp. 3-9 (7).
    4. See Niditch, *Underdogs and Tricksters*, p. 2.

motifs'.[1] In summation, the key characteristic of folklore, as Niditch states,[2] is 'patterned repetition'.

Before we can examine the previous excerpts in terms of one of the motifs in Thompson's *Motif-Index of Folk-Literature*,[3] we must first ascertain if they fulfill most of the following features:

1. Can the tale be isolated in the narrative; does it have a beginning? Is the tale introduced?
2. Does it have a clear ending?
3. Is it then exploited for its main purpose, namely, does the author of the full narrative use the tale for admonition, edification, or amusement?
4. Does it illustrate a point being made in the narrative?
5. Is it possible to see the tale functioning separately as a self-contained story in an oral-audio setting? Does it contain an element that is distinct and different from the ordinary and hence memorable? Does it serve the function of entertaining, exhorting, edifying, or embellishing sacred traditions? Could the tale have been successfully communicated to others ('performed')?

When a possible folktale is discovered it can then be compared with—or seen in terms of—the motifs prominent in the great folklore of the world.

Apocalypse of Abraham

1. The tale in the *Apoc. Abr.* 2.1-9 can be isolated. To a certain extent it is introduced by Abraham's testing of the gods of his father.
2. The story ends in the last verse of ch. 2; the gods disappear in the river Gur.
3. The tale is exploited by the author of the apocalypse. Abraham is disturbed, and reflects on the absurdity of idols. Using irony the author has Abraham ask if Terah is not in fact 'god for his gods' (3.3). The reader is urged to raise the selfsame question, if in fact it has not already sprung forth in

---

1. Niditch, *Underdogs and Tricksters*, p. 7.
2. Niditch, *Underdogs and Tricksters*, p. xiv.
3. S. Thompson, *Motif-Index of Folk-Literature: A Classification of Narrative Elements in Folktales, Ballads, Myths, Fables, Mediaeval Romances, Exempla, Fabliaux, Jest-Books and Local Legends* (rev. and enlarged edn; 6 vols.; Bloomington, IN, 1955–58).

the reader's mind from the ridiculous dimensions of the tale
itself.

4. The brief tale illustrates the major point in the *Apocalypse of
    Abraham;* idols result from the human's utter foolishness.

5. The tale could easily have functioned in an oral-audio setting.
    Hearing a tale about stone 'gods' smashing on the ground or
    sinking in a river is extraordinarily memorable. One can
    imagine this tale being performed at night around a fire, to
    entertain, but also to teach and admonish.

(1–2) The humorous tale in 5.1-17 also fits all of the five requirements. It is a self-contained tale (5.1 is the beginning, 5.17 is the end).

(3–4) The tale is exploited when the author of the apocalypse
illustrates the proper response to the palpable absurdities of making
idols into gods. He emphasizes Abraham's laughter, which is mentioned twice in the tale (5.10 and 5.11). The folktale is then used to
illustrate serious reflections; Abraham is made to say, 'I laughed in my
mind, and I groaned in the bitterness and anger of my soul' (6.1). The
serious agonizing reflections then lead to an altercation with Terah and
a kerygmatic statement: 'But hear this, Terah my father, let me
proclaim to you the God who created all things' (7.10 according to A
B C K in *OTP,* I). The dialogue ends, and Abraham is told by God to
leave Terah, who subsequently is destroyed along with his entire
house. The depth of thought is not missed by listeners who know the
importance of succession, especially from father to son, and the devotion demanded of father by son.

(5) It is easy to imagine this entertaining, didactic, and paranetic
tale, and others in the beginning of the *Apocalypse of Abraham*,
circulating among the early Jews as folk tales.

In the *Apocalypse of Abraham* we confront what might be called
'the creative folk ego of the Jewish people'.[1] The literature of Early
Judaism and not only 'the talmudic-midrashic literature of the *tannaim*
and the *amoraim*' are 'a mine of information of ancient Jewish folklore...handed down by word of mouth for hundreds of years before
it was formulated'.[2] To understand the origin and also the essence of
Jewish apocalyptic literature, it is helpful to study the phenomenon of
folklore in Early Judaism.

---

1. Dov Noy, *Encyclopaedia Judaica* 6 (1971), col. 1376.
2. Dov Noy, *Encyclopaedia Judaica* 6 (1971), col. 1375.

Pre-Sixth-Century Inscribed Seals

Ruth Hestrin and Michal Dayagi-Mendels have recently published some beautifully inscribed seals preserved in the Israel Museum in Jerusalem.[1] Significant for the study of the origin of Jewish apocalyptic thought are the iconographies on the seals.[2] The types of stones on which the seals are preserved are reminiscent themselves of the precious stones that play a symbolic role in the Apocalypse of John. More important are the depictions of winged creatures.

Two seals are particularly important for a perception of the origin and evolution of Jewish apocalyptic thought. The Seal of Shallum, Number 136 (p. 173), contains a depiction of a cult scene. Represented is a worshiper with his hand raised in prayer and standing beside a stylized tree. Above it is a winged solar disk 'with the head of a deity rising from its center and from each of the wings'. The latter are supported by 'bull-men'. This bluish chalcedony seal is of Assyrian origin and is dated to the late eighth or early seventh centuries BCE.

The winged solar disk and the portrayal of men in animal forms is reminiscent of many passages in the Jewish apocalypses. The popular use of the iconography of such seals would have made the bizarre images in the apocalypses less foreign, perhaps even familiar, certainly more intelligible. Compare the iconography in the Seal of Shallum, for example, with the well-known first vision of Daniel (7.2-5).

A creature that looks like a lion with eagles' wings—perhaps a Sphinx—is portrayed on a Phoenician scarab that has been dated to the late fifth or early fourth century BCE.[3] Long ago E.R. Goodenough drew attention to many similar, ancient psychopomps and other fantastic creatures.[4]

1. R. Hestrin and M. Dayagi-Mendels, *Inscribed Seals* (Jerusalem, 1979).
2. The elephants that play such a major role in *3 Maccabees* are portrayed in cylinder seals and scarabs, although they are extremely rare. One is found in the Black Obelisk of Shalmaneser III (see J.B. Pritchard, *The Ancient Near East in Pictures Relating to the Old Testament* [Princeton, 1954], pp. 121 and 290-91 [= no. 353]). Another is on a Sassanide seal (see M.-L. Vollenweider, *Catalogue raisonné des sceaux cylindres et intailles* [Geneva, 1967], I, pp. 83-84 and pl. 42 [no. 95]).
3. Vollenweider, *Catalogue*, I, pp. 123-24 and pl. 64, nos. 158 and 159. Also, see the odd creature—with the head of a Sphinx, with two raised arms, a beetle's body (?), and four wings—in pl. 61 (no. 151) which is also a Phoenician scarab and dates from the late seventh or early eighth century BCE.
4. E.R. Goodenough, *Jewish Symbols in the Greco-Roman Period* (13 vols.; New York, 1953-68), esp. XI, nos. 58, 111, 227, 228, 265, 278, 296, 307, 309, 348; I, p. 195; II, p. 252; and XIII, pp. 126, 127, 135-37.

The most impressive link[1] with the fantastic imagery of the apocalypses is found on the Seal of Shema', Number 98 (p. 125). This green
jasper Ammonite seal from the seventh century contains the following
iconography:

> In the upper register, a stylized fantastic creature with four wings, a
> jackal's head (Anubis) and a bird's tail. The semicircular body is shaped
> like the Egyptian sign *nb*. In the lowest register, a two-winged scarab and
> in the middle register, the name of the owner.[2]

One should not dismiss this iconography as insignificant because it is
Ammonite.[3] Although little research has been prosecuted on the
iconography of seals, it is virtually certain that we must not think
about separate, isolated schools, like the Ammonites versus the
Hebrews; rather there was much sharing of symbolic figures. The
iconography of the seals probably mirrors the symbolism of the
ancient Near East, and I am convinced that it is in that direction, and
not in the free imagination of the scribe, that we should look for the
origin of the apocalyptist's angelological symbolism. As D. Collon has
recently shown, seals were ubiquitous in the ancient Near East for
about 3,000 years before the time of the *Apocalypse of Abraham*.[4]

Of special significance in our search for the origins of Jewish apocalyptic thought is the depiction of 'the fantastic creature with four
wings'. It has a jackal's head with a bird's tail and possesses four
wings. One is reminded of Daniel's vision of the third (Tetrapleryx)
beast: 'After this as I gazed I saw another, a beast like a leopard with
four bird's wings on its back' (7.6 NEB). Also, one is reminded of 'the
four wings of the Lord of the Spirits' mentioned in *1 En.* 40.2.

The iconography in these seals brings to mind two well-known phenomena in the ancient Near East: the depiction of figures that are like

---

1. See also in Hestrin and Dayagi-Mendels, *Inscribed Seals*, the Seal of Yaḥziba'al
(No. 118, p. 152), and the Seal of Bat'eshem (No. 30, p. 47).

2. Hestrin and Dayagi-Mendels, *Inscribed Seals*, p. 125.

3. Examine, for example, the winged lion-griffin (no. 451, Early Akkadian),
Sphinx (no. 1254), and especially the lion-headed eagle with wings (no. 284, Early
Dynastic III, Mesopotamia) in B. Buchanan and W.W. Hallo, *Early Near Eastern
Seals in the Yale Babylonian Collection* (ed. U. Kasten; New Haven, 1981). Also see
nos. 7, 49, 50 (two human-headed and winged ibexes!), 54 (four-winged goddess),
60-63 (winged goddesses) in E.W. Forte, *Ancient Near Eastern Seals: A Selection of
Stamp and Cylinder-Seals from the Collection of Mrs William H. Moore* (New York,
1976).

4. D. Collon, *First Impressions: Cylinder Seals in the Ancient Near East* (Chicago,
1988).

the Cherubim and of the demons. Only a brief reference to each is sufficient.

The Cherubim are described in 1 Kgs 8.6-7 (also see *1 En.* 20.7; 71.7; *2 En.* 12.1-3; *Apoc. Abr.* 10.9); they have wings, and beneath these wings in the inner shrine of the Temple rests the Ark of the Covenant. Similar creatures are portrayed in artifacts preserved from the ancient Near East.[1] For example, G.E. Wright identified a Phoenician work of art as 'Cherubim guarding a sacred tree'; and he associated these winged Cherubim with the Solomonic Temple.[2] O. Keel draws attention to another Phoenician work of the first century BCE; this artifact portrays a woman, perhaps the sun, with two large wings that are outstretched with a lotus in each hand.[3] In Solomon's Temple the Cherubim were certainly winged and probably etched in olive wood, and perhaps in the Holy of Holies the Cherubim statues were overlaid with gold.[4]

Popular Iconography

Winged creatures (gods or goddesses) are found throughout the ancient Near East; for example, they are depicted in the magnificent bas-reliefs in Assyria and at Pergamum, the cylinder seal found in a Late Bronze tomb near Acre,[5] the ivory plaque from Samaria, perhaps from Ahab's palace, depicting a sphinx in a lotus thicket.[6] Winged victories from the Hellenistic and Roman periods, showing a mixture of eastern and western art, have been found in Israel at er Rama, the ed Dikke synagogue, a tomb at Qaloniye, a rock chamber near the

---

1. See the photograph of the winged animals found at the Palace of Arslan Tash in F.I. Sarkis, *Les Phéniciens: Panorama d'une civilisation* (Beirut, 1980), p. 236; and in A. Parrot, M.H. Chéhab, S. Moscati, *Die Phönizier: Die Entwicklung der phönizischen Kunst von den Anfängen bis zum Ende des dritten punisches Krieges* (Munich, 1977), p. 95.

2. G.E. Wright, *Biblical Archaeology* (rev. edn; Philadelphia, 1962), p. 138; also see Wright's discussion on pp. 139-42.

3. O. Keel, *Die Welt der altorientalischen Bildsymbolik und das Alte Testament: Am Beispiel der Psalmen* (3rd edn; Zürich, 1980); see illustration no. 222 and the discussion on pp. 126-44.

4. H.T. Frank, *An Archaeological Companion to the Bible* (London, 1972), p. 139.

5. See the photographs in A. Mazar, *Archaeology of the Land of the Bible 10,000–586 BCE* (Anchor Bible Reference Library, 2; New York, 1990), p. 268.

6. See the excellent photographs in Mazar, *Archaeology of the Land of the Bible*, p. 503, and in *The Cambridge Encyclopedia of Archaeology* (ed. A. Sherratt; Cambridge, 1980), p. 198.

Jerusalem Syrian Orphanage, and elsewhere.[1] These winged figures and sphinxes remind us of Isaiah's vision when he sees 'the Lord seated on a throne... About him were attendant seraphim, and each had six wings' (Isa. 6.1-4 [NEB]; cf. the six-winged creatures described in *2 En.* 11.4 [J] and Rev. 4.8).[2]

In the Near Eastern Museum of the Staatliche Museen in Berlin one is astounded by the neo-Babylonian architecture from the time of Nebuchadnezzar and by the Assyrian bas-reliefs. One in particular caught my eye during a visit to this museum in June 1984; it was an Assyrian relief of about 885–883 BCE, which depicts an 'Adlermensch'. He has a falcon head, human hands in front, two wings in back, and human feet.

There are many other examples of similar figures. Without doubt the folk in the streets and the international merchants would have been impressed consciously and subconsciously by such memorable and majestic images.[3] Through trade routes and oral-audio transmission these ideas would have become common property in the symbolism of the ancient Near East.

It is from this store of ancient symbols—I am convinced—that the author of *4 Ezra* developed the vision in which the eagle has twelve wings and three heads (*4 Ezra* 11), that the compiler of *2 Enoch* conceived of the solar elements as having a 'form like that of a lion', a tail, a head like that of a crocodile, and twelve wings (*2 En.* 12.1–13.2), that the composer of the *Apocalypse of Zephaniah* evolved the description of the good angels, who had mixed grotesque animal forms (4.1-7), and that the author of the *Apocalypse of Abraham* depicted the dragon with twelve wings and hands and feet like a man (ch. 23).

In the great altar of Pergamum (c. 180–160 BCE), so magnificently presented in the Staatliche Museen, we are confronted with a frieze portraying a battle between the gods and giants. One scene is particularly apt for our present search. It depicts Athena, the protectress of Pergamum, wrestling successfully with the male giant, Alkyoneus, who has large, powerful wings. Behind this iconography is the ancient

1. See M. Avi-Yonah, *Art in Ancient Palestine: Selected Studies* (ed. H. Katzenstein and Y. Tsafrir; Jerusalem, 1981), p. 27 (see fig. 2), p. 238 (see fig. 5), pl. 27.

2. Examine the pictorial celebration of Isaiah's career reproduced in Goodenough, *Jewish Symbols*, XI, no. 307.

3. Especially in Egypt the mixed animal and human forms are popular. They are depicted richly and with great imagination in the Book of the Dead. See especially the marvelous examples on display in Cairo, Turin, and—of course—the Metropolitan Museum in New York.

myth of the battle between the Titans, or giants, and Zeus, a symbolism that influenced the authors of *1 Enoch* and the *Sibylline Oracles* 1 and 3, who described the evil spirits in terms of the primordial giants (*1 En.* 15.8-12; *Sib. Or.* 1.305-10; 3.110-61). The link here between this myth and its symbolism and *Sibylline Oracle* 3 is obvious; it celebrates it.

The Römanisch-Germanisches Museum der Stadt Köln preserves some examples of ancient iconography which help us perceive more clearly the extent and depth of popular images in the ancient Near East. The early date of the winged creatures and their worldwide popularity in Hellenistic and Roman times is confirmed. The Roman wall paintings found in 1969 near the Cologne Dom are spectacular. On Wand A is depicted a two-winged creature with human features. Also to the right of Bacchus is a two-winged male with a bird's body and nondescript arms.

Most impressive for our present research are the two figures depicted below the lions that are beneath Bacchus. Here are painted two creatures that have two wings on the back, a man's (?) face, arms and chest, a bird's legs, feet and tail (another wing?). Other fantastic creatures—sphinxes and sirens—are seen, if only partially visible now, on Wand A and Wand B. These are popular works (one would not call them refined or elegant); they are paintings from the northern Roman provinces; and they date from the second century CE.[1]

We are not dealing with images found only in one locale; they are found throughout the Hellenistic world. Similarly winged fantastic creatures, for example, were also painted on the walls of houses in Pompeii (cf. the Villa Imperiale), and in Rome (cf. the House of Farnesina).

It is possible that similar winged fantastic creatures—with mixed human and animal forms—were also painted on the walls of Hellenistic and Roman buildings in pre-70 Palestine. The art work found recently in Roman Jerusalem, Masada, the Herodium, and at Roman Jericho are undeniable witnesses to the presence of Hellenistic and Roman art work in Palestine. The iconographical background to many of the 'bizarre' images in Jewish apocalyptic thought and the apocalypses is becoming clear and obvious; it deserves a full and separate study.

The demons, long before the first century CE, were often portrayed with wings and with forms of more than one animal, including *homo sapiens*. An Assyrian bronze plaque, which dates from the first half of

---

1. See Kölner, *Jahrbuch für Vor- und Frühgeschichte*, 13 (1972–73); and A. Linfert, *Römische Wandmalerei der nordwestlichen Provinzen* (2nd edn; Cologne, 1979).

the first millennium BCE, depicts on the back side[1] a demon with four wings, or two pairs of wings. It has an animal-like head with the body and feet of something like an eagle; the phallus and tail are represented having a serpent's head. The front part of the tablet[2] depicts two priests exorcising a demon from a person in bed. The demon Pazuzu—'the king of the evil spirits of the air'—is impressively sculptured in a bronze statue from the seventh century BCE. He has a grotesque face, human body, four wings (or two pairs of wings), and an eagle's feet.[3]

It was from such a store of grotesque images that the author of the Apocalypse of John probably mined his fantastic pictorial representations of evil. Most notably, he depicted a demon as a beast with ten horns and seven heads, and like a leopard with feet like a bear, and a mouth like a lion (Rev. 13.1-2).

The ancient inconography of sphinxes, griffins, psychopomps, and anguipedes is only partially preserved and it has only been sketched out above (cf. also 2 *En.* 11.4 [J] in which six-winged [Hexapheryx] angels are described, and Rev. 4 in which the four living creatures around God's throne each has six wings). There should be little doubt now that the Jewish apocalypses inherit very ancient symbols and fantastic imagery. The iconography and symbolism, I am convinced, were transmitted to the Jews through numerous means, including trade and oral-audio folklore.

When one sees the human figures depicted with wings,[4] and Hermes, the messenger of the gods, who is portrayed sometimes as a human with wings, as I have shown elsewhere,[5] it is difficult to endorse J.T. Milik's claim (à propos of *1 En.* 61.1 and the *Book of the Parables*) that 'early Jewish literature is not familiar with any winged angels' and that in Christianity winged angels do not appear before the end of the

1. See Keel, *Die Welt*, no. 92.

2. See Keel, *Die Welt*, esp. no. 97; but also Pritchard, *The Ancient Near East in Pictures*, no. 658 and the discussion on p. 328.

3. See Keel, *Die Welt*, no. 93 and Pritchard, *The Ancient Near East in Pictures*, no. 659 and discussion on p. 328.

4. It has been misleadingly reported that wings 'werden erst seit dem 4. Jh. Attribut der Engel' (G. Heinz-Mohr, *Lexikon der Symbole: Bilder und Zeichen der christlichen Kunst* [Cologne, 1983], p. 110). See, however, the excellent discussions of the mixed animal and human forms placed under 'Greif' (pp. 120-21), 'Hund' (pp. 140-41), 'Kentaur' (pp. 140-41), 'Kentaur' (pp. 156-57), and 'Sphinx' (p. 270).

5. Charlesworth, 'Literature in Early Judaism', in *Judaism, 200 BC–AD 200* (ed. Charlesworth; Evanston, IL, 1983); see the discussion and slide in *J2-20*.

fourth century.[1] It is easy, on the other hand, to re-emphasize the main points in the following statement by F.M. Cross:

> The evolution of late biblical religion has not been adequately traced: the decline and transformation of prophecy, the recrudescence of mythic themes stemming in part from decadent royal ideologies and from archaic lore preserved in the wisdom schools, and the new synthesis of these elements which should be designated 'proto-apocalyptic'.
>
> The origins of the apocalyptic must be searched for as early as the sixth century BC. In the catastrophe of the Exile the older forms of the faith and tradition came into crisis, and Israel's institutions, including her religious institutions, collapsed or were transformed.[2]

We must endeavor to understand that what is bizarre and exotic to the modern mind was sometimes normal and popular to the ancients. The logic of symbols is complex, and images are multivalent. Sometimes an apparently meaningless comment has deep and profound symbolic meanings. For example, J.-G. Heintz has shown that the imaginative language of a sword coming out of the mouth of the Messiah is to be understood in terms of a real iconographical symbol. In the royal imagery of the ancient Near East are found depictions of a lion, a symbol of the king, with a sword coming out of his mouth.[3] Here is profound evidence for the position I am attempting to introduce; it is singularly important for interpreting the well-known passages in Isaiah, the *Psalms of Solomon*, and *4 Ezra*, in which the Lord, or his Messiah, is described as destroying the enemies of the Jews with the 'sword of his mouth'. Early iconography is sometimes essential to exegesis. Apocalyptic language is expressive and imaginative;[4] and it is grounded in social realities and ancient symbolic intentionalities.

---

1. J.T. Milik, with M. Black, *The Books of Enoch: Aramaic Fragments of Qumrân Cave 4*, (Oxford, 1976), p. 97. Milik—in the discussion noted—tends to minimize the interrelationship between the Jewish and non-Jewish worlds, and to overemphasize the significance of what little has been preserved from antiquity. Also, his interpretation of *1 En.* 61.1 falls because the reference to angel wings is only in manuscripts B and C (see *OTP*, I, p. 42).

2. F.M. Cross, 'A Note on the Study of Apocalyptic Origins', in *Canaanite Myth and Hebrew Epic: Essays in the History of the Religion of Israel* (Cambridge, MA, 1973), p. 343.

3. See J.-G. Heintz, 'Royal Traits and Messianic Figures: A Thematic and Iconographical Approach (Mesopotamian Elements)', in *The Messiah: The First Princeton Symposium on Judaism and Christian Origins* (ed. J. Charlesworth, with J. Brownson, S.J. Kraftchick and A.F. Segal; Augsburgh: Fortress, 1992).

4. See Collins's comments in *The Apocalyptic Imagination* (New York, 1984), p. 14.

Conclusion

The foregoing discussion reveals that the search for the origin of Jewish apocalypticism, and for the earliest prototypes of the apocalypses themselves, must be attuned not only to Prophecy and Wisdom, but also to the social matrix of humor, the motifs in folklore, and the symbolic consciousness of the ancient Near East.

Jewish theology—especially during the period of Early Judaism (250 BCE to CE 200)—was historical theology. Apocalyptic thought was not only concerned with portraying the future in terms of ancient symbolic and pictorial language. It was sociologically based and conditioned by the crises of the present. As G. Scholem stated, 'in the work of the apocalyptists themselves, motifs of *current* history, which refer to *contemporary conditions and needs*, are closely interwined with those of an apocalyptic, eschatological nature, in which not only the experiences of the *present* exercise an influence, but often enough *ancient mythical images* are filled with utopian content'.[1]

Retrospect
The force of the present prolegomenous study is twofold:

1.   We must try to perceive the importance of the folktale in the study of the origins of Jewish apocalyptic thought. After all—as Thompson stated—the oral tale is 'the most universal of all narrative forms'; hence we must 'understand its relation to the literary stories of our own civilization'.[2] The psychic dimension of the story in *Geistesgeschichte* is indicated by R. Price's following comment: 'A need to tell and hear stories is essential to the species *homo sapiens*—second in necessity apparently after nourishment and before love and shelter'.[3]

2.   We must allow for the impact of all ideas, symbols, and especially the prevalence of popular pictorial reliefs and other art forms on the collective Hellenistic consciousness. Long before the beginnings of Jewish apocalyptic thought, the forms of animals and humans were mixed in many cultures in the ancient Near East. Men, women, gods, goddesses, types of humanlike animals, and demons were portrayed with two or more wings. It is no wonder, then, that in apocalyptic thought

---

1. G. Scholem, *The Messianic Idea in Judaism, And Other Essays on Jewish Spirituality* (New York, 1977), pp. 5-6 (the essay quoted was translated by M.A. Meyer; italics mine).
2. S. Thompson, *The Folktale* (Berkeley, 1977), p. vii.
3. R. Price, *A Palpable God* (New York, 1978), p. 3.

the bizarre and obscure aspects of our world—especially during times of anxiety or conquest—were depicted in supra-human, supra-animalistic, and ethereal forms. Jewish apocalyptic thought—if it is to be understood in terms of all its grandeur and complexity—must also be studied in terms of ancient art and the pictorial representations of the products of human fears, hopes, and imaginations.

Prospects

Among the desiderata in the study of Early Judaism is an exploration of the whole domain of folklore. The present essay calls for at least the following major works: (1) folklore in Early Jewish literature, (2) classifying motifs and types in Early Jewish folklore, and (3) perceiving and classifying the element of performance in Early Jewish folklore.

The increased sensitivity to the sociological dimensions of Early Judaism and Earliest Christianity should help open the way for an examination of the performance of tales among folk, in family groups, in social gatherings (both sophisticated and spontaneous), and in pauses in the rhythm in the average day. As W.H. Jansen states, 'verbal folklore, however insignificant, implies an auditor, frequently a group of auditors, and, of course, some person or occasionally persons to "do" that piece of folklore for that audience'.[1] Jansen perceives 'three aims or something very akin to them' in all folklore: 'didacticism, admonition, or entertainment'.[2] Each of these dimensions is evident in traditions preserved at the beginning of the *Apocalypse of Abraham*.

As one thinks of the function of folklore in Early Judaism, and the oppression by the Persians, Greeks, Syrians, and then Romans, perhaps other functions of these traditions can be perceived. For example, there is a *catharsis* which relieves the pressure of life, and *recitation* or *celebration* of the sacred text by imaginative embellishments on it. The laughter accompanying the story of Abraham's troubles with idols, in the *Apocalypse of Abraham*, is an example of catharsis; reflections on the Torah account of Abraham and Terah is an example of celebration of sacred text.

Comparative analysis of folk-motifs will also produce disparities, and these may help us find an answer to the question wherein lies the

---

1. W.H. Jansen, 'Classifying Performance in the Study of Verbal Folklore', in *Studies in Folklore: In Honor of Distinguished Service of Professor Stith Thompson* (ed. W.E. Richmond; Bloomington, IN, 1957) p. 112.
2. Jansen, 'Classsifying Performance in the Study of Verbal Folklore', in *Studies in Folklore*, p. 113.

uniqueness and essence of Jewish apocalyptic thought. Experts in Early Judaism will probably be surprised to discover a type of folklore titled 'Journeys to the Other World'.[1] Though there may be some functional similarity between the Ladder of Jacob and the motif of The Arrow Chain,[2] the Jewish apocalypses seem remote from such motifs as The Star Husband, according to which a young woman, finding herself in heaven, marries a Star but is forbidden to 'dig'. She disobeys, of course, sees her earthly home, and with the aid of a rope, descends back to it.

Even here there may be more similarity than a *prima facie* reading suggests. According to *1 Enoch* 21 (cf. *1 En.* 88) and Rev. 1.20, the stars can be identified as angels. An examination of the function and elasticity, indeed the non-systematic nature, of symbols and concepts is a dimension of diachronic historical research.

If the specialists in the field of folklore are correct that folktales are a vital art in our culture, past and present, and that such tales lie behind all literary narratives[3]—they certainly lie behind Goethe's *Faust*[4]—then we must examine early Jewish literature in light of this important unexplored dimension of our historical-critical research.[5] Seeking to discover folktales, their function, performance, and place among and within social phenomena will help us draw closer to the inherited meanings of quasi-sacred narratives and their significance for the life of the early Jew.

Finally, the world of myths and symbols prior to the Jewish apocalypses remains full of data that will help us understand early Jewish thought. For example, Assyrian omen texts, especially *Šumma izbu*, are unexplored yet significant sources for comprehending the dawning and developing of Jewish apocalyptic thought. Note the following omen: 'If the anomaly of a mare has the face of a human (and) the tail

---

1. Thompson, 'Journeys to the Other World', in *The Folktale*, pp. 345-52.

2. Defined by Thompson as follows: 'The hero makes a huge quantity of arrows which he shoots toward the sky, one after the other, so rapidly that they form a chain' ('Journeys to the Other World', in *The Folktale*, p. 348).

3. Thompson wrote that one of the goals of his *The Folktale* was 'to present the folktale as an important art, vital to most of the race and underlying all literary narrative forms' (p. viii).

4. See the popular summary of Faustforschung and photographs and facsimiles in L. Geiges, *Faust's Tod in Staufen: Sage—Dokumente* (Freiburg, n.d. [c. 1982]).

5. As W.H. Kelber points out, 'neither European nor American biblical scholarship has profited in depth from the Anglo-American oralist school'. See Kelber, *The Oral and the Written Gospel* (Philadelphia, 1983), p. 2, and the bibliography given in n. 12.

of a dog—the land will draw near to struggle'.[1] Such conceptual possibilities certainly help us see into the intellectual and social world of the Jewish apocalyptic thinkers who describe a cosmos full of anguipedes, griffins, psychopomps, and sphinxes.

The Jewish apocalypses certainly reflect the brilliance and erudition of the scribal schools—in that sense they represent scribal phenomena—but they also inherit ancient myths, symbols, and folklore—in that sense they preserve popular (perhaps religious) phenomena. We have found another key that will open for us another door to that mysterious and enchanting world of two thousand years ago in and around Judea and Galilee.

1. Tablet XXI 46´. in E. Leichty, The Omen Series *Šumma Izbu* (Texts from Cuneiform Sources, 4; Locust Valley, NY, 1970), p. 188; see also esp. pp. 38, 45, 52, 56, 77-81, 91, 178, 181-83, 185-89. Also see P.A. Porter, *Metaphors and Monsters: A Literary-Critical Study of Daniel 7 and 8* (ConBib OTSeries, 20; Lund, 1983). I am grateful to Professor J.J.M. Roberts for pointing out the importance of the omen texts for Jewish apocalyptic thought.

7

BAHMAN YASHT: A PERSIAN APOCALYPSE

Anders Hultgård

The aim of this contribution is to discuss problems of transmission and interpretation of an important but much disputed Persian apocalyptic document known as the *Bahman Yasht* (*BYt*) or the *Zand i Vahuman Yasn*.[1] In doing this I shall pay particular attention to the state of present scholarly research. The relevance of *Bahman Yasht* for the study of early Jewish and Christian religions lies in the importance commonly attributed to Iranian ideas in understanding the origins of Jewish and Christian apocalyptic. In the present discussion of *Bahman Yasht* I will keep sight of its relationship to early Jewish traditions. The views put forward in this article are based on a forthcoming, more detailed study.[2]

The interest of *Bahman Yasht* lies in the fact that it presents most of the themes generally connected with apocalyptic and universal eschatology. We find variants of a serial periodization into ages and reigns that are symbolized by different metals. There is a detailed instruction of the manner in which the capacity of divine vision is transmitted to a human recipient, providing at the same time an allusion to a heavenly ascent. A considerable portion of *Bahman Yasht* is made up of an elaborate description of the signs announcing the end of the world: disasters affecting the country, cosmic upheavals, and the general

---

1. Both titles are in current use, but are secondary, since the text is transmitted without any title in the manuscripts: *bahman* (New Persian) < *vahuman* (Middle Iranian) < *vohu-manah-* (Avestan) meaning 'good thinking', the foremost of the Amesha Spentas, hypostases or minor deities associated with Ahura Mazdah. As to the word *yašt,* it denotes a sacrificial hymn to a particular deity or deities; in the Pahlavi texts *yašt* is often used synonymously with *yasn* (Avestan *yasna-*). The word *zand* means in this context a Pahlavi translation with glosses based on an Avestan text.

2. A. Hultgård: 'Mythe et histoire dans l'Iran ancien—une étude de Bahman Yasht'; to be published in *Apocalyptique iranienne et dualisme juif* (ed. G. Widengren). This volume will also contain a study by Widengren on the ages of the world and a study by M. Philonenko on Jewish dualism and its Iranian background.

deterioration of humankind and the earth. The account of the ultimate events concentrates on the restoration of Mazdean Iran and the defeat of its enemies, and the coming of the eschatological saviors.

The *Bahman Yasht* is a comparatively short text compiled in the ninth or tenth century CE among Zoroastrians of Iran who were living as a minority group in a predominantly Muslim environment. It is written in Pahlavi, the Middle-Iranian language which was in use by Zoroastrians during the Sassanian and early Islamic periods for composing religious literature.

Bahman Yasht *in Scholarly Debate*

The humble origins of *Bahman Yasht* make a sharp contrast with the impact it has had on Western scholarship. This impact can be seen from four different viewpoints: (1) that of classical scholarship and history of religions in the Greco-Roman world, (2) that of biblical studies and Jewish-Christian apocalypticism, (3) that of comparative religion, and (4) that of the study of ancient Iranian religion. An exhaustive survey cannot be given here, but I shall present an overview illustrating each of the four aspects mentioned.

1.   For R. Reitzenstein as a classical scholar and a proponent of the 'religionsgeschichtliche Schule', *Bahman Yasht* was a central text in elucidating the origins of the ancient Greek and Platonic world-view as well as Hellenistic apocalyptic literature.[1] Hesiod's well-known myth of the metallic ages was according to Reitzenstein ultimately derived from an ancient Persian-Babylonian tradition that survived in *Bahman Yasht*. The same line of reasoning is today followed by M.L. West in his edition of and commentary on Hesiod's *Works and Days*.[2] West adduces *Bahman Yasht* as a striking oriental parallel to Hesiod's myth of the ages. The myth in Plato's *Politikos* (269c–273e) was, according to Reitzenstein, influenced by the Iranian tradition behind *Bahman Yasht*, which thus could be put far back in antiquity with the help of Plato.

Furthermore, exploring the remnants of the Hellenistic apocalyptic literature such as the *Oracle of the Potter and Asclepius*, chs. 24–26, Reitzenstein found the clue to their

---

1. R. Reitzenstein, 'Vom Töpferorakel zu Hesiod', *Studien zum antiken Synkretismus aus Iran und Griechenland* (ed. R. Reitzenstein and H.H. Schaeder; Leipzig, 1926), pp. 38-68.
2. M.L. West, *Hesiod, Works and Days* (Oxford, 1978), pp. 172-77.

background in Iranian apocalypticism, in particular the
Bahman Yasht. F. Cumont and E. Benveniste supported their
interpretation of the *Oracles of Hystaspes* as an originally
Iranian apocalypse largely on a comparison with *Bahman
Yasht*: and, in the case of Benveniste, also the Jāmāsp Nāmak,
another Pahlavi text.[1] This approach has since then dominated
the study of the *Oracles of Hystaspes* by scholars like G.
Widengren, C. Colpe, J. Hinnells and H. Kippenberg.[2] The
Iranian character of the *Oracles of Hystaspes* is thus
established primarily by comparison with *Bahman Yasht*.
This in turn opens the way for proposing Iranian influence on
Jewish traditions that has come through the *Oracles of
Hystaspes*, as is done by M. Philonenko.[3] Colpe has furthermore pointed to the fact that different periodizations are
fused together in a strongly similar way in Sethinan gnostic
texts and in the *Bahman Yasht*, suggesting a historical
interrelation.[4]

2.　　In 1855 F. Delitzsch made the first reference to *Bahman
Yasht* as a parallel to the book of Daniel with its description
of the metallic statue seen by Nebuchnadnezzar (Dan. 2.31-
45).[5] Since then there has been a widespread opinion among
biblical scholars that the author of Daniel was indebted to a
Persian or, more generally speaking, an Oriental source,

　　1.　F. Cumont, 'La fin du monde selon les mages occidentaux', *RHR* 103 (1931),
pp. 29-96, esp. pp. 66-68, 72-82, 86, and 92; Benveniste, 'Une apocalypse
pehlevie: le Žāmāsp Nāmak', *RHR* 104 (1932), pp. 337-80.
　　2.　G. Widengren, *Die Religionen Irans* (Stuttgart, 1965), pp. 199-207; *idem*,
'Leitende Ideen und Quellen der iranischen Apokalyptik', *Apocalypticism in the
Mediterranean World and the Near East* (ed. D. Hellholm; Tübingen, 1983; 2nd edn
1989, enlarged by a supplementary bibliography), pp. 77-162, esp. pp. 119-29; C.
Colpe, 'Der Begriff "Menschensohn" und die Methode der Erforschung
messianischer Prototypen', *Kairos* 12 (1970), pp. 81-112; J. Hinnells, 'The Zoro-
astrian Doctrine of Salvation in the Roman World: A Study of the Oracles of
Hystaspes', in *Man and his Salvation, Essays in Memory of S.G.F. Brandon* (ed.
E.J. Sharpe and J. Hinnells; Manchester, 1973), pp. 125-48; H.G. Kippenberg,
'Die Geschichte der mittelpersischen apokalyptischen Traditionen', *Studia Iranica* 7
(1978), pp. 49-80, esp. p. 51.
　　3.　M. Philonenko, 'La sixième vision de IV Esdras et les Oracles d'Hystaspe',
L'apocalyptique (ed. M. Philonenko and M. Simon; Etudes d'histoire des religions,
3; Paris, 1977), pp. 129-35.
　　4.　C. Colpe, 'Sethian and Zoroastrian Ages of the World', in *The Rediscovery of
Gnosticism* (ed. B. Layton; Leiden, 1981), II, pp. 540-52.
　　5.　F. Delitzsch, 'Daniel', *Realencyklopädie für protestantische Theologie und
Kirche* (1855), III, pp. 271-87.

which is epitomized in *Bahman Yasht*.[1] However, voices
pleading for a dependence of *Bahman Yasht* upon Daniel[2] or
expressing prudence in reaching definitive conclusions have
not been missing.[3] Most notable in reversing the evidence for
the priority of Daniel is the attempt of J. Duchesne-Guillemin
to apply the remarks of E. Bickerman on the method of
casting a metal statue in antiquity to the problem of Daniel
and *Bahman Yasht*.[4] Other aspects of the question of Iranian
influence on early Judaism have also been brought up with
reference to *Bahman Yasht*.[5] In this connection one should
note the suggestions of W. Bousset that Jewish-Christian
eschatological legends current in late antiquity may have
influenced *Bahman Yasht*.[6]

The discussion of the literary genre apocalypse, in which
mainly biblical scholars have taken part, has so far centered
on Jewish and Christian texts; but it should be noticed that J.
Collins has referred to Persian material, particularly *Bahman
Yasht*.[7]

1. E. Meyer, *Ursprung und Anfänge des Christentums. 2. Die Entwicklung des Judentums und Jesus von Nazaret* (Stuttgart, 1921), pp. 189-93; D. Winston, 'The Iranian Component in the Bible, Apocrypha, and Qumran: A Review of the Evidence', *HR* 5 (1966), pp. 183-216, esp. p. 190 n. 19; J.J. Collins, *The Apocalyptic Vision of the Book of Daniel* (Missoula, MT, 1977), pp. 39-43; K. Koch, *Das Buch Daniel* (Erträge der Forschung, 144; Darmstadt, 1980), pp. 196-97; *idem*, 'Die Bedeutung der Apokalyptik für die Interpretation der Schrift', in *Mitte der Schrift? Ein christliches-jüdisches Gespräch: Texte des Berner Symposiums vom 6–12 Januar 1985* (ed. M. Klopfenstein, U. Luz, S. Talmon, and E. Tov; Bern, 1987), pp. 201-209.

2. The first one was Delitzsch himself; furthermore I. Scheftelowitz, *Die altpersiche Religion und das Judentum* (Giessen, 1920), pp. 220-21.

3. The statement of M. Hengel, *Judentum und Hellenismus* (2nd edn, Tübingen, 1973), p. 333 n. 481, on the metallic ages in the Iranian texts, is typical of this opinion: 'Diese Nachrichten stammen jedoch aus sehr späten Quellen, die kaum älter sind als das 9. Jh. n. Chr., das Alter der dahinterliegenden Traditionen ist schwer bestimmbar'.

4. J. Duchesne-Guillemin, 'Apocalypse juive et apocalypse iranienne', *La soteriologie dei culti orientali nell'impero romano* (ed. U. Bianchi and M. Vermaseren; Leiden, 1982), pp. 753-59.

5. Winston, 'The Iranian Component', pp. 191, 192, 195.

6. W. Bousset, *Der Antichrist: Ein Beitrag zur Auslegung der Apocalypse* (Göttingen, 1895), p. 73; *idem*, 'Beiträge zur Geschichte der Eschatologie', *ZKG* 20 (1900), pp. 103-31, esp. pp. 120-24.

7. Collins, 'Persian Apocalypses', in *Apocalypse: The Morphology of a Genre* (*Semeia* 14 [1979]), pp. 207-17; *idem*, 'Apocalypse. An Overview', in *The Encyclopedia of Religion* (ed. M. Eliade; New York, 1987), pp. 334-36.

3.   In studies of comparative religion, *Bahman Yasht* is cited as
      an important document for illustrating themes like 'ages of
      the world', 'cosmic cycles', 'universal eschatology', and for
      reconstructing a common Indo-Iranian apocalyptic world-
      view.[1] References are also made to *Bahman Yasht* in studies
      of ancient Scandinavian eschatology and its wider religio-
      historical context.[2]

4.   For scholars in the field of Iranian studies, *Bahman Yasht* is
      naturally recognized as a central specimen of apocalypticism
      and eschatology in the Pahlavi books. But besides this,
      Bahman Yasht takes on particular significance in the efforts to
      elucidate the type of religious personality represented by
      Zarathustra.[3] It has also been used to supplement our knowl-
      edge of the ancient period of Zoroastrian apocalypticism, as
      evidenced by some early Avestan texts.[4]

The origins and transmission history of *Bahman Yasht* have been
commented upon by several scholars. The work of E.W. West during
the 1870s became influential in this respect and contributed strongly to
the consensus which up to now has prevailed in Iranian studies on the
issue of *Bahman Yasht*.[5] This consensus gives the following picture.
Bahman Yasht is basically a Pahlavi adaptation of Avestan materials
and it is even considered to reproduce to a large extent an Avestan
yasht dedicated to Vohu Manah, one of the Amesha Spentas ('Holy
Immortals'). This Avestan composition was translated into Middle
Iranian and included in that vast but vague corpus known as the *Sassanian Avesta* in Pahlavi, the contents of which are summarized in the
Dēnkart. It is from this Pahlavi version that the present text of

1. N. Söderblom, 'Ages of the World (Zoroastrian)', *Encyclopaedia of Religion
and Ethics* (ed. J. Hastings; Edinburgh, 1908), I, pp. 205-10; *idem, La vie future
d'après le mazdéisme: étude d'eschatologie comparée* (Paris, 1901), pp. 270-74; E.
Abegg, *Der Messiasglaube in Indien und Iran* (Berlin, 1928), pp. 208-40; M. Eliade,
The Myth of the Eternal Return (New York, 1965), pp. 112-30, esp. pp. 124-27;
G. Widengren, *Religionsphänomenologie* (Berlin, 1969), pp. 456-66.
2. A. Olrik, *Ragnarök: Die Sagen vom Weltuntergang* (Berlin, 1922), pp. 345-
46, 390-92; R. Reitzenstein, 'Weltuntergangsvorstellungen', *Kyrkohistorisk
Årsskrift* 24 (1924), pp. 129-212, esp. pp. 143, 146, and 200.
3. Widengren, *Die Religionen Irans*, pp. 67-74; *idem*, 'Révélation et prédication
dans les Gathas', in *Iranica* (ed. G. Gnoli; Naples, 1979), pp. 339-64.
4. M. Boyce, 'On the Antiquity of Zoroastrian Apocalyptic', *BSOAS* 47 (1984),
pp. 57-75, esp. pp. 66-68.
5. E.W. West, 'Bahman Yasht', in *Sacred Books of the East. V. Pahlavi Texts
part I* (ed. M. Müller; Oxford, 1880), pp. l-lix (introduction), pp. 191-235
(translation and notes).

Bahman Yasht is thought to have been compiled in the post-Sassanian period, augmented with allusions to the Sassanian and Islamic epochs. With the presupposition that genuine religious traditions ceased to be composed in the Avestan language long before the rise of the Sassanian empire in the third century, most of the material in *Bahman Yasht* can thus be assigned to a period considerably earlier than the actual time of the compilation of the work. The underlying Avestan text is usually dated to the period of crisis following the fall of the Achaemenian empire in the late fourth century BCE, and is moreover seen in relation with a growing Oriental resistance to the Hellenistic rulers who became the heirs of Alexander the Great. The adherents of this view on the origins and transmission history of *Bahman Yasht* include A. Christensen, E. Benveniste, M. Boyce, J. de Menasce, S.K. Eddy, H.G. Kippenberg, and above all G. Widengren, who has presented additional evidence.[1]

However, the traditional view on *Bahman Yasht* and its proposed influence on Jewish and Hellenistic apocalyptic traditions has been vehemently criticized by Ph. Gignoux. In no less than five articles, all published in recent years, the French scholar attempts to prove that there has never been an Avestan yasht dedicated to Vohu Manah and that the contents of *Bahman Yasht*, though built up around a core of eschatological commonplaces, are largely post-Sassanian.[2] The reasons put forward by Gignoux may be summarized as follows:

1. A. Christensen, *Les Kayanides* (Det Kgl. Danske Vidensk. Selskab. Hist.-fil. meddel. 19.2; København, 1931), esp. p. 39; G. Widengren, *Iranische Geisteswelt* (Baden-Baden, 1961), pp. 181-95, 197-208; *idem*, 'Leitende Ideen und Quellen', pp. 105-27; M. Boyce, 'Middle Persian Literature', in *Handbuch der Orientalistik. 2. Literatur* (ed. B. Spuler; Leiden, 1968), pp. 31-66, esp. pp. 48-50; *idem*, 'On the Antiquity of Zoroastrian Apocalyptic', esp. p. 68; J. de Menasce, 'Zoroastrian Pahlavi Writings', in *The Cambridge History of Iran, vol. III (II). The Seleucid, Parthian and Sassanian Periods* (ed. E. Yarshater; Cambridge, 1983), pp. 1166-95, esp. pp. 1171, 1194-95; S.K. Eddy, *The King is Dead: Studies in the Near Eastern Resistance to Hellenism* (Lincoln, NB, 1961); H.G. Kippenberg, 'Die Geschichte. . .', p. 51.

2. Ph. Gignoux, 'Nouveaux regards sur l'apocalyptique iranienne', *CRAIBL* (1986), pp. 334-36; *idem*, 'Sur l'inexistence d'un Bahman Yasht avestique', *Journal of Asian and African Studies* 32 (1986), pp. 53-64; *idem*, 'Apocalypses et voyages extra-terrestres dans l'Iran mazdéen', *Apocalypses et voyages dans l'au-delà* (ed. C. Kappler; Paris, 1987), pp. 351-74; *idem*, 'L'apocalyptique iranienne est-elle vraiment la source d'autres apocalypses?', *Acta Antiqua Academiae Scientiarum Hungaricae* 31 (1988), pp. 67-78; *idem*, 'Bahman, ii. In the Pahlavi Texts', *Encyclopaedia Iranica*, III (ed. E. Yarshater; 1988), p. 488.

a.   The style, the genre and the literary devices of *Bahman Yasht* reveal that it is a late and secondary product with many borrowings.

b.   The sources on which the compiler claims to have based his work are largely fictitious, and the existence of an Avestan yasht for Vohu Manah or of its supposed Pahlavi translation is dubious to say the least.

c.   The contents of *Bahman Yasht* reflect the fall of the Sassanian empire and the invasion of the Arabs in the seventh century and other events affecting Iran in the turmoil of the eighth and ninth centuries.

It should also be noted that Gignoux presents a definition of 'apocalyptic' which is in my opinion too narrow. According to Gignoux, the terms 'apocalyptic' and 'apocalypse' should be restricted to historical events recast in the form of predictions, that is to say prophecies *ex eventu*. Much of his argument can be understood from that viewpoint.

I am not going to discuss the above arguments in detail here, since this will be done elsewhere, but some of my criticisms against the conclusions of Gignoux will implicitly appear from the standpoints taken in this contribution. As to the meaning of 'apocalyptic', I can only state here that a definition which excludes eschatology (both universal and individual) from apocalyptic runs against the common usage of the concept and is, therefore, less appropriate.

It is nonetheless to the credit of Gignoux that his articles have inspired a reconsideration of the *Bahman Yasht* also on the part of those scholars who take a different position.

The main issue in the study of *Bahman Yasht* can be traced all through the hundred years of scholarly debate and is this: Can we really use a text unanimously held to have been compiled in the ninth and tenth centuries CE as a source for Iranian beliefs a thousand years previously? With this central problem in mind I shall briefly discuss the following matters pertaining to *Bahman Yasht*: (1) genre, transmission and sources, (2) the revelatory setting, and (3) the interpretation of the eschatological traditions.

Genre, Transmission and Composition

It should be noted at the outset that the literary genre of *Bahman Yasht* is not that of a fully developed apocalypse like the book of Revelation in the New Testament, or the Jewish apocalypses of *4 Ezra* and *2 Baruch*. *Bahman Yasht* has the appearance of a secondary compilation, it lacks a narrative setting and title, and the apocalyptic materials recorded are put together with a minimum of redactional changes. Surely this diminishes its literary quality but increases instead its value as a vehicle of inherited traditions. However, the intention of the compiler seems to have been to create a coherent apocalypse, since he orders his materials so as to form a consistent narrative, starting with an account of the manner in which divine revelation comes to Zarathushtra, and ending with the description of the final renewal of the world.

What makes *Bahman Yasht* distinguishable as a literary unit in its own right is the fact that it appears with an identical framework in all manuscripts[1] and that all Pahlavi manuscripts present a uniform text with few substantial differences. The introductory piece of the framework consists of three elements: a praise to the creator Ohrmazd, a blessing for the Mazdean religion, and a wish of happiness for the anonymous person to whom the compilation is dedicated. *Bahman Yasht* ends with a short prayer that the eschatological event (*frazaft*) might come in joy and happiness according to the will of God (*yazdān*).

The textual transmission of *Bahman Yasht* is solid, since it is found in the earliest and most important Pahlavi manuscripts.[2] Compared with classical and early Christian literature, the Zoroastrian manuscript tradition for both the Avestan and Pahlavi texts is late. The fourteenth to the sixteenth centuries, with one manuscript of the *Avestan Yasna* from the end of the thirteenth century, constitute the first and main period of preserved Zoroastrian manuscripts. *Bahman Yasht* is regularly copied together with the *Bundahishn* and belongs to the same type of writings, in which authoritative traditional materials have been collected.

There is no modern and critical edition of the Pahlavi text. West based his pioneering translation on the Copenhagen MS. K20, which was the only one known to him at that time (1880). For his translation West also consulted a Pazand version,[3] in itself less reliable, but con-

---

1. The two incomplete manuscripts have only the introduction.
2. The entire text of *Bahman Yasht* is preserved in two manuscripts, K20 (from the late 14th century) and DH (end of the 16th century). In addition, a large portion of the text is found in MS. K43 from the 16th century, and a fragment in MS. K20b. The last mentioned manuscript containing the *Bundahishn* and the beginning of *Bahman Yasht* dates from the 16th century, but preserves one folio from its 'Vorlage' which can be assigned to the early 14th century.
3. The term *pazand* denotes a transcription of a Pahlavi text in Avestan characters (which includes a linguistic interpretation!).

taining a more complete text in a few passages.[1] In 1899 K.A.
Noshervan published a facsimile edition of the manuscript DH, and
facsimile editions of the other manuscripts are available in the Copenhagen series.[2] The first one to use two manuscripts (K20 and DH) in
establishing a printed text was B.T. Anklesaria. His edition with
transcription and translation, although printed already in 1919 in
Bombay, was not published until 1957.[3] Complete translations in
English are thus available only in West (1880) and Anklesaria (1957),
but G. Widengren has made a translation into German, which in many
passages is more accurate than the older ones.[4] A critical edition with
introduction, translation and commentary is being prepared by the
present author.[5]

Two different divisions into chapters and paragraphs are found in
the literature and editions. One was introduced by E.W. West in his
translation, the other by B.T. Anklesaria for his edition. When citing
the *Bahman Yasht*, I suppose that one follows the division of West,
because it has priority and is printed in the margin of the text in Noshervan's facsimile edition.

Before discussing the tradition history of some materials included in
Bahman Yasht, it may be useful to outline the contents and structure of
the work. Five different sections of varying length can be distinguished, and they also appear to be compiled from different sources.

Bahman Yasht opens with a short description of the four ages
(*āvām*) symbolized by a tree with four metallic branches (*BYt* I, 1-5).
These are seen by Zarathushtra in a vision and are explained by Ahura
Mazdah as four different periods (*xvatāyīh*) in the religious history of
Iran. The golden one is when Zarathushtra meets Ahura Mazdah and
Vishtāspa receives the Mazdean religion, the one of silver is the reign
of Artashir, the *kavi* king (*kai-šāh*), the one of steel is the reign of
Xōsrōv Anōshurvān, the great Sassanian king (531–79 CE) and the one
of mixed iron represents the last evil time when enemies, catastrophes
and dissolution shall hit the lands of Iran.

The following passage (*BYt* I, 6-8) first mentions three sources, all
of which the compiler considers to have predicted the appearance of

---

1. West, 'Bahman Yasht', p. lvii.
2. K.A. Noshervan, *The Text of the Pahlavi Zand-i Vohuman Yasht* (Poona,
1899).
3. B.T. Anklesaria, *Zand-î Vohûman Yasn and Two Pahlavi Fragments with Text,
Transliteration and Translation in English* (Bombay, 1957).
4. Widengren, *Iranische Geisteswelt*, pp. 183-95, 198-208.
5. A. Hultgård, *The* Bahman Yasht. *A Critical Edition with Introduction, Translation and Commentary* (Uppsala, forthcoming).

the heretic Mazdak 'in that period'; the reference is probably to the third period, that of steel, mentioned in the preceding passage. *BYt* I, 6-8 also contains a reminiscence of a council of Zoroastrian sages summoned by Xōsrōv Anōshurvān to settle the issue on the *zand* and its teaching.

The third section (*BYt* II, 1-22) is parallel to the first but is more elaborate. It is likewise introduced by a source reference. The vision of the ages, here seven in number, is preceded by a description of how Zarathushtra asked for immortality from Ahura Mazdah. It was denied to him but he was instead granted the divine capacity of omniscience. This enables him to see the seven regions of the world, paradise and hell, and finally a tree with seven metallic branches, symbolizing seven different periods. Only the passage with the vision of the tree is explained by Ahura Mazdah.

The fourth section (*BYt* II, 23-63) describes with much detail the apocalyptic woes announcing the end of 'Zarathushtra's millennium', that is the period of present history. Hordes of enemies, 'the demons of Wrath', will ravage the lands of Iran, the Mazdean religion will decline, general disorder will break up society, and cosmic changes will cause the life of human beings to deteriorate.

The fifth and last section (*BYt* III, 1-62) is essentially concerned with the defeat of the forces of evil, the restoration of Iran and the final renewal of the world. However, a short passage (*BYt* III, 3-11) presents traditions that are partly parallel to the apocalyptic woes described in the preceding section. These traditions are in all probability derived from another source than that or those underlying the fourth section (*BYt* II, 23-62).

The three source references found in *Bahman Yasht* raise intricate questions. Are the sources indicated largely fictitious or can we in any way verify the claim made by the compiler to have based his account on real traditions or texts?

Bahman Yasht opens with the following statement: 'as is evident from the Sūtkar', introducing section one (I, 1-5). What is the Sūtkar? In the encyclopedic writing known as the *Dēnkart* and compiled in the ninth or tenth century CE,[1] a survey is given of the so-called *Sassanian Avesta*. The term denotes the body of Zoroastrian sacred traditions that was finally authorized during the reign of Xōsrōv Anōshurvān (531–79). The *Sassanian Avesta* contained traditions transmitted in the Avestan language, as well as in a Middle Iranian or Pahlavi translation,

---

1. J. de Menasce, *Une encyclopédie mazdéenne, le Dēnkart* (Paris, 1958), pp. 110-12.

with glosses and commentaries. By the late Sassanian period this Pahlavi version was known as the *zand*. *Dēnkart* informs us that the *Sassanian Avesta* was divided into 21 sections, called *nasks*, and that one of the 21 *nasks* was the Sūtkar. The Sūtkar *nask* had, according to the *Dēnkart*, a passage dealing with the four ages of Zarathushtra's millennium.[1] The very brief summary that is given by the *Dēnkart* in IX, 8 contains no mention of the mythical episodes which introduce the corresponding material in *Bahman Yasht* (sections 1 and 3). These mythical introductions have simply been omitted by the redactor of the *Dēnkart* version. In comparison with *Bahman Yasht*, the summary in *Dēnkart* reveals more redactional reworking. The description of the first three periods in the *Dēnkart* version have been put in the retrospective, and the fourth and last is presented as contemporary with the author of this particular version. All this is clearly secondary compared to *Bahman Yasht*, where the periods of the dreamvision are described as lying in the future, with exception of the first one, thought to represent Zarathushtra's own time. Furthermore, we are not told that the different periods are symbolized by a tree with four or seven branches as in *Bahman Yasht*. Both *Dēnkart* and *Bahman Yasht* base their summaries on Pahlavi *zand* versions, which are in turn founded on an original Avestan tradition, the wording of which is beyond recovery.

We may assume, then, that the Sūtkar *nask* as claimed by the compiler of *Bahman Yasht* contained an account in Avestan of the world ages as well as an an elaborate Pahlavi version adapted to the Sassanian historical context. Compared with the *Dēnkart*, the summary given in *Bahman Yasht* is more faithful to the *Vorlage* in the Sassanian Avesta.

The source reference for section two (*BYt* I, 6-8) runs: 'from the zand of Vahuman yasn, Hordāt yasn and Aštāt yasn it is evident that. . .', followed by the mention of Mazdak and the council summoned by Xōsrōv Anōshurvān. Mazdak is known for having attempted a thoroughgoing reformation of the social and religious structure in the Sassanian empire of the sixth century, and it was precisely Xōsrōv Anōshurvān who crushed the rebellion of Mazdak and his followers. The council mentioned was most probably part of an endeavor to consolidate the Zoroastrian 'state church' after the disorder created by the Mazdakite movement.

---

1. *Dēnkart* IX, 8. Division into books (in quotations denoted with Roman figures) is made by the compiler of *Dēnkart*, while chapters and paragraphs have been introduced by E.W. West.

The Hordād and Ashtād liturgies in an Avestan form are still extant as *Yashts* 4 and 18 in the *Avesta* that has come down to us. Both these texts seem to include heterogeneous elements and are considered to be late compositions although they may transmit older materials.[1] These *Yashts* contain no mention of Mazdak nor of King Xōsrōv Anōshurvān. This fact is taken by Gignoux as an indication of the compiler's use of dubious or fictitious source references.

The issue is not so simple, however. The two Avestan texts, although late, would nonetheless have been composed several centuries before the appearance of Mazdak. The compiler of *Bahman Yasht* quite correctly states that he has not based his account on the Avestan texts themselves but on the *zand*, their Pahlavi version. Since there are no traces of such a *zand* for these two Avestan texts in the material that has survived, one might, with Gignoux, still dismiss the claim made by the compiler.

There is, however, evidence that points to the existence of a now lost *zand* to the Hordād and Ashtād Yashts. In every religion that possesses a body of sacred, authoritative writings or traditions, a process of interpretation and reinterpretation is generated to understand them in new historical and cultural contexts. What is left of the Pahlavi *zand* texts clearly shows this development.[2] Although the methods of interpretation and explanation may vary in detail from one text to another,[3] the main intention to reinterpret and to actualize is nonetheless the same.

The comparison with the genre of Qumran writings denoted *pesher* is highly illuminating. As is well known, in these *pesher* texts biblical prophecies are interpreted in the light of contemporary events and key figures which were of particular significance to the Qumran community. In a very similar way Zoroastrian sages of the Sassanian period found in the sacred Avestan traditions clear allusions to the contemporary history of their own community and recorded them in their *zand* texts, which in form and function clearly correspond to the Qumran *pesher* texts. A good example is given in the *Dēnkart,* Book 7.

---

1. Cf. I. Gershewitz, 'Old Iranian Literature', in *Handbuch der Orientalistik. IV. Iranistik. 2. Literatur* (ed. B. Spuler; Leiden, 1968), pp. 1-30, esp. p. 20; H. Lommel, *Die Yäst's des Awesta* (Leipzig, 1927), pp. 166-67.

2. Pahlavi versions of the Yasna with the Vispered, the Vidēvdāt and the Nirangistan have come down to us, these Avestan texts being frequently used in the Zoroastrian liturgy. Of the yashts which gradually became less used in post-Sassanian ritual, no Pahlavi translations have survived except a few short fragments primarily found in the *Dēnkart*.

3. J. de Menasce, 'Zoroastrian Pahlavi Writings. . .', p. 1167.

The compiler describes in ch. 7 the events from the conversion of Vishtāspa to the downfall of the Iranian empire (*ērān šahr*). Coming to speak about the glorious period of the first Sassanian king he supports his interpretation by quoting in Pahlavi a stanza from *Yasht* 13 introduced by the statement 'among the reformers of the period (*āvām*) is Artašīr, son of Pāpak, of whom it is said. . .' Then follows the Pahlavi version of *Yt* 134.106-107. But here the name of the Avestan figure has been replaced by Artashīr. For this passage in *Dēnkart* (VII, 7.12-13) we have consequently three stages: (a) the Avestan text, (b) the Pahlavi version, the *zand*, and (c) the compiler's restatement. In the second stage (b) the reinterpretation has been introduced into the text proper by replacing the Avestan figure with the Sassanian king. It is then reaffirmed more explicitly by the post-Sassanian redactor in stage three (c).

In the following passage (*Dk* VII, 7.14-18) we find a similar reinterpretation of earlier traditions with the purpose of applying them to Tōsar or Tansar, another Sassanian figure purported to be contemporary with Artashīr. In this case, however, the Avestan text has not survived, and we are left with the two younger stages: the *zand* and the redactor's introducing statement. In the *Hordād Yasht*, one of the Avestan texts referred to by the compiler of *Bahman Yasht*, one prays for the divine beings to be liberated from enemies, demons and 'the evil man' (*Yt* 4.3). For the Zoroastrian clergy in the late Sassanian period 'the evil man' meant in the first place Mazdak, who in the Pahlavi books stands out as the great heretic and is given epithets that are clear equivalents to the Avestan words used for 'the evil man' in Hordād yasht. No doubt the Sassanian commentators found allusions to this Mazdak in *Hordād Yasht* 4.3 as well as in other Avestan texts. There are further concordances of that kind between the Avestan text and the passage of *Bahman Yasht* with which we are concerned. This suggests that the compiler of *Bahman Yasht* actually knew a *zand* text of *Hordād Yasht* as he himself explicitly states. In this case we have the Avestan tradition (a) and the restatement of the post-Sassanian compiler (c), but the intermediary *zand* text (b), in which the identification with Mazdak was made, is no longer extant.

The third and last reference to a previous source is found in *Bahman Yasht* II, 1 (section 3 above) and refers only to 'the zand of Vahuman yasn' which was also mentioned in the preceding section (*BYt* I, 6-8). It is somewhat surprising that the doctrine of the metallic ages is here stated to derive from another source than in the parallel passage (*BYt* I, 1-5) where it was said to come from the Sūtkar nask. As we have seen, the compiler of the *Dēnkart* also referred to this source. The problem with the reference to a 'zand of Vahuman yasn' is that we have independent evidence neither for the existence of an Avestan composition dedicated to Vohu Manah nor of its *zand*. It is to the credit of Gignoux that this fact, which was too easily passed over by previous scholars, has been brought up as an important issue.

However, it is difficult to believe that this reference is entirely fictitious. The following circumstances point to the contrary. First, the other two source references found in *Bahman Yasht* can be shown to have a factual basis. Second, it is hard to believe that a Zoroastrian compiler of the ninth or tenth centuries, when more extensive traditional materials were available than today, would have had recourse to forgery by inventing titles of nonexistent writings. Third, there are actually some liturgical formulas in the present text of the *Bahman Yasht* which may be hints to the compiler's use of a ritual 'Vorlage' for parts of his work.[1] Fourth, the literary character of much of section five in *Bahman Yasht* (III, 1-62) strongly suggests an underlying *zand* text of the same type as the Pahlavi *Vidēvdāt* which actually survives. In addition the same section preserves epic fragments originally belonging to an Avestan source, as demonstrated by Widengren.[2]

Furthermore, that two different source writings are referred to for the same material is in itself not surprising, since variants of the same basic tradition also occurred in different passages of the *Sassanian Avesta*, to judge from the summaries presented in the *Dēnkart*. In *Bahman Yasht* the two accounts of Zarathushtra's dreamvision are far from being identical, a fact that can be explained by the use of two different sources as also claimed by the compiler.

What is, then, the conclusion to be drawn from our discussion of the source references in *Bahman Yasht*? First, the compiler no doubt based much of his work on earlier sources, but these sources, the *zand* texts, do not as such carry us beyond the Sassanian period, that is roughly the third to the sixth centuries CE. However, the *zand* texts were themselves based on Avestan texts now largely lost. The problem is that in most cases we can reconstruct the contents of these lost Avestan traditions only in outline without much certainty of detail. There is a further complication. We must face the possibility that Zoroastrian priests might have been able to compose Avestan texts long after Avestan ceased to be a living language. But whether they

---

1. Cf. J. Tavadia, *Die mittelpersische Sprache und Literatur der Zarathustrier* (Leipzig, 1956), p. 122; A. Hultgård, 'Forms and Origins of Iranian Apocalypticism', *Apocalypticism*, pp. 387-411, esp. p. 408.

2. Widengren, 'Leitenden Ideen. . .', pp. 105-11.

actually did so remains to be shown. Anyway, a typical *zand* text with inserted glosses indicates, in my opinion, a genuine Avestan substratum, since it is hard to imagine that Zoroastrian priests composed explanatory remarks to their own Avestan imitations.

The Revelatory Setting

The modes of revelation found in *Bahman Yasht* deserve a closer study since they are central to the understanding of Iranian visionary traditions. In my contribution to the Uppsala Colloquium ten years ago, I made a preliminary analysis of the various forms of apocalyptic communication underlying the Pahlavi texts.[1] Two such original forms were distinguished: (a) the *hampursakīh* form, most conveniently explained as a kind of oracular session held in a particular place to which the inquirer is brought by the guidance of a divine messenger, and (b) the dreamvision form, in which the vision is given to a human recipient but interpreted by a deity or a divinely inspired person. The problem is to know whether these two forms presupposed an otherworldly revelatory journey and in what way they are related to each other.

Otherworldly journeys undertaken by an individual in his lifetime are known from a wide area in the Mediterranean region and the Near East. The morphology, origins and interdependence of these traditions and religious practices have been much discussed. They were a central issue for the 'religionsgeschichtliche Schule' and they continue to be in the focus of scholarly attention.[2]

---

1. Hultgård, 'Forms and Origins. . .', pp. 392-400.
2. More recent literature includes (A) for ancient Iran: G. Widengren, 'Stand und Aufgaben der iranischen Religionsgeschichte II', *Numen* 2 (1955), pp. 47-134, esp. pp. 66-72; *idem*, *Die Religion Irans*, pp. 67-74; *idem*, 'Révélation et prédication. . .', pp. 346-51; Ph. Gignoux, 'La signification du voyage extra-terrestre dans l'eschatologie mazdéenne', in *Mélanges d'histoire des religions offerts à Henri-Ch. Puech* (Paris, 1974), pp. 63-69; *idem*, ' "Corps osseux et âme osseuse": essai sur le chamanisme dans l'Iran ancien', *JA* 267 (1979), pp. 54-67; *idem*, 'Les voyages chamaniques dans le monde iranien', *Monumentum Georg Morgenstierne I* (Acta Iranica, 21; Leiden, 1981), pp. 244-65; *idem*, 'Apocalypses et voyages extra-terrestres. . .'; J. Kellens, 'Mythes et conceptions avestiques sous les Sassanides', in *Monumentum H.S. Nyberg I* (Acta Iranica, 4; Leiden, 1975), pp. 457-70; P. Calmeyer and H. Gaube, 'Eine edlere Frau als sie habe ich nie gesehen', *Papers in Honour of Professor Mary Boyce* (Acta Iranica, 24; Leiden, 1985), pp. 43-60. (B) Generally and in Judaism, early Christianity and Hellenistic religions: C. Colpe, 'Die "Himmelsreise der Seele" als philosophie- und religionsgeschichtliches Problem', in *Festschrift J. Klein* (ed. E. Fries; Göttingen, 1967), pp. 85-104; J. Schwartz, 'Le

Zoroastrian tradition has recorded three such journeys, which all have a revelatory aim; two are found in ninth century Pahlavi books and one in an early Sassanian inscription from the third century. The most elaborate and well known is that made by the pious Artāi Virāz. The other two concern Vishtāspa, the royal protector of Zarathushtra, and the Sassanian highpriest Kartīr. These otherworldly journeys represent genuine Iranian ideas and ecstatic practices. This is admitted, although not wholly unambiguously, also by Gignoux, who has made an important contribution to their study.[1] The tendency to discard the Iranian otherworldly journeys as late products influenced by Jewish, Christian or even Islamic apocalyptic ideas has been stated most clearly by I.P. Culianu, and is best seen in his article 'Ascension' for *The Encyclopedia of Religion*.[2]

Although the dreamvision of Zarathushtra in *Bahman Yasht* bears every sign of an otherworldly revelatory journey, it has gone unnoticed as such in the scholarly discussion, probably because there is no explicit mention of Zarathushtra's soul leaving his body. However, the ritual procedure inducing the ecstatic vision is quite similar to that found in the accounts of Artāi Virāz's and Vishtāspa's heavenly ascents. In addition the present text of *Bahman Yasht*, though incomplete, has preserved the detail that Zarathushtra during his ecstatic vision looks down at the seven world regions with that supernatural clairvoyance which enables him to distinguish, as it is told, every single hair on the back of the cattle. Besides the description of the four or seven world periods symbolized by different metals, the second version of Zarathushtra's journey also includes elements of a vision of heaven and hell. These are by no means extraneous to the account, but

voyage au ciel dans la littérature apocalyptique', in *L'apocalyptique* (ed. M. Philonenko and M. Simon; Paris, 1977), pp. 91-126; A.F. Segal, 'Heavenly Ascent in Hellenistic Judaism, Early Christianity and their Environment', *ANRW* 23 (1980), pp. 1333-94; I.P. Culianu, *Psychanodia I: A Survey of the Evidence concerning the Ascension of the Soul and its Relevance* (Leiden, 1983); *idem, Expériences de l'extase: extase, ascension et récit visionnaire de l'Hellénisme au Moyen-Age* (Paris, 1984); J.D. Tabor, *Things Unutterable: Paul's Ascent to Paradise in its Greco-Roman, Judaic and Early Christian Contexts* (Landover, MD, 1986); M. Himmelfarb, 'From Prophecy to Apocalypse: The Book of the Watchers and Tours of Heaven', in *Jewish Spirituality: From the Bible to the Middle Ages* (ed. A. Green; New York, 1986).

1. In addition to the studies of Gignoux previously listed, mention should be made of Ph. Gignoux, 'L'inscription de Kirdir à Naqs-i Rustam', *Studia Iranica* 1 (1972), pp. 177-205.

2. I.P. Culianu, 'Ascension', in *The Encyclopedia of Religion* (ed. M. Eliade; New York, 1987), pp. 435-41.

are in good agreement with the Iranian tradition of the otherworldly journey. Already Kartīr states in his inscription that the main purpose of his visit to the otherworld is to get a divine affirmation of his having been chosen for paradise and not for hell. And there is no reason to suppose that the otherworldly journey of Kartīr composed in third century CE and in the Middle-Iranian language represents an innovation in the religious history of Iran. The evidence points to the contrary. Although preserved only in two Pahlavi versions from the ninth or tenth century, one in the *Dēnkart* (*Dk* VII 4.84-86 and the other in the *Pahlavi Rivāyat* (*PR* 47.27-32), the account of Vishtāspa's ecstatic journey to heaven is obviously based on an Avestan text, as pointed out by M. Molé and G. Widengren.[1] Hence it testifies to an Old-Iranian tradition. The ecstatic otherworldly journey can be shown to have deep roots in an Indo-Iranian 'shamanistic' tradition. The evidence has been presented by G.M. Bongard-Levin and E.A. Grantovskij from a wide range of Indo-Iranian cultures.[2]

Furthermore, the mythical episode in *Bahman Yasht* which introduces the otherworldly journey of Zarathushtra is part of well-established Zoroastrian tradition on the relationship between immortality and posterity that can be traced back to Indo-Iranian times.[3] Thus, it seems clear to me that the revelation of the different ages of the world is conveyed to Zarathushtra through an ecstatic otherworldly journey and set in an ancient mythical and ritual framework.

A particular problem is raised by the literary characteristics of the two modes of revelation in *Bahman Yasht*. In the dreamvision, the human recipient is asked by the deity to retell what he saw, and thereupon the deity interprets the things seen in the vision. In the *hampursakīh* form—the oracular consultation—Zarathushtra poses questions to Ahura Mazdah who answers at length.

The question and answer pattern is considered by Gignoux to be a late innovation in Zoroastrianism and he compares it with similar

---

1. M. Molé, *Culte, mythe et cosmologie dans l'Iran ancien* (Paris, 1963), pp. 378-79; *idem, La légende de Zoroastre selon les textes pehlevis* (Paris, 1967), pp. 189-91; G. Widengren, 'Stand und Aufgaben. . .', p. 67; *idem, Die Religionen Irans*, p. 69; *idem*, 'Révélation et prédication. . .', pp. 347-49.

2. G.M. Bongard-Levin and E.A. Grantovskij, *De la Scythie à l'Inde: énigmes de l'histoire des anciens Aryens* (trans. Ph. Gignoux; Paris, 1981; Russian original, Moscow, 1974), pp. 83-113. As pointed out by Gignoux, these authors were the first ones to interpret Kartir's otherworldly journey in a shamanistic context.

3. A. Hultgård, 'Zoroastrian Myth in the Bahman Yasht', in *Nordic Studies on the Middle East* (ed. B. Utas and M. Laanatza; Uppsala, 1991).

forms in Christian, patristic literature.[1] The pattern is, however, found in the Younger Avesta, with Zarathushtra asking questions and Ahura Mazdah giving the answers, and it can be confidently put back at least to the late Achaemenian period.[2] It is most probably modeled after the *Gathahymns* with their many question and answer passages (e.g. Yasna 31 and 44). The question and answer pattern with its *hampursakīh* background appears to have been the chief revelatory framework in which the Zoroastrian priests put most of the Younger Avesta. An independent witness is provided by the Hellenistic writer Diodorus Siculus (1.94.2), who parallels the revelation given to Moses by the god of the Jews with that given to Zarathushtra by the deity of the eastern Iranians. The reliability of this information on the revelatory setting of the *Avesta* has rightly been emphasized by Gh. Gnoli.[3] On this point too, the literary framework, there is no reason to mistrust the continuity of Iranian tradition.

The Interpretation of the Eschatological Traditions

Before concluding, I will make some general observations on the two last sections of *Bahman Yasht*. They constitute the bulk of the book and contain eschatological traditions presented as elements of an apocalyptic scheme. The periodization that dominates in *Bahman Yasht* is the traditional Zoroastrian one. The world is divided into four periods, each lasting 3000 years, but it is only the last one that interests the compiler of *Bahman Yasht*. This last period begins with the mission of Zarathushtra and ends with the coming of the Saoshyant, the final savior. His appearance marks the end of the present world and the beginning of the cosmic renewal, the *fraso.kərəti* of the *Avesta*. Between the time of Zarathushtra and the coming of the Saoshyant two other savior figures will appear, each one at the turn of a millennium. The peculiar thing with this subperiodization is its cyclical tendency. The first and third millennia begin as a time of happiness but end with

---

1. Gignoux, 'Nouveaux regards...', p. 338; 'Sur l'inexistence...', p. 56 n. 17; 'L'apocalyptique iranienne...', p. 72.

2. This 'question–answer' pattern is attested already in the yashts dedicated to Mithra and Verethragna (*Yt* 10, 1 and 121; 14, 1); also in Yasna 19, 1-3 and the whole of Vidēvdāt, which is cast in the same pattern. Explicit references to the *humpursakīh* consultation itself occur in Vidēvdāt 2; 1-2 and Yasna 12, 6. A 'question–answer' form is also found in Yasna 9, 1-15 (Zarathushtra–Haoma deified) and in 71, 1-2 (Frashaoshtra–Zarathushtra).

3. Gh. Gnoli, *Zoroaster's Time and Homeland: A Study on the Origins of Mazdeism and Related Problems* (Naples, 1980), pp. 144-46.

apocalyptic disasters. The last two millennia are, however, essentially an improvement on the first one. Expectations naturally concentrated on the savior who was next to come, Hushetar, as he is named in the Pahlavi texts. By the end of the Sassanian period his advent should be very close, according to Zoroastrian time reckoning. But as time went by, the need for corrections in the apocalyptic scheme was felt, and thus we find in some ninth-century Pahlavi books that the coming of Hushetar has been postponed for several centuries.[1] In *Bahman Yasht* his appearance is set to 600 or 800 years after the end of Zarathushtra's millennium.[2]

Underlying the two accounts of the metallic ages is another scheme in which the world is symbolized by the cosmic tree and the ages by the branches. On this scheme, however, is superimposed a periodization of Zarathushtra's millennium in different historical reigns (*xvatāyīh*). Here we have clearly to do with prophecies *ex eventu*, except for the last evil period, that of mixed iron, which is thought to manifest itself towards the end of that millennium. The invasion of hostile peoples, the cosmic and social disorders, are, according to the compiler and his immediate sources, 'signs' (*daxšak*) announcing the end of Zarathushtra's millennium. In interpreting the descriptions of the 'signs of the end' in *Bahman Yasht*, one has to account for the diversity of elements of which these descriptions are composed. Traditions from different times and contexts have been merged together and given an actualizing tendency reflecting in the main the late Sassanian period.[3]

The elaborate description of the signs of the end found in *Bahman Yasht* II, 23-63, and III, 3-11 presents many similarities with corresponding passages in Jewish and Christian apocalypses, including those from the early Middle Ages. However, the most notable affinity is with the Indian doctrine of the world ages, as first witnessed by the *Mahābhārata* and its descriptions of the Kali-yuga.[4] Previous authors have noted that the accounts of the social disorders and the

---

1. Cf. Söderblom, *La vie future*, p. 274; Kippenberg, *Geschichte*, p. 57; E. Yarshater, 'Iranian National History,' *The Cambridge History of Iran* (ed. E. Yarshater; Cambridge, 1983), III, pp. 359-480, esp. p. 387.

2. In MS. K20 the figure is 600 and in MS. DH it is 800. It is to be noted that K20 is written about 200 years before DH!

3. The passages describing the assault of the demons of the race of Wrath (*hešm*) constitute a significant example. They reflect cultic conflicts in the early religious history of Iran as shown by G. Widengren, *Hochgottglaube im alten Iran* (Uppsala, 1938), pp. 342-45; S. Wikander, *Vayu: Texte und Untersuchungen zur indo-iranischen Religionsgeschichte,* I (Uppsala, 1941), pp. 136-37.

4. *Mahābhārata* III, 148; and above all III, 186-89.

degeneration of nature show clear similarities.[1] Besides these there are other striking concordances. In *Bahman Yasht* the account of the signs of the end is characterized by the recurrent formula (found with minor variants) 'at the lowest age' (*pat hān ī nitom āvām*) intended as it were constantly to remind the reader (or listener) of what period is being described. A very similar formula with the same function runs like a refrain through the description of Kali-yuga in *Mahābhārata,* 'at the end of the age' *(yugānta).* In both texts historical peoples are introduced into the description of eschatological evils in a closely parallel manner. These hostile peoples will rule over Iran and India respectively, and they are compared to 'serfs', *bandak* in *Bahman Yasht* and *śūdra* in *Mahābhārata.*[2] The lists enumerating historical peoples give a hint to the time in which the accounts of the apocalyptic woes underwent their final redaction. Turks, Byzantines, Arabs and Hephtalites in *Bahman Yasht* point to the late Sassanian period.[3] In *Mahābhārata* we find, among others, Greeks (*yavanās*) and Sakas (*śakās*), indicating a redaction of the materials in III, 186 during the first centuries CE.[4]

The affinities between *Bahman Yasht* and the Indian teaching of the world ages can be interpreted in different ways. They indicate a historical connection, the nature of which is however still open to question.

The passages dealing with the eschatological restoration present similar problems of interpretation to those concerned with the signs of the end. Different traditions with a different transmission history are juxtaposed. They are partly of Sassanian origin, but more ancient mythical and legendary materials have been collected and put into a new historical context.[5] The same process of actualization and reinterpretation of old materials can be observed in other Middle-Iranian texts of an apocalyptic character.[6]

In conclusion, there is, in my opinion, clear evidence of an ancient mythical and apocalyptic core in *Bahman Yasht*. For that text, as for

---

1. Olrik, *Ragnarök*, pp. 389-93; Reitzenstein, 'Vom Töpferorakel. . .', p. 53.

2. *BYt* II, 49 and *Mahābhārata* III, 186:30.

3. The Arabs are called *tāǰīk* in the ninth century Pahlavi books. This term is already used in classical Armenian sources of the fifth century to denote Arabs. In the late Sassanian period Arab tribes made several incursions into southern Iran.

4. This is the period in which the Sakas became overlords of northwestern India.

5. Cf. Widengren, 'Leitende Ideen. . .', pp. 105-19; Boyce, 'On the Antiquity. . .', p. 69.

6. Cf. in particular the J̌āmāsp Nāmak, another apocalyptic Pahlavi text, and the study of T. Olsson, 'The Apocalyptic Activity. The case of J̌āmāsp Nāmag', in *Apocalypticism*, pp. 21-49, esp. pp. 35-46.

other Pahlavi books, distinction must be made between the actual date of compilation and the age of the wide variety of traditions included in these writings. With respect to form and content it cannot be discarded as an exclusively ninth century product. However, scholars who want to use *Bahman Yasht* for comparative purposes must be aware of the different tradition layers and their background.

Generally speaking, *Bahman Yasht* can be studied in two main contexts. One is ancient Iranian mythology and Hellenistic-Parthian apocalyptic, the other is the late Sassanian and early Islamic period. It is in the first context that early Jewish apocalypticism and Indian classical doctrine of the world ages belong as comparative materials. The second context is medieval apocalypticism in its various expressions: Zoroastrian, Byzantine, eastern Christian, Jewish, and early Islamic. The study of both contexts is necessary in order to understand *Bahman Yasht* as a genuine apocalyptic work.

8

METHODOLOGICAL REFLECTIONS
ON THE PROBLEM OF DEFINITION OF GENERIC TEXTS*

David Hellholm

One of the issues discussed most vigorously at the Uppsala Colloquium on Apocalypticism was the question of definition. A proposal presented by a committee assigned by the Colloquium to submit an acceptable definition was turned down, as were individually designed suggestions. Thus, contrary to the Messina Conference on Gnosticism, we were unable to present any kind of definition, with the result that practically every contributor to the Volume of Proceedings delivered his or her own definition as the starting point for their subsequent deliberations.

In retrospect I believe that this was the best that could have happened to apocalyptic research, since evidently the time was not ripe for an overall definition, and a premature one could easily have resulted in a straitjacket that could have prevented new incentives and more sophisticated attempts from coming to grips with the difficult task of defining at one and the same time a 'World of Concepts', a 'Literary Genre', and a 'Historical and Sociological Phenomenon'.[1]

In this essay I will limit myself to addressing only one problem of definition, namely the one pertaining to the question of how to define

* For help with computer drawings and technical advice I express my gratitude to my son, Christer D. Hellholm.

1. See the corresponding three parts of the Volume of Proceedings: D. Hellholm (ed.), *Apocalypticism in the Mediterranean World and the Near East: Proceedings of the International Colloquium on Apocalypticism. Uppsala, August 12–17, 1979* (Tübingen, 1983; 2nd edn, 1989): The Phenomenon of Apocalypticism, The Literary Genre of Apocalypses, and The Sociology of Apocalypticism and the Sitz im Leben of Apocalypses, as well as the groupings of *semes* in *idem*, 'The Problem of Apocalyptic Genre and the Apocalypse of John', in A. Yarbro Collins (ed.), *Early Christian Apocalypticism. Genre and Social Setting (Semeia* 36; Atlanta, 1986), pp. 13-64: 'A. Content—Propositions and Themes (text-semantic aspect). . . B. Form—Style (text-syntactic aspect). . . C. Function–Communication function (text-pragmatic aspect)' (pp. 22-23).

generic texts in general and the literary genre called Apocalypse in particular. In so doing I will try to substantiate some of the suggestions given already in my article 'The Problem of Apocalyptic Genre and the Apocalypse of John'.[1]

1. *Analyses of Genre versus Analyses of Individual Texts*

The question of genre is in principle a question of virtual abstraction, or better: of a hierarchy of different virtual abstraction levels, for example Mode of writing, Type of text, Genre, Sub-genres of different ranks.[2]

When discussing the relationship between analyses pertaining to genres and analyses pertaining to individual texts, I will limit myself to doing so by referring to two related fields of research: text-linguistics, and biblical, especially New Testament, form criticism.[3]

a. In *linguistics* one differentiates, since Georg von der Gabelentz and later Ferdinand de Saussure, between three abstraction levels: (1) *Sprachvermögen* or *faculté de langage,* as language competence in general, i.e. language as system, (2) *Einzelsprache* or *langue* as struc-

---

1. Hellholm, 'The Problem of Apocalyptic Genre'.
2. See Hellholm, 'The Problem of Apocalyptic Genre', pp. 28-30.
3. Also in literary criticism the question of genre has always been pertinently and vigorously discussed. I can here only refer to six recent works of great importance: first, the informative and illuminating synthesis by K. Hempfer, *Gattungstheorie* (Uni-Taschenbücher, 133; Munich, 1973); second, the investigation of the classical German theory of genre by G. Willems, *Das Konzept der literarischen Gattung* (Hermaea, 42; Tübingen, 1981); further, the important article by E.-R. Schwinge, 'Griechische Poesie und die Lehre von der Gattungstrinität in der Moderne', in *Antike und Abendland* 27 (1981), pp. 130-62; the comprehensive work by A. Fowler, *Kinds of Literature* (Oxford, 1982); and finally the collections of essays in Vorstand der Vereinigung der deutschen Hochschulgermanisten (ed.), *Textsorten und literarische Gattungen* (Berlin, 1983); as well as in T.A. van Dijk (ed.), *Discourse and Literature: New Approaches to the Analysis of Literary Genres* (Critical Theory, 3; Amsterdam, 1985).

For the affinity between literary criticism and linguistics, cf. e.g. H. Steger, 'Sprachgeschichte und Geschichte der Textsorten/Texttypen und ihrer kommunikativen Bezugsbereiche', in W. Besch *et al.* (eds.), *Sprachgeschichte* (Handbücher der Sprach- und Kommunikationswissenschaft, 2:1; Berlin, 1984), p. 187: 'In der Beschäftigung mit Texttypen bewegen sich Sprach- und Literaturwissenschaft gegenwärtig aufeinander zu. Voraussetzung ist, daß die Sprachwissenschaft jetzt stark semantische und pragmatische Fragestellungen einbezieht, während die Literaturwissenschaft berücksichtigt, daß Gattungen/Texttypen aus virtuellen satzübergreifenden sprachstrukturellen Ganzheiten bestehen, die auf Konventionen oder Normierungen beruhen'.

ture of a particular language, and (3) *Rede* or *parole* as concrete actualization.[1] Eugenio Coseriu in his interpretation of de Saussure has introduced the middle-term 'norm', or better, 'social norm' and 'individual norm', as a resolution to the dichotomic opposition between *langue* and *parole*.[2] These three concepts relate to each other differently depending on the kind of opposition between *langue* and *parole* that is actualized: (1) 'Wenn die Opposition zwischen *System* und *Verwirklichung* besteht, umfaßt die *langue* nur das *System* und die *parole* alle anderen Begriffe...'; (2) 'Wenn dagegen die Opposition zwischen *Konkretem* und *Abstraktem* besteht, fällt die *parole* mit den konkreten Redeakten zusammen und die *langue* umfaßt alle anderen Begriffe...'; (3) 'Wenn die Opposition zwischen *Sozialem* und *Individuellem* besteht, umfaßt die *langue das System* und die *Norm*, und die *parole* demgegenüber die *individuelle Norm* und das konkrete Sprechen...'; (4) 'Besteht schließlich die Opposition zwischen *Originalität des Ausdrucks* und *Wiederholung*, umfaßt die *parole* ausschließlich die noch nie geäußerten und okkasionellen Elemente des

---

1. G. von der Gabelentz, *Die Sprachwissenschaft: Ihre Aufgaben, Methoden und bisherigen Ergebnisse* (Tübinger Beiträge zur Linguistik, 1; 3rd edn [2nd edn Leipzig 1901], Tübingen, 1984), pp. 3, 8-9, 49f., 59, 138-39; F. de Saussure, *Course in General Linguistics* (London, 1966), pp. 9 and 13f. (French original: Geneva, 1915). Cf. E. Coseriu, *Einführung in die allgemeine Sprachwissenschaft* (Uni-Taschenbücher, 1372; Tübingen, 1988), pp. 16-18; *idem, Sprachkompetenz* (Uni-Taschenbücher, 1481; Tübingen, 1988), pp. 15-22. For the influence of Gabelentz on Saussure, see esp. Coseriu, 'Georg von der Gabelentz und die synchronische Sprachwissenschaft', in von der Gabelentz, *Die Sprachwissenschaft*, pp. 3-35. Cf. J.K. Baldinger, *Semantic Theory* (New York, 1980), pp. 150f.: 'The structure or structures are always the structure or structures of a given language. The system is always of a conceptual order, going beyond any given language.' See also the precise dichotomic distinction between *langue* and *parole* by Klaus Heger, 'Die Semantik und die Dichotomie von Langue und Parole', *Zeitschrift für romanische Philologie* 85 (1969), pp. 144-215: 'In diesem Sinne sei bestimmt, daß...unter "langue" Sprache als virtuelles und abstraktes System und unter "parole" Sprache als konkrete (gesprochene oder geschriebene), das heißt an ein jeweiliges hic et nunc gebundene Aktualisierung verstanden werden soll' (p. 147).

2. Coseriu, 'System, Norm und "Rede"', in *Sprache, Strukturen und Funktionen* (Tübinger Beiträge zur Linguistik, 2; Tübingen, 1979), pp. 45-59. On the definition of *langue* as a 'fait sociale' in de Saussure, *Course* (1966) and on the question of the relationship between *langue* and idiolect, see H. Kubczak, 'Zum Verhältnis von "Langue" und "Idiolekt"', *Zeitschrift für romanische Philologie* 105 (1989), pp. 1-27. Kubczak, in agreement with Coseriu, does not include the 'individual norm', i.e. the idiolect, in the *langue*, but defines, contrary to Coseriu, the idiolect as the basis of a diasystem (p. 26); *langue* is thus defined as 'ein synchronisch zu erfassendes Diasystem' (p. 25).

konkreten Sprechens, und die *langue* alle anderen Begriffe. . .'[1] As far
as *generic* investigations are concerned, the issue applies to two kinds
of opposition: (a) first, to the opposition between *concrete* and *abstract*
notions, in which case the oppositional relationship between *langue* and
parole obtains the following structure:[2]

concrete speech	individual norm	social norm	functional system
PAROLE		LANGUE	

(b) second, to the opposition between *social* and *individual* notions, in
which case the oppositional relationship between *langue* and *parole*
obtains a different structure:[3]

concrete speech	individual norm	social norm	functional system
PAROLE		LANGUE	

The problem that arises from these two different *langue*-concepts with
regard to definition and analyses of generic texts will have to be
reflected upon further in future investigations.[4]

From a somewhat different point of view Klaus Heger has pointed to
the fact that the designation of 'langue' as a virtual and abstract system
is a considerably simplified definition, which causes misunderstandings
and misinterpretations, because it conceals the fact that the transition
from *langue* to *parole* does not consist of one but of many levels of
abstraction.[5] Heger, following Hans-Heinrich Lieb,[6] therefore distinguishes between three levels of abstraction. In connection with the
question of the relationship between quantitative and qualitative
analyses of language Heger distinguishes between the levels: *parole, Σ-
parole* and *langue*, and those are characterized as follows:[7] (1) the
level of parole as *concrete actualization* in form of manifestation rep-

---

1. Coseriu, 'System, Norm, und "Rede" ', pp. 57f. Cf. also his *Einführung*,
pp. 293-94.
2. The figure is an adaptation from Coseriu, 'System', p. 197.
3. Coseriu, 'System'. Cf. also the similar double opposition in the quotation from
R. Bultmann, *Die Geschichte der synoptischen Tradition* (FRLANT, 29; 6th edn;
Göttingen, 1964), p. 40, below p. 140.
4. Regarding literary genres as *langue*-entities, see the quotation from Heger,
'Temporale Deixis und Vorgangsquantität ("Aspekt" und "Aktionsart")', *Zeitschrift
für romanische Philologie* 83 (1967), p. 516, below p. 155 n. 2.
5. Heger, *Monem, Wort, Satz und Text* (Konzepte, 8; Tübingen, 1976), pp. 16-
19.
6. H.H. Lieb, *Sprachstudium und Sprachsystem* (Stuttgart, 1970).
7. The Σ in Σ–*parole* stands for 'sum'; see Heger, *Monem*, p. 342.

resents individual entities (occurrences) bound to their *hic et nunc* realizations; (2) the *level of Σ-parole* as *quantitatively measurable amounts* of manifestations (types) abstracted from the *hic et nunc* realizations as described in (1); (3) the *level of langue* as a *qualitative dimension* (linguemes) constitutes a virtual abstract system.[1] From the point of view of *generic* investigations, the most interesting phenomenon in Heger's distinction between *Σ-parole* and *langue* concerns the paradigmatic classes, which are defined as follows: 'die Häufigkeitsklasse (bildet) eine Klasse von Typen und das Paradigma eine Klasse von Linguemen. . . Damit definieren sich gleichzeitig die *Σ-parole* als System von Häufigkeitsklassen und die Langue als System der Paradigmen'.[2] This definition is important, because it takes into account that 'types' on the level of *Σ-parole* cannot stand in syntagmatic relations, while this is the case with regard to 'text-occurrences' on the level of *parole* as well as with regard to 'linguemes' on the level of *langue*. Thus—in spite of the somewhat confusing terminology—we observe the affinity between generic paradigmatic analyses[3] and 'type' analyses on the level of *Σ-parole* on the one hand, and generic syntagmatic analyses and 'lingueme' analyses on the level of *langue* on the other.[4]

For my purpose, with regard to generic investigations, the distinction between *Σ-parole* and *langue* is important as the quantitatively and paradigmatically defined 'types' on the level of *Σ-parole* can be one or more (1–n) without changing the generic structure of a text. For instance, a text containing one vision can belong to the generic entity 'Apocalypse' as well as a text containing four visions, as is the case in the *Book of Visions* in the present text of the *Shepherd of Hermas*.[5]

1. Heger, 'Temporale Deixis', pp. 152-57; *Monem*, pp. 24-28.
2. Heger, 'Temporale Deixis', p. 158; *Monem*, p. 29.
3. See below, section 2 and Hellholm, 'The Problem of Apocalyptic Genre', pp. 22-33. The *semes/noemes* listed in Hellholm, pp. 22-23, cannot, as paradigmatic 'types' on the level of *Σ-parole* (or as 'social or individual norms'; cf. Coseriu, *Einführung*, pp. 293f.), stand in a syntagmatic relationship. As 'text-occurrences' on the level of *parole*, however, they stand in syntagmatic surroundings which we know as 'textual contexts' or 'co-texts', and as 'linguemes' on the level of *langue* they stand in a syntagmatic surrounding which Heger names 'Katena' ('Die Semantik und die Dichotomie', p. 159) or 'lingueme of rank Rn+1' in ascending or 'lingueme of rank Rn-1' in descending analyses (see e.g. Heger, *Monem*, p. 30; further below section 2.1).
4. See further the discussion of this issue in section 2.
5. See my analysis of 'The Book of Visions', in Hellholm, *Das Visionenbuch des Hermas als Apokalypse* (CBNT 13.1; Lund, 1980).

b. In the early stages of New Testament form criticism one can already discover a similar differentiation between the analyses of *individual* texts and that of *generic* texts. Rudolf Bultmann spells this out in the following words in connection with his analysis of the form 'Controversy dialogue' (*Streitgespräch*): 'Aber die methodisch zuerst zu beantwortende Frage ist die nach der literarischen Art des Streitgesprächs und seinem Ursprung als literarischer Größe. Das ist die Frage nach dem *"Sitz im Leben"*; *denn diese fragt nicht nach dem Ursprung eines einzelnen Berichtes in einer einzelnen geschichtlichen Begebenheit, sondern nach dem Ursprung und der Zugehörigkeit einer bestimmten literarischen Gattung in und zu typischen Situationen und Verhaltungen einer Gemeinschaft'*.[1] Bultmann here first makes a distinction between a particular text as a text-occurrence or text-manifestation on the level of *parole* and a literary form or genre as a virtual system on the level of *langue!*[2] Consequently Bultmann here—when correlating *Genres/Forms* and *Sitze im Leben*—also differentiates between *specific* and *typical* situations, of which only the latter can function as *Sitze im Leben*, i.e. can constitute—in de Saussure's words—'faits sociales'.[3] Thus, Bultmann, like Coseriu as we have seen

1. R. Bultmann, *Die Geschichte*, p. 40 (see notes below; italics mine); cf. also the description of the form-critical method of Bultmann's student H. Koester, 'One Jesus and Four Primitive Gospels', in H. Koester and J.M. Robinson, *Trajectories through Early Christianity* (Philadelphia, 1971), pp. 158-204: 'It is often overlooked that the real purpose and aim of the form-critical method is not quite identical with the humble attempt to determine objectively what Jesus said or did in a particular moment of his ministry. . . Rather, form criticism seeks to identify basic patterns in the history of the tradition and to determine their *Sitz im Leben*, i.e. to determine the function of traditional material in the life of people and communities. This, however, is a sociological and theological question, and the determination of the *Sitz im Leben* must not be identified with the determination of the place, time, and situation in which Jesus said or did one thing or another' (pp. 159-60).

2. Cf. also E. Güttgemanns, *Offene Fragen zur Formgeschichte des Evangeliums* (BEvTh, 54; München, 1970), p. 53: 'Methodologisch bedeutet das, *daß die Formen grundsätzlich nach den Prinzipien der Linguistik der langue analysiert werden müssen*, nicht nach den Prinzipien der Linguistik der parole'.

3. See above p. 137 n. 2 and this page n. 1. Bultmann (*Geschichte*, p. 4) spells this out explicitly, when he writes: 'Wie der "Sitz im Leben" nicht ein einzelnes historisches Ereignis, sondern eine typische Situation oder Verhaltungsweise im Leben einer Gemeinschaft ist, so ist auch die literarische "Gattung", bzw. die "Form", durch die ein Einzelstück einer Gattung zugeordnet wird, ein *soziologischer Begriff*. . .' (italics mine). Cf. also G. Theissen, 'Die soziologische Auswertung religiöser Überlieferungen. Ihre methodologischen Probleme am Beispiel des Urchristentums', in *idem*, *Studien zur Soziologie des Urchristentums* (WUNT, 19; Tübingen 1979), pp. 35-54: 'Die *soziologische* Frage richtet sich also erstens

earlier, in fact distinguishes between concrete and abstract concepts on the one hand and between social and individual concepts on the other. At the same time, however, Bultmann also—at least indirectly—observes the interrelationship and interdependence of the two pairs of opposition.

Furthermore, Philipp Vielhauer, in modifying Bultmann's somewhat inexact classification of the synoptic material, carries through a consequent *hierarchy of abstractions,* insofar as he—starting from the genre Gospel—divides the synoptic form-material into: (1) Forms of the Sayings of Jesus; (2) Middle-forms: Apophthegmata; (3) Forms of the Narrative Materials. Within these '*ahistoric* Modes of Writing', or better perhaps, 'Types of Texts', Vielhauer discusses the '*historical* forms', i.e. (a) within the 'Sayings of Jesus' he lists 'Logia', 'Prophetic and Apocalyptic Sayings', 'Legal Sayings', 'I-Sayings' and 'Similitudes' or similar forms; (b) within the 'Apophthegmata as Middle-forms' he lists 'Conflict Sayings', 'Didactic Sayings', and 'Biographical Apophthegmata'; and finally (c) within the 'Narrative Materials' he lists 'Miracle Stories', 'Historical Stories', 'Legends', etc.[1]

This abstraction hierarchy of the Synoptic material is arrived at by means of *paradigmatic* analyses, and consequently it can only to a certain degree contribute to the analysis of the Gospel genre, since for that purpose there is need for a *syntagmatic approach* complementing the paradigmatic type of analysis as well. I cannot, however, agree with Hendrikus Boers[2] in his criticism of the approach by Gerd Theissen in his work on the Miracle Stories[3] for the very reason that

---

weniger auf Individuelles als auf *Typisches, Wiederkehrendes, Generelles,* zweitens weniger auf singuläre Bedingungen einer besonderen Situation als auf *strukturelle Zusammenhänge,* die für viele Situationen zutreffen' (p. 36; italics mine); also K. Koch, *Was ist Formgeschichte?* (3rd edn; Neukirchen-Vluyn, 1974), p. 314: 'Denn Gattungen sind—um auf formgeschichtliche Ergebnisse zurückzugreifen—*soziologische* Tatsachen, gehören in einen Sitz im Leben und im weiteren Sinn in einen Lebensbereich' (italics mine).

1. P. Vielhauer, *Geschichte der urchristlichen Literatur* (Berlin, 1975), pp. 191-310. Cf. also the somewhat different hierarchical classification by G. Sellin, ' "Gattung" und "Sitz im Leben" auf dem Hintergrund der Problematik von Mündlichkeit und Schriftlichkeit synoptischer Erzählungen', *Evangelische Theologie* 50 (1990), pp. 311-31: I Spruch; II Erzählung; III 'Geredete Erzählung'; IV 'ezählte Rede' (pp. 322-23).

2. H.W. Boers, 'Sisyphus and his Rock: Concerning Gerd Theissen, *Urchristliche Wundergeschichten*', in R.W. Funk (ed.), *Early Christian Miracle Stories (Semeia* 11; Missoula, MT, 1978), pp. 1-48.

3. G. Theissen, *Urchristliche Wundergeschichten: Ein Beitrag zur formgeschichtlichen Erforschung der synoptischen Evangelien* (StNT, 8; Gütersloh, 1974). For a syntagmatic approach with regard to the function of Miracle Stories within the Gospel

Theissen did not attempt an analysis of the importance of Miracle Stories either for the Gospel genre or for any particular Gospel. Theissen's sole interest was in the form 'Miracle Story', not in its function within a genre or within a larger text unit as such. A paradigmatic analysis of Miracle Stories, for example, is in itself as legitimate as a syntagmatic analysis of how Miracle Stories function within a literary genre that can be an Epitome of Miracle Stories or a literary genre of a totally different kind, like a Gospel or a Novel.

It can thus be stated that investigations of genres within various disciplines work on different levels of abstraction. This distinction between various abstraction levels is so significant for *generic* investigations, since here the 'law of reciprocity' applies to the effect that the larger the *intension*, the smaller the *extension*, and vice versa.[1] This means that generic structures with few common characteristics (i.e. *semes/noemes*) delineate categories of supreme concepts such as 'Mode of Writing', 'Type of Text', 'Genre', while generic structures with a large density of common characteristics delineate categories of subconcepts such as 'Sub-genres' of different sorts all the way down to the individual text.

c. In connection with the question of how to establish characteristic markers (*semes/noemes*[2]) for genres, two factors have to be taken into consideration: (1) the distinction between *essential*, i.e. invariant, markers on the one hand and *accidental*, i.e. variant, markers on the other;[3] (2) the distinction between divisive *differentiae specificae*[4] or

of Mark, see D.-A. Koch, *Die Bedeutung der Wundererzählungen für die Christologie des Markusevangeliums* (BZNW, 42; Berlin, 1975).

1. So W. Raible, 'Was sind Gattungen? Eine Antwort aus semiotischer und text-linguistischer Sicht', *Poetica* 12 (1980), p. 340. Cf. further K. Oehler, *Aristoteles Kategorien* (2nd edn; Darmstadt, 1986), p. 239: 'Während beim Übergang vom Einzelnen zur Gattung die Menge der möglichen Eigenschaften, die der jeweilige Gegenstandsbereich zuläßt, wächst, nimmt die Menge der charakteristischen Eigenschaften ab'. Concerning the 'law of reciprocity' and its limitation, see A. Menne, *Einführung in die Methodologie* (Darmstadt, 1980), p. 27: 'Inhalt und Umfang eines Begriffes verhielten sich reziprok. Diese Ansicht, die häufig stimmt und sich durch viele Beispiele belegen läßt, wurde vor allem durch die kantische Logik verbreitet. Als allgemeines Gesetz aber ist sie falsch, wie schon Bernard Bolzano durch Gegenbeispiele belegt hat.'

2. For *semes/noemes* in connection with generic analyses, see Hellholm, 'The Problem of Apocalyptic Genre', pp. 14ff., 22ff.

3. Cf. E. Stump, *Boethius's De topicis differentiis* (Ithaca, NY, 1978), p. 250, who—following Aristotle (see below p. 147 n. 3) and Porphyry, *Isagoge* 8.19-20—rightly distinguishes between (a) 'characteristics that belong to the essence of the subject' (*in eo quod quid est*) and (b) 'characteristics that are only accidental to the subject' (*in eo quod quale est*). The former constitute differentiae, the latter are

differentiae divisivae[1] on the one hand and constitutive *differentiae specificae* or *differentiae constitutivae* on the other.[2] These two types of *differentiae*, the constitutive and the divisive, are already discussed by Aristotle, but in the third chapter of his Categories, where he deals with genera and subordinate species, he in fact has only the *differentiae constitutivae* in mind.[3] This has, as far as I can see, been argued

'characteristics that are not part of the subject's essence'; Stump, *Boethius's In Ciceronis Topica* (Ithaca, NY, 1988), p. 249; cf. further Menne, *Einführung*, p. 28: 'Die zufälligen Eigenschaften (Akzidenzien) einer Sache. . . sind ungeeignet zur Definition'.

4. For the usage of *divisive differentiae specificae* in linguistics, see Heger, 'Die methodologischen Voraussetzungen von Onomasiologie und begrifflicher Gliederung', *Zeitschrift für romanische Philologie* 80 (1964), pp. 486-516, esp. 501 and 504.

1. Cf. Oehler, *Aristoteles Kategorien*, pp. 235ff.

2. See Oehler, *ibid.*; G. Hilty, 'Der disjunktive und referentielle Charakter semantischer Komponenten', in H. Stimm and W. Raible (eds.), *Zur Semantik des Französischen* (Zeitschrift für französische Sprache und Literatur Beiheft, 9; Wiesbaden, 1983), pp. 30-39, who at the end of his essay states: 'In diesem Beitrag lag es mir daran, die Bedeutung referentieller semantischer Komponenten gegenüber rein distinktiver zu betonen und damit vor der Gefahr einer gewissen Einseitigkeit zu warnen, welche der strukturellen Semantik innewohnt' (p. 39); also Raible, 'Zur Einleitung', *Zur Semantik*, pp. 4-7 and 11-12, where he distinguishes between 'similarity' and 'contrast'. Cf. further Coseriu, *Einführung*, p. 148: 'So gibt es in der funktionellen (semantischen) Struktur jeweils einen Basiswert für das ganze Paradigma, eine "Vergleichsgrundlage", sowie für jede Einheit unterscheidende semantische Elemente bzw. solche, die bei den verschiedenen Einheiten in unterschiedlicher Weise miteinander kombiniert werden. . . Bei dt. *Schwager* ist der gemeinsame Wert des ihm entsprechenden Paradigmas etwa "Verwandschaftsbeziehung", "Verwandter", und das Unterscheidende ist all das, was das *signifié* von *Schwager* von denen bei *Sohn, Bruder, Vater* usw. absetzt.' Cf. already the distinction in W. Lorenz and G. Wotjak, *Zum Verhältnis von Abbild und Bedeutung* (Sammlung Akademie-Verlag, 39: Sprache; Berlin, 1977), pp. 389-90, between *Genusseme* and *Differentiaseme* and their attribution to different levels of abstraction respectively (see further p. 247). The 'Master-Paradigm' for establishing a genre 'Apocalypse' created by 'the Apocalypse Group of the SBL Genres Project' is conceived of as a set of constitutive differences only; see esp. J. Collins, 'Introduction: Towards the Morphology of a Genre', in *idem* (ed.), *Apocalypse: The Morphology of a Genre* (*Semeia* 14; Missoula, MT, 1979), pp. 1-19: 'By "Literary Genre" we mean of group of texts marked by distinctive recurring characteristics which constitute a recognizable and coherent type of writing' (p. 1).

3. Aristotle, *Cat.* 1b.20-24: 'There is nothing, however, to prevent genera subordinate one to the other from having the same differentiae. For the higher genera are predicated by the genera below them so that all differentiae of the predicated genus will be differentiae of the underlying genus also' [τῶν δέ γε ὑπ' ἄλληλα γενῶν οὐδὲν κωλύει τὰς αὐτὰς διαφορὰς εἶναι· τὰ γὰρ ἐπάνω τῶν ὑπ' αὐτὰ γενῶν

persuasively by Klaus Oehler, who in his commentary concludes by stating: 'Aristoteles kann daher sinnvollerweise in diesem Zusammenhang nur "differentiae constitutivae" gemeint haben...'[1] This statement is true, though, only as far as the species, not as far as the genus, is concerned, since of those *differentiae constitutivae* on the level of the species, at least one is a *differentia divisiva* on the level of the *genus proximum*.[2] With regard to Porphyry[3] as well as Boethius,[4]

κατηγορεῖται, ὥστε ὅσαι τοῦ κατηγορουμένου διαφοραί εἰσι, τοσαῦται καὶ τοῦ ὑποκειμένου ἔσονται]'; trans. J.L. Ackrill, *Aristotle's Categories and De Interpretatione* (Oxford, 1963), p. 77; text by L. Minio-Paluello, *Aristotelis Categoriae et Liber de Interpretatione* (Oxford, 1949). Aristotle here uses *differentiae* in the sense of *differentiae constitutivae* and not in the sense of *differentiae divisivae*, against J.L. Ackrill: 'Only *differentiae divisivae* are in question', and in agreement with Oehler, *Aristoteles Kategorien*, pp. 238ff., who against Ackrill rightly observes (1) that an argument 'für eine Interpretation der Differenz als "differentia constitutiva" auch bezüglich des prädizierten Genus... sich in dem ausdrücklichen Hinweis (findet), daß *alle* Differenzen der prädizierten Gattung auch Differenzen der untergeordneten Gattung (d.h. implizit jedes einzelnen Subgenus) sein müssen' (p. 238), and (2) that Aristotle 'auch hier, analog zum ersten Teil dieses Kapitels, *vom Allgemeineren auf das Speziellere* (schließt) und nicht umgekehrt' (p. 239; italics mine).

    1. Oehler, *Aristoteles Kategorien*, p. 238. So also Stump, *Boethius's In Ciceronis*, p. 246: 'Definitions define species and are composed of the proximate genus and constitutive differentia of the species they define'.

    2. See the statement by Stump, *Boethius's De Topicis*, below on p. 145 n. 4 and in the text on p. 145 nn. 1 and 2. Much of the confusion regarding the two types of *differentiae* derives from the inability to ascribe different status to the same *differentiae specificae* on different abstraction levels: the level of genus and the level of species. An explanation for this may lie in the fact that 'both Porphyry and Boethius seem to use "constitutive differentia" in a broad and a narrow sense, the former being much more common than the latter. In the broad sense, a constitutive differentia is any differentia that is part of the composition of a species; in the narrow sense, it is that differentia which, when added to the proximate genus, yields the definition of the species' (Stump, *Boethius's De topicis*, p. 259 n. 22).

    3. *Isagoge,* 10.1ff. Translation of all texts from the *Isagoge* is by E.W. Warren, *Porphyry the Phoenician: Isagoge* (Toronto, 1975, *ad loc.*). The Greek text in all quotations is the one by A. Busse, *Porphyrii Isagoge et in Aristotelis Categorias Commentarium* (Berlin, 1887), *ad loc.* 'We should also say that among differences per se there are some by which we divide genera into species and some by which the divided genera are constituted as species...' [πάλιν τῶν καθ' αὑτὰς διαφορῶν αἱ μέν εἰσι καθ' ἃς διαιρούμεθα τὰ γένη εἰς τὰ εἴδη, αἱ δὲ καθ' ἃς τὰ διαιρεθέντα εἰδοποιεῖται]; further *Isagoge* 10.9-10 '... these dividing differences, however, complete the genera and become constitutive of the species...' [... ἀλλ' αὑταί γε αἱ διαιρετικαὶ διαφοραὶ τῶν γενῶν συμπληρωτικαὶ γίνονται καὶ συστατικαὶ τῶν εἰδῶν...]; cf. in conclusion also *Isagoge* 10.18-19: 'Since, therefore, the same differences understood in one way become constitutive and in

both types of *differentiae* are described, but they function on different abstraction levels, as has been pointed out by Eleonore Stump in her work on Boethius's *De topicis differentiis*: 'Differentiae can be thought of in two different ways: either they *divide a genus,* in which case they are divisive differentiae; or they *constitute a species,* in which case they are constitutive differentiae. *The same differentia is both divisive and constitutive,* but it is divisive of one thing and constitutive of another.'[1] The same differentia is thus operational on two different levels of abstraction at one and the same time, first in the form of a *divisive differentia* on the more abstract level of the *genus proximum* and then in the form of a *constitutive differentia* on the less abstract level of the *species.* This relationship is further elaborated upon, when Dr Stump continues: 'Except for the lowest species and highest genera, all genera are subaltern genera—that is, they can all be described also as species; all species are subaltern species—that is, they can all be described also as genera. A subaltern genus or species has two different sets of differentiae, those that divide it (its divisive differentiae) and those that constitute it (its constitutive differentiae).'[2] Which constitutive and distinguishing characteristics respectively are *essential,* that is, invariant markers for the various abstraction levels in connection with investigations trying to establish generic apocalyptic texts is still, however, a matter of controversy.[3]

Graphically this twofold function of the *differentiae specificae* can—as I understand it—be described as in the partial pyramid below,

---

another way become divisive, they are all called specific' [ἐπεὶ οὖν αἱ αὐταὶ πώς μὲν ληφθεῖσαι γίνονται συστατικαί, πώς δὲ διαιρετικαί, εἰδοποιοὶ πᾶσαι κέκληνται]. On Porphyry, cf. U. Eco, *Semiotics and the Philosophy of Language* (Bloomington, IN, 1984), pp. 48-68.

4. *De topicis differentiis* 1178B: 'For the differentia will be either constitutive or divisive. If it is constitutive, it stands as it were in place of the genus. . . but if it is divisive, it is considered as a species, for every species occurs with a dividing differentia [aut enim constitutiva erit differentia, aut divisiva: sed si constitutiva fuerit, quasi generis obtinet locum. . . at si divisiva fuerit, velut species consideratur, omnis enim species cum divisibili differentia est]' (trans. Stump, *Boethius's De topicis,* p. 36; text in J.P. Migne, *Patrologia Latina, LXIV. Boetii opera omnia* [Paris, 1860]). Cf. Stump's note on this passage: 'When a differentia is thought of as composing a species, it is a constitutive differentia. When it is thought of as dividing a genus into its species, it is a divisive differentia' (*Boethius's De topicis,* p. 105 n. 55).

1. Stump, *Boethius's De topicis,* p. 239 (italics mine).
2. *Boethius's De topicis, ibid.* Cf. also below p. 150 n. 6.
3. Cf. Hellholm, 'The Problem of Apocalyptic Genre', pp. 22-23.

which takes its departure from the ahistoric abstraction level 'type of text':[1]

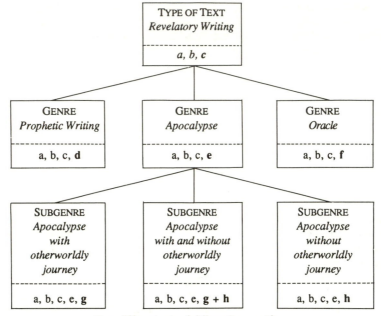

Two different sets of *differentiae specificae*
plain letters = *differentiae constitutivae*
bold letters = *differentiae divisivae*

On the level 'type of texts', the *semes* a and b are *differentiae constitutivae*[2] while the *seme* c constitutes a *differentia divisiva*[3] with regard to the next higher level, i.e. the even more abstract level 'mode of writing'; on the less abstract level 'genre' *all three semes* from the

---

1. Cf. the diagram in Hellholm, 'The Problem of Apocalyptic Genre', p. 30, which, however, did not include any sets of *differentiae specificae*.
2. Cf. Oehler, *Aristoteles Kategorien*, p. 238: 'Differenzen, die ein Genus nicht vollständig umfassen, sondern dieses "nur" in Subgenera aufteilen, können von diesem Genus nicht ausgesagt werden...Die Differenz muß daher auch für das höhere Genus eine definierende Funktion haben, das heißt, jeder Repräsentant muß das charakteristische Merkmal der Differenz aufweisen, mit anderen Worten: die Differenz muß das Genus vollständig umfassen'; see also the quotation from Oehler, p. 239, in the following note.
3. Cf. Oehler, *Aristoteles Kategorien*, p. 239: 'Die Differenzen der Gattung finden sich jeweils als Differenzen der zugehörigen Arten wieder'.

previous level make up constitutive differentiae[1] while the *semes* **d, e,** and **f** respectively constitute divisive differentiae distinguishing (1) the less abstract 'genre' from the more abstract 'type of text', and (2) at the same time various genres of the same 'type of text' from each other;[2] by analogy on the level of 'sub-genre' *all four semes* from the previous level make up constitutive differentiae, while the *semes*, **g, h,** and **g+h** respectively constitute divisive differentiae distinguishing (1) the less abstract 'sub-genre' from the more abstract 'genre', and (2) at the same time various sub-genres of the same 'genre' from each other.[3] If a **d** or an **f** should occur in any of the sub-genres in the diagram above, they were not to be regarded as differentiae there but either as 'properties' or as 'accidentals'.[4]

For the purpose of comparative analyses of so-called Apocalyptic texts—with the aim of arriving at a proper definition of the literary concept 'Apocalypse'—this means that we will have to concentrate on two kinds of characteristics: (a) partly *common semantic constituents*, and (b) partly *divisive differentiae specificae* for the postulated genre 'Apocalypse'. This also means that we have to leave aside other equally

1. Cf. Stump, *Boethius's De topicis*, p. 255: 'So the constitutive differentia (. . .) is also constitutive of the two [or more—DH] species under that genus'.

2. Cf. Porphyry, *Isagoge*, 11.18-19: 'They (sc. our predecessors) also indicate such differences as follows: difference is what naturally separates the species under the same genus' ['Υπογράφουσι δὲ τὰς τοιαύτας διαφορὰς καὶ οὕτως· διαφορά ἐστιν τὸ χωρίζειν πεφυκὸς τὰ ὑπὸ τὸ αὐτὸ γένος].

3. This is my interpretation of a partial Porphyrian tree in accordance with Boethius's interpretation (see the previous note); cf. also the critical discussion of the Porphyrian tree by Eco, *Semiotics*, pp. 57-68.

4. See Aristotle, *Topica*, 102a.18ff.: 'A "property" is a predicate which does not indicate the essence of a thing, but yet belongs to that thing alone, and is predicated convertibly of it. Thus it is a property of man to be capable of learning grammar' ['Ίδιον δ' ἐστὶν ὃ μὴ δηλοῖ μὲν τὸ τί ἦν εἶναι, μόνῳ δ' ὑπάρχει καὶ ἀντικατηγορεῖται τοῦ πράγματος. οἷον ἴδιον ἀνθρώπου τὸ γραμματικῆς εἶναι δεκτικόν]; trans. W.A. Pickard-Cambridge, *The Works of Aristotle* (Oxford, 1928); text by W.D. Ross, *Aristotelis Topica et Sophistici Elenchi* (Oxford, 1958). Cf. Stump, *Boethius's In Ciceronis Topica*, p. 245: 'A property is what belongs to one particular species and to no other and is predicated convertibly (interchangeably) of the species, without being part of the essence of the species. One property of man, for example, is *capable of learning grammar*'; further, Aristotle, *Topica* 102b.4ff.: 'An accident is something which, though it is none of the foregoing—i.e. neither a definition nor a property nor a genus—yet belongs to the thing' [Συμβεβηκὸς δέ ἐστιν ὃ μηδὲν μὲν τούτων ἐστί, μήτε ὅρος μήτε ἴδιον μήτε γένος, ὑπάρχει δὲ τῷ πράγματι]; for trans. and text, see above in this note. Cf. Stump, *Boethius's In Ciceronis Topica*: 'An accident is what can belong or not belong to a thing: sitting, for example, or whiteness can belong or not belong to something' (p. 245); cf. also above p. 142 n. 3

interesting and important phenomena[1] that merely concern the understanding of the individual text-manifestations *per se*.[2]

For the sake of clarification it should be noted that our interpretation of the *differentiae specificae*, as shown in the diagram above, has a bearing on the interpretation of the difficult passage in Boethius's *In Ciceronis Topica* IV. 350/1127 which, according to Eleonore Stump,[3] reads either: '(a) a genus always follows from a species, and a species always precedes a genus' (so *Vat. lat.* 567 and *Reg. lat.* 1649: *Nam genus semper speciem sequitur, species genus praecedit*), or: '(b) a species always follows from a genus, and a genus always precedes a species' (so the text in C. Orelli's edition: *Nam genus semper species sequitur, speciem genus praecedit*). A solution to the textual problem as well as to the interpretation can be arrived at, if we analyze Stump's commentary on that passage, when she, in the light of the context, gives the following alternative:[4] '(a′) if something is a member of species *x*, it is a member of genus *y*; (b′) if something is a member of genus *y*, it is a member of species *x*'. Stump continues her commentary by stating that 'according to Boethius's own metaphysical and logical views, conditional inferences of the form (a′) are acceptable but those of form (b′) are not'. This is a valid interpretation only if we substitute 'something' with a 'representative of a species' and for instance with regard to the question of literary genres read: (a″) if a text is a member of species *x*, it is a member of genus *y*, since an 'Apocalypse' as *species* is also a member of the *genus* 'Revelatory Writing', but not every member of the *genus* 'Revelatory Writing' is a member of the *species* 'Apocalypse', as can be deduced from the diagram above. If we, however, substitute 'something' with '*differentia(e) specifica(e)*' the alternative interpretation is true and we must read: (b″) if a *differentia* is a member of genus *y*, it is a member of species *x*. This is on the one hand in accord with the 'law of reciprocity' referred to above,[5] and on the other a consequence of the fact that not all *semes/noemes* of a *species* are included in a *genus*, but that all *semes/*

---

1. Cf. Heger, 'Temporale Deixis', p. 515: 'Es sei deshalb hier nur wiederholt, daß ich nicht den geringsten Zweifel daran habe, daß die wissenschaftliche Beschäftigung mit Problemen, die sich auf der Ebene der *parole* stellen, ebenso legitim ist wie die mit Problemen, die sich auf der Ebene der *langue* stellen. Ebensowenig erscheint es mir zweifelhaft, daß jeder die Freiheit hat, sich der Beschäftigung zu widmen, die ihm interessanter und lohnender erscheint.'

2. I.e. in Aristotle's terminology: 'properties' and 'accidentals'. See above p. 142 n. 3 and p. 147 n. 4.

3. Stump, *Boethius's In Ciceronis Topica*, pp. 127 and 222f. n. 70.

4. Stump, *Boethius's In Ciceronis Topica*, p. 222 n. 70.

5. See above p. 142 n. 1.

noemes of a *genus* are included in a *species*, as likewise shown in the diagram above. This is due, of course, to the fact that the *divisive* differentia of a species cannot be a member of the *genus proximum*. In my view, the two different textual traditions in Boethius's text, and thus the two possible interpretations, depend on two different assumptions: in case (a) that species in fact stands for 'representatives of the species', and in case (b) that species is understood to be made up of *differentiae specificae* over against the *genus proximum*.

Apocalypse	=	*genus proximum*: Revelatory writing	+	*differentiae specificae*	*syntactics* narrative framework in which a revelation is communicated by other-worldly beings *semantics* transcendent reality: temporal and spatial *pragmatics* (a) generative setting: crisis (b) teleological intention: consolation, authorization
definiendum	=		*definiens*		

From what has been said so far, it is evident that the definition of generic concepts on various abstraction levels has to be made according to the rule of 'real definition'[1] formulated by Aristotle,[2] Porphyry,[3] Boethius,[4] Johannes Damaskenos[5] and others:[6] *Definitio potest fieri per genus proximum et differentias specificas.*[7]

1. See the definition on p. 149. For 'real definitions', see the quotation from I.M. Bocheński, *Die Zeitgenössischen Denkmethoden* (Uni-Taschenbücher, 6; 8th edn; Munich, 1980), p. 90, below p. 159 n. 1; G. Klaus, *Philosophisches Wörterbuch* (Leipzig, 1975), I, pp. 248-49; Menne, *Einführung*, pp. 15, 28.
2. *Topica* 103b.15: 'since the definition is composed of genus and differentiae' [. . . ἐπειδὴ ὁ ὁρισμὸς ἐκ γένους καὶ διαφορῶν ἐστίν]; cf. Stump, *Boethius's De topicis*, p. 238 and n. 3 with Greek text and translation.
3. *Isagoge* 9.2-4: 'Thus, from essential differences the division of genera into species arise and definitions are expressed, since they are composed of a genus and such differences. . .' [κατὰ μὲν οὖν τὰς ἄλλο ποιούσας διαφορὰς αἵ τε διαιρέσεις γίνονται τῶν γενῶν εἰς τὰ εἴδη, οἵ τε ὅροι ἀποδίδονται ἐκ γένους ὄντες καὶ τῶν τοιούτων διαφορῶν. . .]. Further, *Isagoge*, 11.12-17. Cf. Eco, *Semiotics*, p. 59: 'The definition Porphyry gives of genus is a purely *formal* one: a genus is that to which the species is subordinate. Likewise the species is what is sub-

ordinate to a genus. Thus genus and species are relative to each other, that is mutually definable.'

4.   *De topicis differentiis*, 1187C: 'Definition differs from description because a definition contains genus and differentiae. . .' [Differt autem diffinitio a descriptione, quod diffinitio genus ac differentias sumit. . .] (trans. Stump, *Boethius's De topicis*, pp. 49-50; text in J.P. Migne, *Patrologia Latina*, LXIV).

5.   *Dialectica*, 8, 16f.

6.   Concerning abstraction hierarchies of general and specific concepts, cf. the *arbor porphyriana*, according to which the superior concepts are called *genera* (γένη) and the inferior *species* (εἴδη). These terms, however, are only relative to each other, as has been pointed out by Oehler, *Aristoteles Kategorien*, p. 235: 'Es sei darauf hingewiesen, daß die hier verwendeten Termini γένος (Genus) und εἶδος (Spezies) Mengen bezeichnen. Sie haben für Aristoteles noch relative Bedeutung. Dabei werden εἶδος für relativ untergeordnete Mengen und γένος für relativ übergeordnete Mengen gebraucht. . . Es hangt aber von dem jeweiligen Kontext ab, ob einer Menge der Ausdruck γένος oder der Ausdruck εἶδος zukommt.' See also the quotation from Eco, *Semiotics*, p. 59, above n. 3. In addition, see Stump, *Boethius's De topicis*, *passim*, esp. pp. 237-61; *idem*, *Boethius's In Ciceronis Topica*, pp. 244-55; G. Richter, *Johannes von Damaskos: Philosophische Kapitel* (Bibliothek der Griechischen Literatur, 15; Stuttgart, 1982), *passim*, esp. ch. 8, ll. 15f., 67f., 90; *Erläuterungen*, nn. 77, 173. Cf. also R. Dieterich, 'Theoriebildung in der Linguistik', in H.L. Arnold and V. Sinemus (eds.), *Grundzüge der Literatur- und Sprachwissenschaft*, 2. *Sprachwissenschaft* (Munich, 1974), p. 48; and Eco, *Semiotics*, pp. 46-86.

7.   Notice the variation of the classical *Definitio fit. . . differentiam specificam*. With regard to the former variation, *potest fieri*, see W. Welte, *Moderne Linguistik: Terminologie/Bibliographie* (Munich, 1974), 1.107 s.v. Definition: 'Anstatt *definitio fit*. . . hieße es besser *definitio potest fieri*. . . Man denke nur an die (oft zitierte) als → Adjunktion von → Prädikaten zu verstehende Definition eines Skandinaviers (Ein Skandinavier (Sk) ist ein Schwede (S) oder ein Däne (D) oder ein Norweger (N) oder ein Isländer (I). Formal: Skx ↔ Sx v Dx v Nx v Ix). . .' With regard to the latter variation, *differentias specificas*, see e.g. A. Wedberg, *Filosofins historia* (2nd edn; Stockholm, 1968), I, p. 111; and Oehler, *Aristoteles Kategorien*, p. 237: 'Der Wunsch des Aristoteles, eine Definition auf die Angabe einer einzigen Differenz reduzieren zu können, bleibt in vielen konkreten Fällen allerdings unerfüllbar, da oft nur eine Kombination von gleichermaßen gültigen Eigenschaften die hinreichende Festellung einer Spezies leisten kann'.

Regarding the three sets of *differentiae specificae* that I—in conformity with earlier suggestions ('The Problem of Apocalyptic Genre', pp. 16-18, 25-27)—propose here: syntactics, semantics, and pragmatics, cf. also H. Kubczak, *Was ist ein Soziolekt?* (Heidelberg, 1979), p. 47: 'Es ist für die Heger'sche Theorie wichtig, daß die Sememe so konzipiert sind, daß ihnen Seme von grundsätzlich *verschiedener.*Art inhärieren. Eben diese Differenzierung hängt wieder mit Bühlers Organonmodell zusammen. Es sollen nämlich symptomfunktionale, signalfunktionale und symbolfunktionale Seme unterschieden werden. Seme aller drei Arten konstituieren also eine "Bedeutung", ein "Semem".' See also Baldinger, *Semantic Theory*, pp. 254-59: 'If we analyse the *signifié* we arrive at each one of the meanings contained in the one

2. *Paradigmatic versus Syntagmatic Approaches*

The relationship between paradigmatic and syntagmatic analyses has most recently been summarized instructively by Eugenio Coseriu, when he writes that 'die Funktionen "der Sprache" sich bei ihrer Realisierung in der Rede [or in a literary genre—DH] wechselseitig durch ihre auf zwei "Achsen" entstehenden Beziehung bestimmen: einmal auf der "syntagmatischen Achse" (Kombinations- oder Reihungsachse), die der Abfolge der Zeichen in der *chaîne parlée* entspricht, und zum anderen auf der "paradigmatischen Achse" (oder Selektionsachse), die den Klassen funktioneller und materieller Spracheinheiten entspricht, unter denen die für die jeweilige Ausdrucksabsicht geeignete Einheit ausgewählt wird'.[1]

Until recently the prevailing approach to apocalyptic texts has been a combination of strict *paradigmatic* investigations, which implies that the relationship between the linguistic elements *in absentia* is *disjunctive* (either x or y but not both of them at the same place/time; either of the elements though can be present [x ⟺ y]; in German: 'statteinander'),[2] and of *classes of syntagmatic distribution* which, however, incorrectly are understood to constitute syntagmatic elements *in absentia*.[3] This becomes evident when one looks, for example, at the volume 'Apocalypse: The Morphology of a Genre', edited by John J. Collins in the *Semeia* series.[4]

The disadvantage of paradigmatic analyses (including quantitatively measurable 'type' analyses)[5] carried out so far is threefold: (a) only tentative suggestions have been made to distinguish between those characteristics that are constitutive or divisive and those that are not,

---

signifié. These meanings are sememes which we can call "full", because the functions of symbol, symptom and signal are still together' (pp. 255f.). In a footnote to the quotation just given, Baldinger—from a (system)linguist's point of view—makes an important concession to semiotics when he writes: 'Thus we come to a new definition of *signification* (*meaning*) = "full sememe", and precision in the relationship between signification (meaning) and sememe'. This is, of course, equally true when we try to establish the 'meaning' or 'sememe' of a generic entity in general or a genre in particular!

1. Coseriu, *Einführung*, p. 141.
2. Cf. Coseriu, *Einführung*, pp. 142-43: 'Zwischen den Gliedern eines Paradigmas (das seinerseits "Glied" eines Paradigmas höherer Ordnung sein kann) besteht. . . eine *paradigmatische* oder *oppositive* Beziehung' (p. 143).
3. Coseriu, *Einführung*, p. 145. This is a misunderstanding of the syntagmatic distribution, since the syntagmatic relation is one *in presentia*; see further below.
4. J. Collins (ed.), *Apocalypse: The Morphology of a Genre* (*Semeia* 14; Missoula, MT, 1979).
5. See above, section 1 (a).

i.e. those which are purely accidental or quantitative in character; in other words, between those characteristics that are true *differentiae specificae* and those which are not; (b) very few semantic characteristics have been tied exclusively to the generic concept 'Apocalypse', i.e. have been designated as *differentiae divisivae* on the specific hierarchic abstraction level named genre; (c) there has been a tendency to neglect the text as it stands and to go behind it in an attempt to reconstruct the development of the genre without having first established the genre by means of its present syntagmatic structure.

There has long been a need for an approach to apocalyptic texts of a *syntagmatic* nature as well, which implies that the relationship between the linguistic elements *in presentia* is *copulative* (x as well as y; neither of the elements can be absent [x ∧ y]; in German: 'nacheinander').[1] Because of these needs, I have in earlier studies[2] presented macro-syntagmatic analyses (i.e. qualitatively lingueme-bound analyses[3]) *as a complement* to the paradigmatic ones[4] and I continue to favor such a complementary approach.[5]

1. Cf. Coseriu, *Einführung*, p. 141; 'Zwischen den Gliedern eines Syntagmas (die ihrerseits wieder Syntagmen sein können) besteht eine *syntagmatische Beziehung*'.

2. Hellholm, *Visionenbuch*; *idem*, 'The Problem of Apocalyptic Genre'. See now also the positive reaction by A. Yarbro Collins in her 'Introduction' to *Semeia* 36 (1986), p. 8: 'A major contribution of David Hellholm's essay is its demonstration of the validity and usefulness of both paradigmatic and syntagmatic studies of the genre and its initial attempt to relate the two.'

3. See above, section 1 (a).

4. On the relationship between paradigmatic and syntagmatic structures, see e.g. H. Schnelle, *Sprachphilosophie und Linguistik* (Reinbek b. Hamburg/Wiesbaden, 1973), p. 168: '. . .(b) Die *Bedeutungen* der Ausdrücke einer Sprache sind nicht unabhängig voneinander. Sie stehen im Gegenteil *in einem systematischen Zusammenhang*, und zwar in doppelter Weise: (b¹) Die Bedeutungen zusammengesetzter Ausdrücke lassen sich durch Bedeutungskombinationen aus den Bedeutungen gewisser Teile der Ausdrücke bestimmen. M.a.W., die Bedeutungen komplexer Ausdrücke bestimmen sich kombinatorisch-auf-der-Grundlage-der-Syntax [i.e. not only sentence-syntax but also text-syntax—DH] oder *syntagmatisch*, wie man dafür auch sagt. (b²) Die Bedeutungen einfacher Ausdrücke lassen sich durch Beziehungen auf andere Ausdrücke, die nicht im gleichen Text vorkommen müssen, partiell bestimmen. . . Man sagt, daß die Bedeutung der Ausdrücke durch ihren Platz im relationalen System der Bedeutungsbeziehungen bestimmt ist (oder im semantischen Beziehungsnetz) oder, wie man auch sagt, *paradigmatisch*.' Cf. further the discussion in Hellholm, *Visionenbuch*, p. 84 with n. 42. In addition, see also the definition of paradigmatic and syntagmatic relations by M.A.K. Halliday, *Language as Social Semiotic* (London, 1978), p. 41: '. . .just as the system is the form of representation of paradigmatic relations, the structure is the form of representation of syntagmatic relations'; and cf. M.A.K. Halliday and R.D. Huddlestone, 'Paradigmatic and Syn-

There is indeed an integral interrelationship between the two approaches, as has rightly been emphasized by Helmut Schnelle,[1] when he states that the definition according to syntagmatic relations and according to paradigmatic relations can be dependent upon each other: the paradigmatic relations can be determined with regard to the syntagmatic framework, and the syntagmatic combinations can be predetermined paradigmatically. That the syntagmatic combinations can be predetermined paradigmatically is also emphasized by Eugenio Coseriu, when he states that 'die paradigmatische Achse bei der Wahl der Ausdruckseinheiten in jedem Fall die primär bestimmende ist; denn sie entspricht dem, was man sagen will'.[2]

The interrelationship between the two approaches applies already to ancient rhetorics, as has been observed by Heinrich Lausberg when he declares that the *dispositio* is the necessary supplement to the *inventio* that without the *dispositio* would be a phenomenon without relations;[3] here the *dispositio* corresponds to the *syntagma* and the *inventio* to the *paradigma*.

Since by definition the paradigmatic analysis of oppositions is disjunctive while the syntagmatic analysis of distribution classes is copulative, a combination of these two procedures constitutes not only a necessary but also a sufficient condition for generic investigations. Thus, in addition to *paradigmatically* defined *differentiae specificae*, there is a need to explore *syntagmatically* defined constitutive and divisive *differentiae specificae* on various abstraction levels with

tagmatic Relations', in M.A.K. Halliday and J.R. Martin (eds.), *Readings in Systemic Linguistics* (London, 1981), pp. 17-53.
    5. Cf. W. Lorenz and G. Wotjak, *Zum Verhältnis vom Abbild und Bedeutung*, p. 257: 'Einen generellen Mangel für die Feldtheorien [or Genre-theories—DH]. . . sehen wir in der Verabsolutierung der paradigmatischen Betrachtung und in der damit einhergehenden Vernachlässigung bzw. Unterschätzung des für die Kommunikation entscheidenden Umstandes, daß die LE [sc. lexikalischen Einheiten—DH] zwar paradigmatisch systemhaft in bestimmter Weise determinierte semantische Mikrostrukturen (LB [sc. langue-Bedeutung—DH]) Semkonfigurationen (SK) und mit diesen ganz spezifische Kontextvorgaben aufweisen, daß durch deren Kombination zu syntagmatischen Makrostrukturen (Satzsemstrukturen) jedoch eine hinreichende Variationsbreite hinsichtlich der Sachverhaltswiderspiegelung gewährleistet ist, um allen Kommunikationserfordernissen gerecht zu werden'.
    1. Thus Schnelle, *Sprachphilosophie*, pp. 168-69. See also the quotation of the preceding section on p. 152 n. 4 above.
    2. Coseriu, *Einführung*, pp. 145-46.
    3. Thus, H. Lausberg, *Handbuch der literarischen Rhetorik* (2nd edn; Munich, 1973), I, p. 244 [§445].

regard to macro-structural text-delimitation on the one hand, and communication embedment hierarchies on the other.

The macro-syntagmatic text-delimitation

In order to establish the textual macro-structure of a text, one has to delimit the text as a whole into sub-texts of different rankings. 'The ranking of sub-texts *per definitionem* leads not only to a sequential order, but also, and more importantly, to the establishment of hierarchically and functionally well-defined interrelationships between various sub-texts, that is to say, to understanding, how sub-texts on higher levels function within the next lower level in rank all the way down to level zero.'[1]

For the reason of text-delimitation there is a need to establish hierarchically defined markers of a pragmatic, semantic and syntactic nature. The question of delimitation markers is discussed extensively in my dissertation[2] and in my article in *Semeia* 36,[3] and will thus not be dealt with here. One question of great importance, however, still has to be discussed, namely how the syntagmatic surroundings on the level of *parole* are related to the syntagmatic surrounding on the level of *langue*.[4] This question is important, since in our comparative macro-syntagmatic analyses of texts we are not concerned primarily with individual texts, but rather with texts as part of generic entities.

In answering the question posed above I will make use of system-linguistics as it is presented by Professor Klaus Heger. By means of distinct terminology he is able to show in a precise way the difference between the two kinds of syntagmatic surroundings.

Biblical as well as classical scholars know that each pericope stands in a syntagmatic relationship to the surrounding text, which we usually call 'context' or sometimes 'co-text'. The importance of the context for the interpretation of words, sentences and pericopes of individual texts is so familiar that I content myself by quoting Professor Coseriu when he writes: 'Eben deshalb ist der Kontext so wichtig, denn nur durch

---

1. Hellholm, 'The Problem of Apocalyptic Genre', p. 38. Cf. also the formulation by Coseriu, *Einführung*, p. 143: 'Die Identifizierung der syntagmatischen Beziehungen in einem Syntagma höherer Ordnung (Syntagma von Syntagmen) gestattet es nun, dessen syntagmatische Struktur ("Form der inneren Beziehungen") zu ermitteln'.

2. Hellholm, *Visionenbuch*, pp. 78-95.

3. Hellholm, 'The Problem of Apocalyptic Genre', pp. 38-42.

4. As stated above (section 1 [a]), there can be no syntagmatic surroundings on the *Σ-parole* level.

ihn, sei es durch den sprachlichen, sei es durch den außersprachlichen Kontext, erhält der Text einen Sinn'.[1]

When pursuing macro-syntagmatic analyses of *generic* texts, we do in fact nothing else than look at different text-parts or sub-texts in their hierarchical relationship to their textual surroundings, but we do so on a higher level of abstraction. In order to distinguish this kind of textual surrounding from the one we call context in a text-occurrence or text-manifestation, Heger uses the term *Lingueme of the rank Rn+1* in ascendent procedures and *Lingueme of the rank Rn-1* in descending procedures. In accordance with his ascendent procedure Heger summarizes his position in the following way: 'Die *Langue*-Entsprechungen [I could specify: *genre* equivalents—DH] solcher Kontexte sind im Rahmen von *Langue*-Analysen insoweit von Interesse, als sie sich in Form von Einheiten beschreiben lassen, die auf dem gegenüber den Ausgangseinheiten nächsthöheren hierarchischen Rang paradigmatisierbar...und somit als *Lingueme des Ranges Rn+1* definierbar sind'.[2] In this way the constitutive rôle of the sub-text hierarchy is scientifically secured, since the delimitation of texts

---

1. Coseriu, *Textlinguistik. Eine Einführung* (Tübinger Beiträge zur Linguistik, 109; 2nd edn; Tübingen, 1981), p. 107. Cf. further below (p. 161 n. 2) the quotation from W. Pannenberg (*Anthropologie*, pp. 362-63).

2. Heger, *Monem*, p. 30 (italics mine). Cf. also the comment by Raible on Heger, 'Signemränge und Textanalyse', in T.A. van Dijk and J.S. Petöfi (eds.), *Grammars and Descriptions* (Research in Text Theory, 1; Berlin, 1977), pp. 260-313; in the article by E. Gülich and W. Raible, 'Überlegungen zu einer makrostrukturellen Textanalyse: J. Thurber, The Lover and His Lass', *Grammars*, p. 163: 'Die zweite Konsequenz besteht darin, daß durch die Konzeption der Signemränge eine Fabel oder beispielsweise ein Roman mit ebenso großer Selbstverständlichkeit Objekt der Sprachwissenschaft sein kann wie etwa die Untersuchung der Wortbildung oder der Nebensätze. Hegers Ansatz macht die Trennung zwischen einer Linguistik, die sich mit satzmäßigen Gebilden befaßt, von einer solchen, die "übersatzmäßige" Einheiten zum Gegenstand hat, ebenso willkürlich wie diejenige zwischen einer Morpholinguistik und einer Syntagmalinguistik...Nun ist es freilich so, daß, wie Heger selbst betont, die Definition von Signemrängen ab Rang 8 [or 12 in later publications by Professor Heger—DH] immer tentativer wird. Dies liegt jedoch nicht etwa daran, daß das auf den drei geschilderten Prinzipien beruhende Verfahren irgendwelche gravierenden Mängel aufzuweisen hätte, sondern daran, daß im Gegensatz zu dem Bereich, der durch die Signeme bis Rang 7 abgedeckt wird, für den Bereich ab Rang 8 [or 12—DH] eine vergleichsweise geringe Zahl sprachwissenschaftlicher Vorarbeiten existiert.' See already Heger's programmatic statement in 'Temporale Deixis', p. 516: 'Im Grunde ist ja auch allgemein bekannt, daß es durchaus möglich ist, sowohl sehr kleine Einheiten als Phänomene der *parole* zu behandeln..., als auch sehr große Einheiten—beispielsweise ganze Kontext-Patterns in Form der sogenannten *literarischen Genera* (italics mine—DH)—unter ihrem Systemaspekt, das heißt als Phänomene der *langue* zu analysieren'.

into text-parts of different grades in my descendent generic analyses aims at constituting *lingueme-*(or, better, *signeme-*) ranks of the rank Rn-1.

A parallel phenomenon within form-criticism is the structural description of sub-texts in, for example, miracle stories: *Exposition, Miracle,* and *Demonstration*.[1] Gerd Theissen thereby distinguishes quite correctly between *individual text-structures* that he names 'compositional sequences' and *generic structures* that he calls 'paradigmatic fields'.[2] Another well-known example is the delimitation of letter prescripts into *superscript, adscript,* and *salutation*.[3] Both of these examples from the exegetical field are primarily of interest not on the level of *parole* but on the two levels of *langue* as described above (section 1 [a]), that is on the level of systemic linguistics. On the level of *parole* they draw the readers'/listeners' attention only in so far as they deviate from the conventionally accepted norm.

The communication-embedment hierarchy

Since in narrative texts in general and in texts adhering to the apocalyptic genre in particular a number of actors, i.e. *dramatis personae,* are present not merely (a) in a passive way as *patiens,*[4] but rather (b) in an active way as *agens,*[5] or even further (c) in an alternating way as *agens* and *patiens* respectively in dialogues or polyorational conversations,[6] or finally (d) in a 'not-participating-not-I-rôle'[7] as *spectators,* it is necessary to distinguish between various levels of communication. In so doing one has to take into account that in narrative texts 'communication takes place not only on the *text-external* level between sender and receiver but also on various *text-internal* levels by means

---

1. Cf. e.g. Bultmann, *Geschichte,* pp. 236-41; J. Jeremias, *Neutestamentliche Theologie* (Gütersloh, 1971), I, pp. 90-96, esp. p. 93; G. Theissen, *Urchristliche Wundergeschichten* (Gütersloh, 1974), *passim,* esp. pp. 82-83; D.-A. Koch, *Die Bedeutung der Wundererzählungen,* pp. 12-26; D. Lührmann, *Das Markusevangelium* (HNT, 3; Tübingen, 1987), pp. 94-95.

2. Theissen, *Urchristliche,* pp. 18f., 21. This observation is correct regardless of whether Theissen's terminology is appropriate or not.

3. See e.g. H. Conzelmann, *1 Corinthians* (Hermeneia; Philadelphia, 1975), pp. 19-24; Vielhauer, *Geschichte,* pp. 64-66; and most recently F. Schnider and W. Stenger, *Studien zum neutestamentlichen Briefformular* (New Testament Tools and Studies, 11; Leiden, 1987).

4. See J. Lyons, *Einführung in die Moderne Linguistik* (Munich, 1973), pp. 347ff., 357ff.

5. See Lyons, *Einführung,* pp. 300ff., 346ff., 357ff.

6. Heger, *Monem,* pp. 307-308, 315.

7. Heger, *Monem,* p. 228.

of the just described rôles of the *dramatis personae*'.[1] The distinction between various levels of communication has already been carried out extensively for *Hermas* and in a preliminary way for the Apocalypse of John in previous works of mine and will be executed even more extensively in my forthcoming analysis of Lucian's *Icaromenippos*.[2]

Of great importance for my purpose of generic investigations is—to state it once more—the fact that such a hierarchy of communication levels has the potential to serve not only 'as a model of concrete, actual acts of communication', that is, on the level of *parole*, but also 'as a model of requirements for the possibility of such acts of communication', that is, on the level of *langue*.[3]

A similar differentiation within New Testament form-criticism is Bultmann's distinction quoted above[4] between the individual origin of an individual text and the typical origin of a literary genre, insofar as 'Sitz im Leben' is a sociological concept that is not a singular historical happening, but a typical situation or way of conduct within the life of a community.[5]

Interpreted in this way, this last criterion also fulfills the scientific requirement of being a possible set of constitutive semantic characteristics as well as of divisive *differentiae specificae* to be used in generic analyses of narrative texts on different abstraction levels.

3. *Synchronic versus Diachronic Analyses*

Among linguists and particularly among New Testament scholars working with structuralistic models, a purely synchronic approach has become increasingly more popular and even absolutized. These scholars often claim that text-linguistics is responsible for their one-sidedness.[6]

One should, however, realize that prominent text-linguists do not see the dichotomy of 'diachrony' and 'synchrony'[7] as two forms of

---

1. Hellholm, *Visionenbuch*, p. 16. Cf. also *idem*, 'The Visions He Saw or: To Encode the Future in Writing. An Analysis of the Prologue of John's Apocalyptic Letter', in T.W. Jennings, Jr (ed.), *Text and Logos. The Humanistic Interpretation of the New Testament* (Festschrift H.W. Boers; Atlanta, GA, 1990), pp. 116-17, 135-38.
2. Hellholm, 'Lucian's Icaromenippus' (forthcoming).
3. Heger, *Monem*, p. 14; cf. also Fowler, *Kinds of Literature*, pp. 48-49.
4. See the quotation above p. 140 n. 1.
5. See the quotation from Bultmann, *Geschichte*, p. 4, above p. 140 n. 3.
6. So e.g. Boers, 'Sisyphus', p. 42
7. For this important distinction, see de Saussure, *Course*, pp. 79ff., 101-39, 140-90, and von der Gabelentz, *Die Sprachwissenschaft*, pp. 58-61. See also the

language, but rather as two ways of looking at one and the same object. Hartmut Kubczak is, in my opinion, right in claiming that a language, in the synchronic way of looking at it (i.e. *langue*), under no circumstances is adherent to change, since we here abstract from its development.[1] His teacher Klaus Heger agrees and gives the following three interpretations of *synchrony*: (a) *syn* refers to an *absolute period of time*, which in most cases is impossible to determine especially when one works with ancient material; (b) *syn* refers to a *relative period of time*, which is very difficult to limit; and (c) *syn* refers to an *abstract point of view*, which is the only reasonable understanding of a synchronic approach.[2]

Synchrony, as understood here, is thus a methodological aspect that has to do with abstraction rather than with chronological limitation.[3] Such a synchronic approach is, of course, without objection from a scientific point of view, but as Kubczak, in agreement with Coseriu, states, it is not the only possible and certainly not the only necessary one.[4]

In addition to the synchronic there is also a diachronic linguistic tradition, the aim of which is to describe the change of language, that is on the level of *langue*. Both kinds are complementary insofar (a) as they correspond in fact to two different perspectives for examining and interpreting the same object; and (b) as changes diachronically, that is, by means of comparison between synchronic related *langue* systems, can be observed. In this way the analysis will not remain synchronic–static but rather diachronic–dynamic in scope.[5]

synopsis in Coseriu, 'Georg von der Gabelentz', pp. 14-17, and also H. Geckeler, *Strukturelle Semantik und Wortfeldtheorie* (Munich, 1971), pp. 184-85.

1. Thus H. Kubczak, *Die Metapher* (Heidelberg, 1978), p. 123; also Coseriu, 'Synchronie, Diachronie und Typologie', in *Sprache, Strukturen und Funktionen*, p. 80: 'Denn so wie F. de Saussure diese Antinomie [sc. von Synchronie und Diachronie—DH] dargestellt hat, gehört sie nicht der Objektebene, sondern der Betrachtungsebene an: es handelt sich hier nur um eine Verschiedenheit der Standpunkte, um eine *methodische Unterscheidung...*'

2. Heger, 'Verhältnis von Theorie und Empirie in der Dialektologie', in W. Besch *et al.* (eds.), *Handbücher der Sprach- und Kommunikationswissenschaft*. I. *Dialektologie* (Berlin, 1984), pp. 428-29.

3. Baldinger, *Semantic Theory*, p. 24.

4. Kubczak, *Die Metapher*, pp. 124f.; *idem, Was ist ein Soziolekt?, passim.* Cf. also Coseriu, 'Vom Primat der Geschichte', *Sprachwissenschaft* 5 (1980), pp. 125-45; and his *Synchronie, Diachronie und Geschichte* (Internationale Bibliothek für allgemeine Linguistik, 3; Munich, 1974).

5. Hempfer, *Gattungstheorie*, pp. 122ff., 131f., 140, 192-220; Raible, *Was sind Gattungen?*, pp. 326f., 340ff.; Hellholm, *Visionenbuch*, p. 64; Baldinger, *Semantic Theory*, pp. 277-309.

Regarding genre-critical and form-critical analyses, this means that we are able not only to investigate innovations in genres and forms, but also to follow changes and developments of a genre or a form from one time to another.[1] This also means that even with regard to analyzing genres and forms, contrary to structuralism, we cannot dispense with historical interpretations of literary phenomena.[2] Here I am in principle in agreement with Rudolf Bultmann and his program for a History of the Synoptic Tradition; I would only add that this goes with equal importance for the History of the Gospel genre or the History of literary genres in general. For instance, the History of the genre 'Apocalypse' has still to be written! It is essential to recognize that form criticism took an interest not primarily in the history (i.e. the diachronic development) of *individual* text-parts (i.e. on the level of *parole*), but of *literary forms* (i.e. on the level of *langue*) and their changes and developments through periods of time within Early Christian communities.[3]

This is a clear indication of how important it is not to neglect the relationship between 'analyses of genre versus analyses of individual texts' on the one hand and 'synchronic versus diachronic analyses' on the other:

1. See the important analysis of the genetic origin and the later development of the genre 'Historiette' (NB as *nominal* definition, on which see e.g. I.M. Bocheński, *Denkmethoden*, p. 90: '. . . die reale Definition sagt was ein *Ding* ist, die nominale bezieht sich nicht auf ein Ding, sondern auf ein *Zeichen*'; further G. Klaus, *Philosophisches Wörterbuch*, p. 249; Menne, *Einführung*, pp. 15, 34;) in France from 1657 onwards by F. Nies, 'Das Ärgernis *Historiette*. Für eine Semiotik der literarischen Gattungen', *Zeitschrift für romanische Philologie* 89 (1973), pp. 421-39, esp. 432-33.

2. See esp. Kubczak, *Die Metapher*, pp. 124ff.; W. Vosskamp, 'Gattungen als literarisch-soziale Institutionen', in W. Hinck (ed.), *Textsortenlehre–Gattungsgeschichte* (Heidelberg, 1977), pp. 27-44; Fowler, *Kinds of Literature*, pp. 48ff.; H. Steger, 'Über Textsorten und andere Textklassen', in Vorstand der Vereinigung der deutschen Hochschulgermanisten (ed.), *Textsorten und literarische Gattungen,* pp. 25-67. As far as biblical texts are concerned, see the discussion in B. Lategan, 'Some Unresolved Methodological Issues in New Testament Hermeneutics', in B. Lategan and W. Vorster (eds.), *Text and Reality, Aspects of Reference in Biblical Texts* (Semeia Studies; Atlanta, GA, 1985), pp. 3-25, esp. 3-12.

3. In order to avoid misunderstanding, it must be made explicit that diachronic analyses are not to be identified or confused with source criticism.

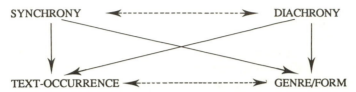

All combinations are scientifically legitimate. Which of the possible options one choses is entirely dependent on the purpose of the investigation. What is required, however, is that the interpreters know what their aims are and what they are doing, so as not to mix the possibilities into a kind of method, which cannot be handled by the interpreters themselves, or which is impossible for others to check.

With regard to the analysis of generic texts, and in our case especially of apocalyptic texts, another aspect that has to be taken into account is the relationship between 'synchrony and/or diachrony' on the one hand and 'syntagmatic and/or paradigmatic approaches' on the other.[1] I will try to illustrate this in two ways:

a. First, with regard to *word-semantics*. With reference to Ludwig Wittgenstein's statement that 'die Bedeutung eines Wortes...sein Gebrauch in der Sprache (ist)',[2] it is often claimed that words obtain their meaning only in texts, that is actually on the level of *parole*. This misunderstanding of Wittgenstein's position[3] has been challenged and corrected by the linguist Peter Hartmann, when he states that everybody knows that words do not only obtain a meaning in the text but that they also bring a meaning to the text, since if they brought nothing, there would be no established texts.[4]

Within philosophy of language Franz von Kutschera[5] and Siegfried J. Schmidt,[6] within linguistics Hartmut Kubczak[7] and Wolfgang

---

1. Cf. E. Brandenburger, *Markus 13 und die Apokalyptik* (FRLANT, 134; Göttingen, 1984), p. 14: 'Eine Apokalypse kann sehr verschiedene, ursprünglich nicht der Apokalyptik enstammende Einzelgattungen in sich aufnehmen und einem neuen Sinngefüge dienstbar machen'.

2. L. Wittgenstein, *Philosophische Untersuchungen* (3rd edn; Suhrkamp Taschenbuch, 14; Frankfurt am Main, 1975), p. 41 [§43]. Cf. Baldinger, *Semantic Theory*, pp. 14ff., 143, 146, 149; Heger, *Monem*, pp. 54, 205.

3. See F. von Kutschera, *Sprachphilosophie* (2nd edn; Uni-Taschenbücher, 80; Munich, 1975), pp. 148-51, esp. 150-51; see the quotation below in n. 5.

4. See P. Hartmann, 'Zum Begriff des sprachlichen Zeichens', *Zeitschrift für Phonetik, Sprachwissenschaft und Kommunikationsforschung* 21 (1968), pp. 211-12.

5. Von Kutschera, *Sprachphilosophie*, pp. 43f., 112-18, 148-51: 'Die These ist also nicht, daß man die Bedeutung erklärend reduzieren kann auf einen Gebrauch, der

Lorenz/Gerd Wotjak,[1] and within systematic theology Wolfhard Pannenberg[2] have taken a similar position.

From a text-linguistic perspective Werner Kallmeyer and his co-authors have taken a similar middle position, when they differentiate between the *potential meaning* of lexical words and the *actualized meaning* of words within a textual context.[3] By means of the textual context a monosemization of the polysemic *signemes* will occur.[4] Here it becomes clear that one of the limitations of system-linguistics is precisely its exclusively text-internal position, since it can account only for the inter-textual, but not for the intra-textual, and situative, context.[5] The same is also true of the so-called text-oriented or text-centered approach within New Testament exegesis in its extreme form. As a complement to the primarily text-internal model of system-linguistics there is need for a pragmatic or text-theoretical approach encompassing the text-external realm, and thus also accounting for the situative context and its interactional aspects.[6]

b. Second, with regard to *text-semantics*. Analogously the same can be said with regard to text-semantics; for when, for example, tradi-

Bedeutung nicht voraussetzt, und diesen auf ein Verhalten, das Sprache nicht voraussetzt. . ., sondern daß sich die sprachlichen Funktionen erst im Sprachgebrauch erschließen, den man lehren und, wenn Sprachverständnis bereits vorausgesetzt werden kann, durch sprachliche Beschreibungen erläutern kann' (pp. 150f.).

6. S.J. Schmidt, *Texttheorie* (2nd edn; Uni-Taschenbücher, 202; Munich, 1976), p. 58.

7. H. Kubczak, *Das Verhältnis von Intension und Extension als sprachwissenschaftliches Problem* (Forschungsberichte des Instituts für deutsche Sprache, 23; Tübingen, 1975), pp. 93-99.

1. Lorenz and Wotjak, *Zum Verhältnis von Abbild und Bedeutung*, pp. 252-53.

2. W. Pannenberg, *Anthropologie in theologischer Perspektive* (Göttingen, 1983), pp. 362-63: 'Das Wort ist also immer durch ein Ineinander von Bestimmtheit und Unbestimmtheit gekennzeichnet. Seine Bestimmtheit erhält es im Zusammenhang des jeweiligen Satzes [i.e. the *textual context*—DH]. . . Auch im Satz aber verliert sich die Unbestimmtheit nicht gänzlich. Darum ist der Sinn des einzelnen Satzes erst durch den Zusammenhang der Rede oder der Situation, in der er gesprochen wurde [i.e. the *situative context*; cf. also the quotation from Coseriu above on pp. 154-55—DH], festgelegt. Dementsprechend muß die Interpretation sich am Kontext der Rede orientieren, und zwar sowohl an ihrem engeren als auch an ihrem weiteren Kontext.'

3. W. Kallmeyer *et al.*, *Lektürkolleg zur Textlinguistik. I: Einführung* (2nd edn; Fischer Athenäum Taschenbücher, 2050; Kronberg, 1977), pp. 115-19.

4. Heger, 'Die Semantik und die Dichotomie von Langue und Parole', *Zeitschrift für romanische Philologie* 85 (1969), pp. 170ff.

5. Heger, 'Die Semantik', pp. 161-62.

6. See esp. Schmidt, *Texttheorie*, and I. Rosengren, 'Texttheorie', in H.P. Althaus *et al.* (eds.), *Lexikon der germanistischen Linguistik* (2nd edn; Tübingen, 1980), pp. 275-86.

tional motifs or forms of different kinds are placed in a syntagmatic surrounding, they certainly bring a meaning with them, though this meaning can, by means of the textual context, be made more precise or under circumstances even altered.[1]

Therefore we must recognize that the context (i.e. on the level of *parole*) or the lingueme ranks (i.e. on the level of *langue*) ultimately determines the precise meaning of a 'motif', a 'form', or, more generally stated, a 'sub-text' within a text as a whole.[2] This is true with regard to pure semantics but even more so on the semantic-pragmatic level of analysis, since with regard to macro-syntagmatic analyses the rule applies that neither sentences nor sub-texts of various degrees 'have *per se* any function but only obtain their function from a superior totality, for example (with regard to tones) within a melody or as far as texts are concerned, within a superior unity of meaning',[3] or in other words 'the meaning of the parts is determined by the structure of the whole'.[4] The importance of the syntagmatic surroundings applies not only—as we have seen—to context-analyses on the level of *parole* when investigating individual texts, but also to *lingueme*-analyses on the level of *langue* when investigating generic entities. With regard to genre-investigations, this insight has been adequately emphasized from the point of view of encodement as well as of decodement by John Kloppenborg, when he states that 'a genre

1. Concerning this aspect of traditio-historical and redaction-critical investigations in connection with (a) genre analyses on the level of *langue* and (b) text-interpretation on the level of *parole*, see first the quotation (above p. 160 n. 1) from Brandenburger, *Markus 13*, p. 14, and further the apt remarks in K. Koch, *Daniel* (BKAT, 22/1; Neukirchen-Vluyn, 1986), p. 18: 'Mit überlieferungs- und redaktionsgeschichtlichen Erwägungen verlassen wir den Horizont dessen, was in der Primärkommunikation der Erstschriftsteller und seine intendierten Leser vorgestellt und bedacht haben. Während die Kennzeichen des Gefüges. . . vom Verfasser beabsichtigt waren und vom Leser wahrgenommen werden sollten, hat diese dritte Dimension des Textes sich weder die eine noch die andere Seite damals vergegenwärtigt. Uns Nachgeborenen aber, denen viele Informationen fehlen, über die damals Schriftsteller und Leser selbstverständlich verfügten, gewährt der überlieferungsgeschichtliche Aspekt eine Hilfe, um den Horizont des damaligen Kommunikationsgeschehens zu rekonstruieren. Ziel solcher Überlegungen ist nicht, von der Endfassung des Textes als exegetischer Aufgabe abzuführen, sondern sie im Gegenteil sachgemäßer zu verstehen.'

2. Cf. the quotations above from Coseriu (*Textlinguistik*, p. 107), p. 154 at n. 5 and from Pannenberg (*Anthropologie*, pp. 362-63) p. 161 n. 2.

3. Thus Raible, 'Zum Textbegriff und zur Textlinguistik', in J.S. Petöfi (ed.), *Text vs. Sentence: Basic Questions of Text Linguistics* (Papiere zur Textlinguistik, 20/1; Hamburg, 1979), p. 69 (translation mine).

4. Boers, 'Sisyphus', p. 38.

conception is that notion of the whole which both controls the production of a literary work in all its individual parts and allows an interpreter to ascertain correctly the sense of each part'.[1]

Even though synchronic and diachronic procedures are equally legitimate, their actual use must in each case be determined by the purpose of the investigation. In my own analysis of apocalyptic texts I have not, however, for reasons of principle, chosen a synchronic procedure for the purpose of investigating the syntagmatic structure of the generic entity 'Apocalypse'. The necessary diachronic complement to this investigation will and must follow within the framework of a comparative analysis of a number of apocalyptic texts.

4. *Conclusion*

As far as *definitions* of generic texts in general and apocalyptic texts in particular are concerned, it is my proposal that these definitions be made on various hierarchical abstraction levels respectively according to the rule of real definition, namely, *per genus proximum et differentias specificas*.

Further, my suggestion concerning the *analyses* of texts as generic entities is that these analyses be understood as investigations on the basis not only of paradigmatic but also of macro-syntagmatic and communication-strategic procedures. Thereby one should take as the starting-point a synchronic view using a descendent method in delimiting the text into sub-texts of various degrees on the one hand and into communication levels of various ranks on the other.

Finally, a diachronic investigation of a specific generic concept should be undertaken with the attempt at writing a *history* of that concept, in our case the history of the Apocalyptic genre.

---

1. J.S. Kloppenborg, 'Tradition and Redaction in the Synoptic Sayings Source', *CBQ* 46 (1984), p. 58.

INDEXES

INDEX OF ANCIENT REFERENCES

OLD TESTAMENT

NEW TESTAMENT

PSEUDEPIGRAPHA

OTHER JEWISH SOURCES

CLASSICAL SOURCES

INDEX OF AUTHORS

JOURNAL FOR THE STUDY OF THE PSEUDEPIGRAPHA

Supplement Series